MILITARY SOCIOLOGY

Collapse of the Israel Defense Forces

R. Raikhlin

ISBN: 1-4392-6549-6
ISBN-13: 9781439265499

Abstract

Roots of terrorism and various wars, including civil and partisan wars, are explained, based on social dynamics. War is bifurcation and constitutes an inseparable part of the evolution of a society. Causes of degradation in the army are explained. Degradation in the Israeli army that has developed in the past forty years, from the brilliant victory over armies of three Arab countries in the Six-Day War in 1967 till the disastrous defeat in the 2006 second Lebanese war, are taken as examples. Degradation in the army is shown to accompany degradation and division in society. Recruitment methods as well as cohesion methods for the army are considered. Cases of using children in military actions are also described. Mistakes in using the army to perform police functions are noted. The use of repression is discussed.

Keywords: *military sociology, social dynamics, division in society, war, civil war, partisan war, army, the armed forces, war rules, terror, terrorism, repression.*

Contents

R. RAIKHLIN
MILITARY SOCIOLOGY:
COLLAPSE OF THE ISRAELI DEFENSE FORCE

IN THE LOVING MEMORY OF MY FATHER
JUDA RAIKHLIN
DIED IN THE FRONT LINES, December 25, 1941

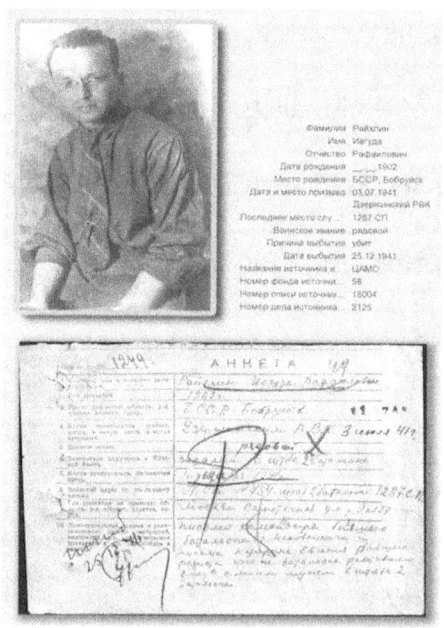

THE CURSED BOOK
Instead of a preface

It seems that both fatal and nonfatal bad luck keeps me from finishing this book. For example, a chapter about international and national war is completely lost. Wars of that kind originated in the age of religious wars. I wanted to use the Second World War as an illustration to the fight of people united by the communist ideology against Nazi Germany. But at the end of the war the communist ideology broke down and all western countries fought for their national interests.

I have not only written a book, but also applied to the newly created committee headed by the Judge Eliyagy Vinograd. The committee was established to investigate the actions of the Israeli government during the war. I proposed that the committee considered my point of view and submitted a summary of my message and a list of issues I had studied. Regretfully, the committee did not want to listen to me. It turned out only when it had finished its work. It was but obvious that the Judge Vinograd played to the tune of the head of the government Mr. Olmert. My continuous attempts to remind about myself did not prevent them from forgetting about me. They simply did not want my view. The committee were wary about the witnesses like me. Instead it listened to Asu Kasher, the leading aesthetic of IDF, completely ignorant and uneducated in sociology and responsible for the Israeli soldiers, speaks demoralization. I consider this fact to be the best illustration of what that committee was worth.

Obviously all the above said explains why the first bad luck came to me in the person of the representative of the Israeli police computer related crimes department from the Northern district. His name was Tsakhi Segal. He came to my doorstep with the search warrant, though he preferred not to take pains with the search. My computer was deplugged and taken to the police office. So was I.

I could have quoted the Mass Media reports to show what kind of person that Tsakhi Segal was. But I do not feel inclined to spend time on him. The reports of Tsakhi Segal are vague and ambiguous and can hardly prove anything.

Before starting to question me Segal ventured a guess that I was an extreme right. It happened that my right arm was just against the wall, which allowed me to answer: "Only the wall is righter than me". Another guess of his: "You are a racist" (gezani in Hebrew). My answer: "Not a gezani, but a gezi" (that's the Hebrew for full-blooded). After all Natan Alterman, an Israeli poet, is my uncle on my mother's side and Berl Katsnelson, a nationalist, is my uncle on the father's side.

A 180-day period, established by law, passed, since my computer had been buried at the police warehouse. Though contrary to the law no one stirred a finger to return it to me. No charges were brought against me either.

Only the investigator told me that I would be charged with something like seditious language. I asked Tsakhi Segal, my investigator, what he thought about my works. To my great surprise he knew nothing about them. He never read anything either in the Internet or on the forfeited computer, event the materials written in Hebrew. "I have no time to read", that's what he told me. It appears that the whole thing was based on my story. I thought that my computer had been forfeited and kept for such a long period due to other reasons. It seemed that someone was weary about my research. The prosecutor's office closed my case. They temporized for a year. But neither the police nor the prosecutor has the right to tell me, a sociologist, what to do and what to write. They have no right to meddle in the way I write. The court held that the computer should have been returned to me immediately.

So, I had to go through the fire and water before I finished my book "Military Sociology: Collapse of the Israeli Defense Forces". There are 10 chapters in the book. I tried to prove that a war is a part of the human evolution that either aims at the enemy destruction, or their full and unconditional surrender.

The next hard stage was to gather reviews of the book both from readers and specialists. Most readers do not understand the world we live in, that's why they ask me naive questions:

"Why aren't NON-GOVERNMENTAL ORGANIZATIONS (or their lawyers) engaged in the author's PROTECTION in our democratic country?"

"WHY did neither Hebrew nor Russian language press nor the show of the channel 9 "YOUR RIGHT" tell anything ABOUT THAT PROSECUTOR'S INVESTIGATION TO THE AUTHOR AND TO THE PUBLIC?"

Vladimir Slavin

Many thanks to Vladimir Slavin.

No organizations of "democratic society" would ever protect the author with the "extremely right" views that shows the demoralization of their "superb army".

I turned to my colleagues, to sociologists and got a reply that my book was out of all bounds. Isn't it enough to make one's mind wild! What bounds?! I ask the professors I know to write a review. They either never reply, or promise to write but never do this. I can understand them. They do not want to be attached to the supporters doomed to be fired. Doctor Larisa Trimbovler has already become a victim of such attitude in Israel. She was fired from the University. I remember that in the USSR my mother and I were chased only because we were Jews.

Let's take the Council for Peace and Security as an example. The Council is very proud of its generals, politicians and diplomats always ready to comment upon any issue free of charge. The Council annually holds expensive conferences in Herzilia. I have applied to this organization and asked to comment my work. Below is the answer:

Dear Mr. Raikhlin

I regret to admit that there are no specialists in the field of military sociology in the Council to provide you with an expert opinion,

Sincerely yours,
Zhenya Livshitz
PR Coordinator of Council for Peace and Security.

That's horrible if such a well-established organization cannot find a qualified specialist among all its generals.

And here is a mournful answer of IDF Press Officer of 15.12.2008. The size of the message is 145 Kbytes. The answer is signed by Avital Leibovich. Below is the translation from Hebrew:

"IDF is subordinate to Politburo and acts in accordance with the orders of the latter. Moreover, I it was already said we cannot comment upon your book."

That's it. Straight and clear. Politburo told us to initiate and to lose the 2nd Libyan War, so we initiated it and lost it. Just as the USSR started and lost the war in Afghanistan by the order of Politburo.

I decided to apply directly to the generals over the head of the press officer and asked them to comment upon my book. Below is the list of generals, I sent my letter to:

General Avi Mizrakhi – Commander-in-Chief of Ground Posture

General Ido Nakhushtan – Commander—n-Chief of Air Forces

General Eli Marom - Commander-in-Chief of Maritime Forces

General Amos Yadlin - Chief of the Intelligence

General Tal Roso - Chief of the Operative Department

General avi Zamir - Head of the Human Resources

General Dan Biton - Head of the Technologies and Logistics Department

General Amir Eshel - head of the designing department

General Ami Shafran - head of the information technologies department

General Ami Aizenkot - Commander-in-Chief of the Northern District

General Gadi Shamni - Commander of the Central District
General Elav Glanti - Commander of the Southern District
General Yair Golan - Commander of the back land
General Meir Khalifi - military secretary of the Israeli government
General Gershun Kogan - Commander of the Academies
General Ishai Bar - Commander of the special subdivision of the Joint Staff
General Shai Yaniv - the Chairman of the military court
Colonel Avikhai Mandelblit - chief military prosecutor
2.

I have received a positive reply only from human resources department (the seventh in the list). But then a short telephone call with a refuse followed. I asked to provide a refuse in a written form but this request was also rejected.

Below is the characteristic for one of those generals, published in the weekly magazine «Eretz Israel Shelanu» and reproduced on the web-site of MAOF on 12.05.2009

When Gadi Shamni was appointed as the commander of the Central District two years ago, many eyebrows were raised. Neither was he a brilliant commander nor a commander of one of those operations that glorified IDF in olden times. He was an officer who climbed the career ladder due to his time in service. So what was behind his appointment to such an important and sensitive position in IDF?

According to the investigations, carried out by «Eretz Israel Shelanu», Gadi Shamni offered a great deal of help to Sharon during cruel and forceful eviction of Gush-Katif and consequently his strive was repaid with the appointment to the high position.

Not everyone in the commandment supported Gush-Katif forceful eviction. Some did it out of sheer necessity, but others played a greater and more active role. At that time Gadi Shamni worked as a military secretary of Arik Sharon, then a Prime Minister. Military secretaries are, in a way, a means of communication between the Prime Minister and the army and other military forces. But Gadi Shamni was different! Shamni exercised continuous pressure on IDF commandment to get them act more aggressively to fulfill the order about the eviction. When the command staff held meetings related to the eviction, Shamni used to call, to know what was going on, to ask why this or that was not being done. He tried to stress that he was acting on behalf of the head of the government Sharon.

When Gush-Katif was evicted, Shamni received most healthful praise from Sharon. Sharon wanted to reward him for his loyalty and included him in the group participated in negotiations with the representatives of American administration, where they discussed the «road map» establishment. There Shamni realized the scale of influence the Americans had over the Sharon government politics. When Sharon was replaced by Olmert, Shamni stayed with the latter and became one of his confidants. The second Libyan War began. It is widely known that Ehud Olmert is not experienced in military affairs that are why he desperately needed the advice of his military secretary - no other than Shamni. Though it turned out that this shadow officer who knew how to be toady before Bush administration

xviii   The Cursed Book

representatives, was useless in war affairs, He was not capable of vivid thinking, he did not have deep understanding of war. Shamni advice was useless, accordingly, Olmert, who relied on him too much, gave useless orders. So the results of the second Libyan War were not unexpected.

After the Libyan War a lot of people responsible for military operations had to quit the army: the minister of defense, his deputy, divisional commanders and many others, but Shamni stayed in the administration of the prime minister, because Olmert and Peretz decided to reward him for his loyalty during Gush-Katif operation and Libyan War. The Minister of defense Peretz ordered to appoint Shamni to the position of the commander of the Central District just before he resigned. And Shamni lived up to their expectations. For two years Shamni has been chasing the faithful to Israel in all spots of Judaea and Samaria. He issues the temporary eviction orders for Judaea and Samaria. He destroys fort posts together with the commander of the territorial division of Judaea and Samaria, brigadier general Noam Tivon. He also did something no other general has ever done. He sent to prison 12 soldiers because they refused to drive the Jews from their homes in Hevron. He is chasing the soldiers who protect the dignity of Israel, like the soldier who fired a rubber bullet at the terrorist who made a riot in Naalin, etc...

When Gadi Shamni was appointed to the post of the commander of the Central District, many people from military circles voiced their opinion about this person as follows: «The authorities of the USA are happy to have Shamni at this position, as he knows perfectly what Americans want of us». That's true! Shamni has never disappointed them. In his interviews to Mass Media he shows his disgust to «lawbreakers» and «bandits», who are no other than mere settlers.

Recently Shamni has been bending over his backward to open the road from Kiryat-Arby to Mearat-a-Makhpela for Arabs. He simply ignores the warnings from the army that this road will be used by Arabs for terror.

Now let's see how the general thrusts his ideology upon his subordinates. (Report of IDF press-office, published on the web-site MIGnews.com http://www.mignews.com/news/society/world/200509_61211_32367.html on 20.05.06)

The major general Gadi Shamni, commander of the Central Military District summoned the Kfir infantry brigadier, the colonel Itay Virtub and reprimanded him for making a stand for the soldiers who assailed the Arabs.

General Shamni stressed that it was vital to prevent the force being applied against the prisoners. He also underlined, that protecting human dignity was one of the key values of the Central Commandment and the whole Israeli Defense Force. He said that the colonel Virtub attempt to excuse the violence of his soldiers distorts the reality and the severity of such incidents. According to the commander, the comments of the colonel Virtub are inconsistent with either the Spirit of IDF (Moral Code of Israeli Defense Army) or its rules.

A stupid careerist tries to show off and pretend to be a humanist. He cares about Arabs while he is ready to sacrifice his soldiers. No wonder that IDF lose even trifle operations like the one in Gaza. The story below explains what the Spirit of IDF and good-for-nothing Codes may lead to. This is a complete report of Israeli 7 channel, published on January 19, 2005, 23:28 19 under the title «The Father of the Killed Captain: Legal System Exposes the

Soldiers to Unnecessary Risk». (http://www.7kanal.com/news.php3?id=77186»)

Dov Vardy - the father of Moran Vardy, the captain of IDF that was killed during the fight with the searched terrorist in Shkhem accused Israeli legal system of his son's death. He said it after his visit to the place where his son was killed in exchange of fire.

Dov Vardy spent a lot of time trying to obtain a permit to visit shkhem, as IDF refused to accompany him there. Though eventually, they had to satisfy his request as the poor father promised to go there by himself. His wife - Moran's mother - knew nothing of his trip. He did not want to hurt her. The place where his son had been killed, and the detail about how it had happened, made a hard impression on him. Having heard everything by his own ears and having seen everything by his own eyes he came to a horrible conclusion: his son's death was in vain, it could have been avoided.

He believes that the Israeli legal system does not provide the soldiers with enough latitude to fight the enemy, avoiding hazards to life. This leads to a waste of soldiers' lives. The Dov says that the soldiers asked for permission to employ massive fire during the operation, but the command said no even without consulting with the higher commanders.

Dov Vardy also claims that the soldiers were not allowed to launch a rocket at the house where the armed terrorist was hiding, the very terrorist that had killed Moran. He says that the decision was absurd, as it was quite obvious that the armed terrorist was hiding in the house; the terrorist that had refused to give up. Had the rocket been launched, Moran would have been alive. He claims that, nowadays, soldiers continue to act in excessively risky conditions.

«I came to the conclusion: if the commander allowed to launch a rocket at the house, everything would have been different», Vardi said, «But there is a legal system that may deprive him from his regalities and put his career at risk. What is the result? We lost the operation that cost Morann his life and made another soldier a disabled.. Someone just did not want to put their position at risk and Moran died».

Dov Vardy appealed for amendments in the existing rules of civil and military legal systems to save other lives. So that the commanders never feared that they would have to answer for their actions in the Israeli High Court of Justice (BAGATZ).

Dov Vardy repeated the words I wrote in my book. It is cheaper to destroy the house with all its inhabitants than to risk a life of IDF captain. Next time the inhabitants won't hide a terrorist among them.

If the general thinks that our children's lives are worthless, then he is gravely mistaken. The Nemesis will come to him just as she came to Itzkhak Rabin, Ariel Sharon, and...

The Israeli general is threatened to be killed for the Jews settlements demolition. Lenta.ru:

http://lenta.ru/news/2009/06/04/threat/ 23.06.9009

According to Agency France-Presse, Gadi Shamni, Israeli general received a letter with threats of severe harm to him and his family. It is suspected that the letter has been sent by the angry Israeli settlers evicted from the Palestine territory,

In the letter the general is called «an anti-Semite hating Jews» and «a son of Satan». Besides the threats to the general, the authors of the letter hinted on possible menace to his children that are also labeled as «sons of Satan». Shamni is in command over the military units on the Western side that are often participate in illegal Jewish settlements eviction from the Palestine territory. It makes the radical settlers angry. On Wednesday, June 4 another settlement of nine shabby buildings was demolished. This settlement has already been demolished several times within the recent months. But the settlers rebuilt their houses. Currently, there are about 100 illegal Jewish settlements on the Western side, while 121 settlements are sanctioned by the government. The International community, and the American administration in the first place demand to demolish all the Jewish settlements on the Palestine territories. The President of the USA Barak Obama declared at the meeting with the Prime minister of Israel Binyamin Netanyahu that the settlements of the Western side should be demolished. On May 31 the Israeli government published the list of illegal settlements to be demolished in the nearest future. The radical forces of Israel encouraged to resist the Washington pressure. But Netanyahu assured that the decision about the settlements demolition was not based on the USA requirements. He also promised that the Jews would not create new ones.

In response to the settlers appeal to stop the demolition operations, Israeli Minister of defense Ehud Barak replied that he stands for the liquidation of the settlements following the negotiations with their inhabitants. Though Barak added that «in cases when the negotiations are deemed impossible, we will act decisively and aggressively to ensure law and order.»

I have described the whole process of the Army degradation in my book. What's more, I have shown how IDF sacrifice its soldiers and officers for the sake of complying with stupid codes, in the name of the ideology. I hope that the reader will understand why I have not received reviews on my book from IDF. «There is no one to read and no one to write». IDF have degraded.

Though there is a ray of light. A dissident from England was brave enough to give his comments against all odds.

Dr. Raikhlin is known to me as a prominent historian and sociologist. His works are widely distributed in the Internet. I find it appalling if someone is being persecuted for merely saying or writing something - as appears to be the case with Dr. Raikhlin.   Vladimir Bukovsky, Cambridge, 3 October 2008.

A New War of Olmert.

Having gained bitter experience during the 2-week 2nd Libyan War in 2006, Israel did not pursuit great aims, declaring war against HAMAS in winter of 2008-2009. The politburo launched a war against the Islamic organization HAMAS, that occupied the territory in the Gaza strip, 20 km in width and 40 km in length, in the South of Israel. Surprisingly, no one ever recalled the Six Days War of 1967. Everyone seemed to forget that HAMAS was created by Israel to oppose Yasser Arafat. If any parallels were drawn, they were the parallels with war against HEZBOLLAH in 2006.

I am not the only one to notice the failure of the Israeli Army. Regretfully, modern analysts tend to point out other reasons for the defeat in the war with Hezbollah and, consequently, draw purely tactical conclusions, not considering sociology.

The military sources thought that the main strategic lesson of the second Lebanon war was the inability to destroy short-range rocket launchers without ground forces. Nonsense. If Israel had dropped more bombs than leaflets, the rockets would have been destroyed. At the beginning of the operation IDF used its Air Forced traditionally. But they did not employed carpet bombing, making only pinpoint strikes.

Who needs their pinpoint strikes on the territory of 40X20 km? The artillery strikes at the area would have been much more effective. Just as the Allies aviation bombed Dresden. Just as the Red Army's artillery cannoned areas before the main attack. But the Israeli commandment divided the people of Gaze into «good guys» and «bad guys», and punished only «bad guys» in spite of all my warnings. A one-ton bomb dropped in a pinpoint strike smashed the house of the Head of the Army of HAMAZ. The commander died. Thousands of its faithful soldiers came to his funerals. Israel got the splendid target and let it pass through its fingers. All police officers wait while the friends and enemies come to the funerals of a big mobster. IDF that performs the police functions lost the opportunity. These funerals once again proved that there is an OUS in Gaza. Any sociologist might have a look at the funeral's photo, conclude that the society is excessively united and advise to strike the area. There are no pinpoint targets there. The whole of Gaza is the pinpoint target. The events in the South of Israel proved the statements in my book. However, there are no military sociologists in Israel. Actually, the same mission was assigned in 2006 with respect to Hezbollah, although it was never achieved through the fault of the Politburo. Soldiers have died, but the Politburo has survived to begin a new losing war.

The Army of internationalists

Just another discovery: the Israeli internationalists (the left wing) are very sensitive to the international reaction to their war. They begin fighting but they do not wait for the enemy to capitulate—they wait for international public opinion instead.

Then I borrow materials from Guy Bechor, Ph.D. of the Interdisciplinary Center Herzilya, the Center where there were no specialists capable of peer reviewing my book. These materials are published on his web site http://www.gplanet.co.il/. Borrowing them, I primarily wish to show the way the Politburo corrupts the army. The society follows the downward path; its systems and the army, in the first place, break down. Regretfully, the Politburo and the Israeli Defense Force refuse to notice it.

The Army of Pacifists.

How did it happen that the famous IDF, the dear creature of Israel, flee in terror from any armed conflict with the Palestinians in the Gaza Strip? How did we abase ourselves so far that our generals beg for a cease-fire extension and the Head of the Joint Staff, General Gaby Ashkenazi, the general that brags about turning IDF into quite a different army, claims that Israel should avoid military actions in Gaza at any cost?

Our army has not become worse; it simply does not want to fight, just as it was during the last war in Libya. The Head of the Joint Staff had a detailed plan of land warfare with Hezbollah locked in his drawer, but the generals preferred to send in air forces to throw bombs on Libya. The same with Gaza: they send air forces, delivering a standard, mediocre, and thoughtless response, with no plan at all.

It is not the army that protects the country; it is the country that protects the army. If rockets strike the army base, the soldiers are evacuated to the deep rear, while the citizens are just left where they are. Israeli society believes that the life of the soldier is more precious than the life of its citizens; that's why they are taken so much care of. However, this is the Force to Defend Israel but not the Israel to Defense Force!

How do we abase ourselves so far as to let IDF become a nearly political establishment that exercises its power over the politicians in order to avoid fights on any front. For example, on the Syrian front, where the military authority pushes the government to negotiations with Asad and retreats from Golan—not to fight—this is their primary aim.

How can it be that our army has lost its killing instinct that used to be a distinctive feature of our self-confident commanders? Those who destroyed the Arab Air Forces so swiftly that not a single airplane managed to take off the ground!

How can it be that the army is petrified by the limited conflict with a small gang of terrorists and demand that the government extend the cease-fire period at any cost, even at cost of the state sovereignty and the peaceful life of its citizens?

Yearly, billions of shekels are spent on the army, so why does it not come up to the mark and its Joint Staff, dissolved in fat and drowsy from the endless budget, not want to take trouble and dream about retiring and about director chairs in private companies?

Legal bodies have interfered with the army too often, which in the end killed the IDF initiative. No one wanted to risk his life only to have his career shot down by the committee of Vinograd or Agranat after the war. Any war will end in investigative committees, as human losses are inevitable. No commander will ever take a risk; what's more, everyone now hurries to hide behind the lawyers. Will "mommy" let us bomb Gaza, or won't she? The Head of the Joint Staff is not in charge of IDF anymore. It obeys the orders of the government legal adviser Meni Mazuaz that dubbed the second Lebanon war as "the legal war." There is no place for ingenious strategic decisions and sudden risky operations in such wars. The lawyers' permission must be obtained in the first place. The Israeli High Court of Justice (BAGATZ) defeated the army.

In the past twenty years, IDF got all the human rights organizations on a string that does not bother about Israeli interests. They haunt the army from inside but are paid from abroad. With BAGATZ's support, the destructive effect of their activity might be enormous.

Nowadays, public opinion of Israel is influenced by the magnitude of human losses. They have become the single measure of military victories and defeats; that is why the army prefers not to fight—it is dangerous. The army is not afraid of the enemy; it is scared to death of mothers, by loud talk-backers, by angry crowds, by Carmela Menashe (army observer of "Voice of Israel" radio station), by newspapers and TV channels. To lynch a general is considered to be a great achievement. Modern Israeli society thinks that the war is lost if there is at least one killed, for example Gilad Shalit.

During the triumphant Six-Day War, about 800 soldiers died within six days. In terms of modern concepts, this war was a catastrophe and a disastrous defeat. We report each death and return to this news every hour, which does not help but only demoralizes people and gives them the feeling of colossal losses. In 1967, the list of dead was announced after the war had been finished—and nothing happened.

The army knows everything, knows who they will have to deal with, and does not want to begin war—neither big nor small. No, it's not the enemy but the cries inside the country that will inevitably arise if, God forbid, there will be dead! Today, IDF tries to develop the strategy that will result in less damage after the loss; no one thinks of winning tactics. Our enemy has noticed the strange feature of ours and successfully uses it against us. Thus, in 2006, when Nasralla hurriedly declared victory, we, overwhelmed by the defeatist feelings, only mournfully nodded to him in response.

We worry only about our personal interests, while the army and the state have moved to the background. Modern society does not believe in patriotism and love of the Motherland; the army has turned into something insignificant; it has become an unnecessary, stupid tool of "invasion." However, it is not only an Israeli phenomenon. It comes from the USA. Pacifism developed in the American mass media and cinema as a reaction to the wars in Korea and Vietnam. Whole layers of our society have drifted apart from the army and from everything it represents. Now, a new group of citizens do their job—they are religious Zionists, notably prominent in the army, and new repatriate that treat the army as a symbol of social mobility. The army command knows the way things are and does not want to get where it found itself in the midst of the second Lebanon war or to spend another eighteen years in the Lebanon marshes, through the stupidity of the political leaders of the country. The generals know that, if the army is stuck in Gaza escapees' settlements, the left wing will oppose them and leave the army at the mercy of the mass media and the numerous committees that will tear it to pieces. They know that the Israeli are ready to sacrifice Sderot, Ashkelon and other cities, so that the bourse go on working and gain profits. The army knows that it has no real support in the rear. Modern Israel is based on personal ego. The hell with solidarity, as though the Israelis do not understand that today they abandon Sderot and tomorrow they will have to flee from Tel-Aviv.

These factors prevent the army from drastic actions. The Modern IDF is not afraid to go forward, but it does not dare to look back, at the rear, as it is afraid to be left alone. IDF is not the people's army any more. It's an army afraid of people. However, we live in the Middle East where people enjoy watching how we destroy and humiliate our army. They do not have to stir a finger—we do the job better, and we do it for them.

Preface

All writings about war abound in descriptions of military hardware and its amount—tanks, planes, ships, and various weaponry. Trends and general lines in weapons development are also highlighted by such writing. By way of illustration, you can read the "Twenty-first-Century Blitzkrieg" section featuring ACEUs—aero-cosmic expeditionary units. All of a sudden, this cosmic idyll is broken by a *shahid*, a suicide bomber wearing an explosive belt. Where do shahids come from? Why don't they ever read about the ACEUs?

In history books, you will find descriptions of battles and feats of valor and biographies of spies, heroes, and outstanding military commanders but not a word about shahids.

What you will not be able to find in such books are the reasons for the behavior of individual officers and men and even entire units. Why, in some cases, are fighting men ready to sacrifice their lives for victory, but in other cases, why are they prone to panic, retreat, or surrender to the enemy? Why do people fight for their faith? Why was the military might of the USA powerless to attain victory in the Vietnam War? Why was it followed by the defeat of the USSR, also a great power, in Afghanistan?

I was prompted to take up this theme because of the defeat suffered by the Israeli armed forces in the second Lebanon war in 2006. How was a well-armed military force, almost an ACEU, defeated by gangs of Muslim fanatics? The fact that the Israeli forces also outnumbered the gangs brings the outcome of the second Lebanon war into the realm of fantasy.

My works in the field of social dynamics enable me to get at the root causes of terrorism and civil and guerilla wars. I am trying to show what caused the dramatic degradation of the Israeli armed forces in the four decades that elapsed from Israel's resounding victory over the armies of three Arab states in the Six-Day War in 1967 to its debacle in the second Lebanon war.

My attempts to bring military science to a higher level often encounter unwillingness or an inability by such detractors to give thought to the issue. In some cases, I have to face ideological problems that cause this unwillingness. My explanations, as in the case of Israeli politicians, are ignored because they run counter to somebody's interests, psychology, or ideology.

Social problems that arise during war and in the periods between wars have never commanded the attention they deserve. This can be attributed to the fact that sociology is still regarded as a kind of *statistics*. If questionnaires can be distributed, polls taken, and then graphs and diagrams constructed, this is seen as sociology. If there are no questionnaires, there is no sociology. My works, however, are based on the principles in the works of Machiavelli, von Clausewitz, Sorokin, and Durkheim, who did not distribute questionnaires. There is a lot of useless works on "sociology" themes, whose only value is that "respectable" people authored them.

I am interested in the social roots of the conflict, and I will try to reveal these roots of conflict, if only in part. This is an uphill task. Terrorist acts are perpetrated without sophisticated military hardware. As for the psychology or sociology of war, lack of objectivity opens possibilities for all kinds of speculation, argument, and refutation.

My work lays bare the causes of military defeat, even when, in the blitzkrieg process, some operations were successful. I predicted the failure of the United States in Iraq and showed how Israel squandered the results of its brilliant victory in the Six-Day War "for the sake of peace" without getting peace.

I am positive that social problems cannot be solved by "technical means." No "Chinese Wall" can protect the country from incompetent political leadership.

Among sociologists or people capable of understanding and discussing the problems I have touched upon, I have tried to find someone who could help solve social and military problems, in particular the shameful inability of Israel to put an end to Arab terrorism. I found neither allies nor opponents. Opponents may associate me with Machiavelli and call me a "Machiavellian." It may be correct.

Niccolo Machiavelli
There are three kinds of mind: a mind that grasps everything by itself; the second mind can understand what the first mind grasped; the third mind cannot understand anything by itself, nor anything that another mind grasped.
– Niccolo Machiavelli

Niccolo Machiavelli worked five hundred years ago. His teachings have been translated into many languages, commented upon, and cited times without number. Some of his expressions have become aphorisms.

In some respects, his works can be compared with pornographic literature—they are very popular, widely read, and widely censured. Critics call them amoral, antihuman, and so on in the same vein that pornography is castigated. A policy based on crude force, cynicism, ignoring moral norms has come to be known as "machiavellianism." Machiavelli was criticized for using the principle of "the end justifies the means" in politics.[1] Bertrand Russell wrote that there was much to be censured in Machiavelli's ideas. And further, that as a connoisseur of the art of state rule, Machiavelli would have appreciated such actions of Hitler's as setting fire to the Reichstag, the purge of the Nazi party in 1934, and the post-Munich perfidy. Why did Bertrand Russell not mention Stalin? Like Hitler, Stalin was not averse to staging provocations, undertaking purges, etc. Why should Bertrand Russell read Machiavelli? Machiavelli must have been very perspicacious indeed to be able to see what Hitler and Stalin would be like five hundred years before they were born.

---

1. Bertrand Arthur William Russell (18 May 1872–2 February 1970). British mathematician, philosopher, and public figure. Russell passed a complex philosophical evolution, which he himself defined as transition from Plato's interpretation of Pythagoreanism to Humism. He created a concept of "logical atomism" and developed a theory of descriptions. Russell believed mathematics could be deducted from logic. In 1950, he was awarded the Nobel Prize in Literature "in recognition of his varied and significant writings in which he champions humanitarian ideals and freedom of thought."

It is worth noting that Machiavelli is not the only victim of the humanists. German sociologist Robert Michels and his *Iron Law of Oligarchy* are mentioned in all sociology books, but never has an attempt been made to put it to practical use. According to this law, the oligarchy of all organizations fighting for "human rights," of pacifists fighting for peace, or of trade unions fighting for better working conditions is a malignant growth on the bodies of these organizations.

It is not the purpose of this work to analyze Machiavelli's ideas, and I am neither going to praise nor blame him. For me, it is as simple as that: Machiavelli is a great sociologist who, five hundred years ago, was able to discern some regularities in the behavior of society and used his knowledge to advise leaders how to govern society. Unfortunately, those he addressed have turned a deaf ear to his advice and have never been able to understand it or benefit from it. Hence, the silly comment about his works. Below, I will discuss some of the regularities Machiavelli discovered.

✿ ✿ ✿

In chapter 1, I lay down the principles of social dynamics and describe the cycle of society's degradation. I already discussed these principles and the degradation cycle. I believe, however, that repeating them at the beginning of this work will help the reader understand the subsequent sections.

Chapter 2 is devoted to the origin and purposes of war. War is an element of society's evolution. I examine the "rules of war," along with its causes. I show that the rules of war are a clumsy attempt to interfere in the evolutionary process.

Chapter 3. The armed forces are an excessively united society. I examine the process of their demoralization and methods of achieving their greater cohesion. Of special significance in this context are the mass media.

Chapter 4. I undertake a case study of the Israeli armed forces, highlighting the impact of the policy and the split in society on the armed forces. I describe the process of the armed forces' degradation and their becoming police squads incapable of protecting the Israeli citizens even from terrorism.

Chapter 5. I show that a regular army evolves from terrorist gangs, which develop into guerilla detachments, ultimately becoming a regular army.

Chapter 6. I examine the expediency of collective and individual punishment, and I show that mass reprisals are in place in a close-knit society where joint responsibility is practiced while, in a low-cohesion society, mass reprisals lead to society's cohesion.

Chapter 7. This chapter is about sacrificing children. I show that children are used as soldiers in an over-united society. They are brought up as patriots and "fighters for a just cause."

Chapter 8. I examine the ways armed forces are formed—by volunteers, mercenaries, or draftees. I then show that society resorts to mercenaries when it is in a state of degradation.

Wars are started at will but ended when it is possible.
– Machiavelli

Chapter 1

Social Dynamics and Degradation of Society

The Hierarchy of Needs

Psychologists have formulated the hierarchy of man's needs. First come physiological needs, without which life is impossible. Such needs include the consumption of food, breathing, etc.

The need for a society comes second. Man is a herd animal, and he needs communication with his own kind, almost as much as he needs air or water. It is this need for a society, for a team, that underlies social dynamics. Among man's sensory organs, such as vision, hearing, etc., there is team spirit, which I referred to as "hevraav." Man can feel "hunger" for society, and the less society is united and the stronger the process of disintegration, the more acute is this feeling. I dwelt in detail on social dynamics and this feeling in my work *Civil War, Terrorism, and Brigandage*. Some diagrams from my previous works are given below. It is shown how the sense of "hevraav" makes people unite into a society.

The Degradation Diagram
None of the great revolutions restores old governments and old aristocracy—they are resigned for good.
– Pitirim Sorokin

Still, ultimately, society loses its cohesion and falls apart. Loosening braces causes the degradation of society and of all its systems, the armed forces included. Braces are physical and spiritual elements that unite people. The physical elements are those that bring pleasure—games, sex, feasts, etc. Spiritual elements are religion or ideology.

Parallel with feeling a need for society, each man or woman wants to get a most advantageous position in it, which leads to the emergence of social hierarchy. Those who are stronger and cleverer than others make their way to the top of the hierarchy and form an oligarchy, pushing the others down. It is this fight for society's boons that erodes its cohesion and causes its collapse. The degradation and collapse of society follow a cyclic pattern.

One of such cycles is shown in fig. 1.

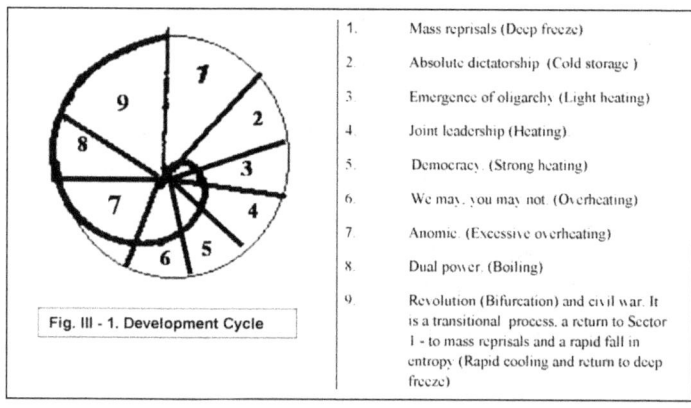

1.	Mass reprisals (Deep freeze)
2.	Absolute dictatorship (Cold storage)
3.	Emergence of oligarchy (Light heating)
4.	Joint leadership (Heating)
5.	Democracy (Strong heating)
6.	We may, you may not (Overheating)
7.	Anomie (Excessive overheating)
8.	Dual power (Boiling)
9.	Revolution (Bifurcation) and civil war. It is a transitional process, a return to Sector 1 - to mass reprisals and a rapid fall in entropy (Rapid cooling and return to deep freeze)

Fig. III - 1. Development Cycle

I will first describe the entire cycle of social dynamics. A single cycle can last for dozens or hundreds of years, depending on a society's leaders, who can slow down or accelerate the process. One cycle is an element of an infinite spiral-like process of society's evolution, the process that started in ancient times. Although the diagram shows borders between the stages, we do not notice how these borders are crossed because, actually, they are vague, and all social phenomena go smoothly and comparatively slowly.

Cyclic development of society is, in a certain sense, like the movement of the minute hand on a watch face. The hand, or rather the angle it makes, shows the degree of cohesion. Society's dynamics can be seen from the typical features, which are the function of society's cohesion. The watch hand goes through and returns to definite positions. The typical sectors on the watch face are like the following:

1. **Mass Reprisals.** They are necessary for shaping society and bringing pressure to bear on it. It is clear that a cycle begins by shaping a new society, and reprisals usually cannot be avoided.

2. **Absolute Dictatorship.** A newly shaped, ascetic society is securely held together both by new ideology and its young, charismatic leader, who becomes an absolute dictator. Those who do not accept this ideology or who do not agree with the dictator or do not want to be part of a closely knit society are exterminated. This society is highly aggressive; it is out to disseminate its ideology and expand its territory—in spite of its isolationism and closed borders. An ascetic society has a weak economy that has been ruined by civil war and reprisals and is geared to munitions production, and only the society's natural resources and pillaging its neighbors keep it alive.

3. **Oligarchy.** An oligarchy is made up of people who want to make the most of power and life. The asceticism and indifference to the good things of life

typical of the former leaders give way to an urge for enrichment. With a new impetus toward economic development, the economy is on the upgrade. Society's membrane becomes more transparent.

4. **Collective Leadership**. The leader's ageing and death militate against society's cohesion. His "comrades-in-arms" are replaced by "collective leadership." It may be a palace guard, political bureau, or anything of this kind.

5. **Democracy.** The "democracy" stage comprises several phases in society's degradation. The stage starts with the creation of parliament and the election of the leader and members of parliament. Some of its phases, such as dual power, are evident, while others remain obscure. It can be said that democracy is the first step to anarchy. This regime is a sign of society's split and degeneration. The split of society—at first hidden—into two halves will steadily grow and culminate in an acute hatred of one half for the other one. The nationalists (rightists) will make up one half, and the internationalists (leftists) will comprise the other half. The leftists will increasingly trample upon the moral principles embedded in religion and tradition, as well as society's laws and symbols. They will have a stronger position, partly owing to the support coming from outside the country. Their criticism of the powers-that-be and their slogans of freedom, equality, and brotherhood lavishly bandied about appeal both to individuals and to the masses because they involve "freedom of the personality" and promise to expand it. The masses do not realize that such slogans lead to anarchy rather than freedom. Even the

nationalists adopt these slogans. The result is that the society's center of gravity continues to slide toward lower cohesion and greater degradation. Previously, the way to power was somehow limited, and the potential leaders had to meet some criteria. Today, everything depends on advertising. Democracy is a stage marked by a flourishing of "class struggle" and terrorism.

6. **We May, You May Not.** This is the name for one of the phases of democracy when everything is trampled underfoot—culture, religion, morals, laws, and traditions. The process of rising amorality and the destruction of the framework and society's legal foundation goes into full swing. The judicial system begins collapsing. Treason, prompted by hatred for society or greed, becomes a commonplace occurrence.

7. **Anomie.** Anomie is a situation when society no longer has any leader worthy of this name. Those who come to power as a result of an advertising campaign or "democratic elections" are demoralized and impotent. The person on top is "impotent" as far as the intellect, personality, and capability to rule are concerned. This person can be a laughingstock; he may be insulted and spit in the face. Other symbols of the state and society—the flag, coat of arms, anthem—lose their meaning, as the person on top loses society's esteem. Society disintegrates into a multitude of sects and parties led by people whose only wish is to rule. A state of mob rule sets in. No religion unites the people, and morals and laws have been trampled underfoot. Patriotism, once a salient feature of the society, is gone.

What we see is the unfolding and flourishing of the "struggle for human rights," of pacifism, feminism, and other "isms," which actually conceal the hatred the internationalists feel for their society. Terrorism and crime, unrest, strikes, and protest marches plague society. At this point, society is falling apart, and its frontiers are disappearing along with its symbols. The economy functions, but the laws governing it are ignored. The situation is conducive to the growth of crime and corrupt practices.

8. **Dual Power.** This is an obvious stage inasmuch as, initially, central power exists parallel with independent local power, which may be exercised by a gang of criminals. However, in compliance with the "Iron Law of Oligarchy," this gang will be concerned about the stability of its position and will maintain order in its area with an iron hand. It is precisely for this reason that a gang may enjoy greater support of the local population than the impotent central power. Yet the main division of power takes place along ideological lines.

9. **Civil War.** The split in society and erosion of power culminates in civil war. The bifurcation [PP9] process starts with a "Revolution" and ends with the "Establishment of a New Society," or what I'm calling mass reprisals. Civil war is the transitional process between these two points.

If the territory occupied by society can be divided and each seceding part given its share, civil war can be avoided [PP10]. If there is no unoccupied territory and its division is physically impossible, "then each half will claim its former place, and civil war will break out."

The end of civil war completes the cycle, and everything returns to the point of departure.

The length of the cycle depends on the leaders or, rather, on the degree of their impotence.

In some cases, the armed forces interfere in the process. This interference takes the form of a fight for power if it occurs at the beginning of the cycle. If it occurs at the end of the process, this is an attempt to put an end to anarchy and halt the degradation process, in which case, it is a welcome development.

As a way helping to understand social dynamics, the above can be briefly laid down in terms of thermodynamics and synergetics as shown in the list that follows:

1. **Reprisals** is the process of deep freezing and entropy emission. Synergy.
2. **Absolute Dictatorship** is the cold-storage process. If the dictatorship is weak, that is, there are no reprisals, and the frontiers are not closed, society gets warmer, and entropy increases.
3. **Oligarchy** consumes energy. Ultimately, it leads to phase changes in society and its split. Oligarchy lays the foundations for the split between the rightists and leftists. The outcome, however, does not become obvious until the "democracy" stage sets in. Entropy continues to grow.
4. **Collective Leadership.** Oligarchy remains at the helm. Everything described in paragraph 3 is true.
5. **Democracy.** Society's split and degradation become obvious. Entropy grows at an accelerated pace. Strong fluctuations occur in the form of class struggle, putsches, and terrorism.

6. **We May, You May Not.** Since this stage is part of democracy, everything said in paragraph 5 remains true. Entropy grows, and hierarchy tumbles.

7. **Anomie.** Entropy reaches its maximum. There are strong fluctuations that can exceed the allowed threshold at any moment and not only stop the degradation process, but turn it in the opposite direction.

8. **Dual Power.** Entropy reaches its maximum. The degradation process gives way to a transitional process, uncertainty, and bifurcation.

9. **Civil War.** Civil war is a transitional process that does not allow any definite characterization.

Machiavelli sees the historical process as proceeding in cycles, that is, a sequence of forms of government in conformity with clear-cut laws. He believes that historical records reveal certain rules and principles in the sequence of these forms and cites examples to show that monarchy—one-man rule—is succeeded by oligarchy, oligarchy by republic, which again gives way to monarchy. Such is the state [power] of evolution, according to him. The cyclic character of the rise and fall of societies stems from the clashes of contradictions and interests, conflicts between small and large groups, which are part of society's life and "the order of things."

As long as you know the laws of society's development, you can make forecasts. In his article, "Cyclic Concepts of the Socio-Historical Process," Pitirim Sorokin says that Machiavelli was the first to advance the idea of cyclic development.

Speaking of the behavior of society, I have always stressed that it depends on the degree of its cohesion.

Cohesion is the main parameter of society, which should determine both the responsibility and the punishment of society. The various rules of war and instructions of all kinds, such as, for instance, concerning action against guerrilla detachments, ignore the nature and behavior of society. This attitude toward social problems can fuel guerilla movements and can even bring defeat to the invader, as was the case with the American troops in Vietnam. During that war, American presidents did not give a thought to the fact that the society inside their country was divided. Moreover, they prevented South Vietnamese leaders from uniting their society. Fifty years later, we see a recurrence of this situation in Iraq after Saddam Hussein, a dictator, was toppled. Three types of societies can be identified according to cohesion-based evaluation.

1. Over-united society (OUS), with a very high degree of cohesion of close to 100 percent.
2. Optimal society, with the degree of cohesion around 50 percent.
3. Anomie, a society with practically no cohesion—close to zero.

The above sequence corresponds to the process of society's degradation from absolute dictatorship, that is, OUS, to its complete disintegration.

OUS—GEMEINSCHAFT

Let us now return to our classification of societies and examine the "over-united society" (OUS) (point 1) in the list, its behavior and its joint responsibility and the possibility of *punishing* it. This examination can be found in many of my previous works. I repeat it here, to make it absolutely clear exactly what is being examined. Sociologists use the German term for this kind of society—*Gemeinschaft*. There are many variants of translation of this word into Russian, but none of these convey its essence. Therefore I prefer "OUS."

Below are some examples of *Gemeinschaft*.

More than a hundred years ago, in an old Russian village, there was an applicable law of joint responsibility. If a villager committed an offense, the entire peasant community was held responsible for it. If a villager refused to join the others in a breach of law, he was nevertheless held responsible according to the rule "one for all and all for one."

Joint responsibility or "guansi" is common in China. It is the guiding principle in dealing with many family or commercial affairs.

Golem

Leonard Broom and Philip Selznick describe the behavior of OUS members in their book *Sociology*. Some of their ideas are as follows:

If a person is bound by a profound sense of solidarity to a closely united group, he accepts the norms and values of this group. He no longer regards his own interests as differing from the interests of the group and does not consider himself an independent personality that can have a life differing from the life of this group or society.

The behavior of an OUS member can be expressed by just one word: "golem." A Japanese kamikaze sending an American aircraft carrier to the bottom of the sea or an Arab shahid blowing himself up in a coach are golems. They sacrifice their lives for the sake of their OUS. This sacrifice may be ostensibly made to God, a leader ("For Stalin!"), or other symbol ("For the Motherland!"). Emil Durkheim qualified such suicides as "altruistic." After their deaths, they are declared heroes and buried in state with crowds of mourners. The leader's death plunges society into a state of mass hysteria.

Our aim, however, is to dissect the behavior of society, rather than that of an individual. Below is another idea expressed in the same book:

A closely united society produces rules and norms governing the behavior of people and relationships between people. This kind of society gives its members a sense of confidence and safety, by establishing clear-cut rules of what is good and what is bad and by keeping daydreams within the limits of reasonable hope and actual possibilities.

The clear-cut rules of what is good and what is bad are reflected in the art of such a society. It bore the name of "classicism" or "socialist realism," depending on the time period. It should be added that OUS is isolated from other societies to a great extent.

Isolation may be caused by nature: forbidding mountains, seas, deserts, dense forests—or created by man: monastery walls, frontier guards, radio jamming, etc. It is the need for isolation that makes various gangs, sects, and lodges act in secrecy, and it drives them underground. Any cooperation of an OUS member with the authorities is cut short. If an OUS member tries to leave this society, he or she is eventually destroyed as a "traitor."

Isolation relieves OUS of any obligations to, and agreements with, other societies and countries. If there happens to be some agreements, honoring them is not considered an obligation.

An important consequence of isolation is the absence of economics (markets included) in an isolated society. Such a society does not progress and marks time at the level it had at the moment of the revolution that gave rise to it. Apposite examples in the world of today are Cuba, North Korea, or Muslim countries. This is why economic blockades as a collective *punishment* to an OUS is hardly of any use. OUS practices self-isolation and is stagnant, even without any blockade. Another argument confirming the ineffectiveness of economic blockades is the asceticism of OUS members. An ascetic does not need anything; he can even do without food as long as his *ego* is suppressed.

Asceticism

Fanatical asceticism of any OUS member and the society in general is a concomitant of isolation and excessive cohesion. It is hard to say which is the cause and which is the effect. Asceticism that leads to excessive cohesion and isolation cannot be excluded. Asceticism is known to have appeared some 500 years BCE. Judaism prohibits it. Ancient Greek sources, at that time, censured asceticism. Yet stoics and Buddhists won the minds by their readiness for self-sacrifice and primarily by their aggressiveness. Such ascetic religions as Christianity, Buddhism, Islam, and later, Communism spread across the world.

A golem's asceticism is manifested in how he prays. Lying prostrate on the ground and bowing incessantly are signs of self-flagellation, which is demonstrated with even greater clarity in martyrdom and other forms of self-torture. Sometimes, backbreaking work and voluntarily uniting in labor squads, *kibbutzes*, farms, etc., are substituted for martyrdom. In such cases, martyrdom is camouflaged.

Aggressiveness

Aggressiveness is a salient feature of OUS. Even when market and economics scale down to zero, OUS continues to manufacture weapons and to keep enormous armed forces, as can be seen in the "axis-of-evil" countries—Iran, some other Arab countries, Cuba, North Korea, and others. All of them hanker for weapons of mass destruction similar to an atom bomb. Even small sects, such as that of David Coresh in the United States or the Japanese Aum Shinri-kyo, had various weapons. In March 1995, this Japanese sect staged a gas attack in the Tokyo subway, killing twelve people and poisoning over five thousand. Isolation and aggressiveness are the breeding ground of bloody religious wars or fierce intergang fighting for territory and power.

In some situations, aggressiveness is viewed favorably, giving rise to stories about the exploits of heroes, knights, kamikazes, shahids, or something of this kind. There is no rationale for looking for examples in the history of the ancient world or the Middle Ages. Modern history abounds with such examples. For all that, I would like to mention two ancient Greek states—Sparta and Athens. Thanks to the Lycurgus laws, Sparta was an OUS and was famous for the feat of its three hundred warriors who, led by King Leonidas, defended the Pass of Thermopylae from a thousands-strong army of Persian King Xerxes. The Greeks had no hope of victory, as they knew that the Persians were outflanking them, but they decided they would rather die than surrender. And they were killed in action. Only one of them survived. He was ill, and Leonidas allowed him to stay in some settlement. Back in Sparta, he was ostracized; nobody would speak to him, and he was labeled a "coward." It was rumored that two more Spartans had survived. One of them was sent to Thessaly as a messenger, and when he returned home, he encountered the same treatment from his fellow townspeople. Ultimately, he hanged himself.

It is worth noting that the feat of the Spartans had no military results, because a traitor helped the Persians outflank Leonidas's detachment. Their feat, however, inspired Greeks to fight the Persians. In the following year, 479 BC, the Persian troops were completely routed in the battle near Plataea in Boeotia.

This story is proof positive that society's cohesion and the willingness of its members to sacrifice their lives is a more powerful factor for victory than the quality and quantity of weapons and even good military leadership.

Patriotism is another salient feature of all OUS members.

In OUS, as its name suggests, there can be **no opposition** or any sects, factions, or other organizations of this kind. Any manifestation of opposition is regarded as treachery and is suppressed.

Absence of morality is one more salient feature of OUS.

"We are not and cannot be guided by the old principles of morality and humaneness. We are not waging war against individuals. We are wiping out bourgeoisie as a class. You should not look in the investigation material for evidence that the accused has by word or deed acted against the Soviets. The first question you should put to him is about the class he belongs to, his background, education, or profession. It is these issues that must determine the fate of the accused. This is the meaning and essence of red terror."

The above is a citation from *Instructions to Checka Men* by Martin Latsis, a close associate of Felix Dzerzhinsky, head of the Cheka.

Relationships among OUS members are guided by the position of its members in the hierarchical pyramid, rather than morality or written laws.

✧ ✧ ✧

Entropy of the Personality

Further, we will show the impact that the degree of cohesion has on the behavior of society and its members. The graph in fig. 2 demonstrates the dependence of each personality's entropy on the degree of society's cohesion.

Entropy   50%   Cohesion   100%

Fig. 2. Entropy of the Personality

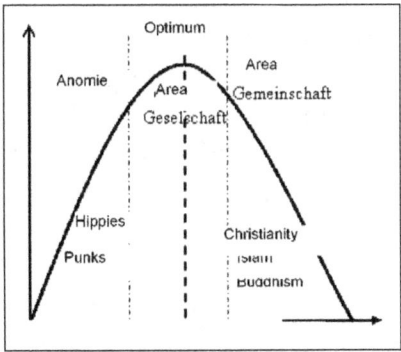

Entropy is a phenomenon of inquiry in the sphere of physics. In our case, it shows the degree of the freedom of personality. The graph shows that maximum entropy is observed in a society with 50 percent cohesion. Inasmuch as society's morals depend on entropy, the same graph illustrates the dependence of society's morals on its cohesion, measured in percent. "Demoralization" in the meaning it has today is not an apt expression in this case. The graph shows that a high-cohesion society and a society with very low cohesion do not have any morals. To avoid ambiguity, we will discuss the degradation of society, rather than demoralization. If cohesion is on the downgrade, society undergoes degradation.

The right-hand part of the graph, where cohesion is close to 100 percent, is separated from the rest by a vertical line. Any society in this area has a very high degree of cohesion. Sociology has a German word—*Gemeinschaft*—for this kind of society.

Religion unites people. Widespread confessions belonging in this area are listed in the graph. They are Christianity, Islam, Buddhism, Communism, etc. These confessions suppress the personality and preach asceticism and self-torture. People worship in prostrate positions.

A 100-percent-united society is a merciless dictatorship with minimal freedom of the personality. The personality is suppressed, turned into a golem, and does everything the leader wants it to do. This type of society breeds shahids, kamikazes, and other volunteers ready to give their lives for the "public weal." Society's cohesion in wartime must be very high.

The opposite end of the graph is anomie—society has fallen apart, and its cohesion is minimal. Instead of enjoying complete freedom, man, as a herd animal, craves society, rather than freedom. His sense of "hevraav" tells him that society is no more, and he tries to make up for it by challenging whatever is left of it. This is how hippies, punks, and similar crowds appear.

Split of Society

When cohesion is below 50 percent, society splits into two antagonistic camps—internationalists (leftists) and nationalists (rightists). Those who have a strong "team spirit" develop hatred for their society, as it does not satisfy their need for a team lifestyle. They make up the leftist camp. The internationalists hate their people and everything related to it—morals, traditions, religion, and culture. Society's degradation intensifies this hatred to a point where such people are ready to betray their country.

The split and degradation of society lead to the emergence in its midst of pacifists, sundry cult followers, and others who cannot be accused of open treason, but they refuse to do their term of military service (those with the conscience of conscientious objectors!) and are actually in opposition to their own country. It should be noted that although the leftists demand freedom and equality, what they need is reliable cohesion, which is the opposite.

In my *The Art of Governing Society*, a manual for leaders, I list the elements a leader must use when governing society.

1.   **Social hierarchy** is the helm in a leader's hands, which he uses to govern society. Social hierarchy is a tool of governance.

2.   Various **economic, political, and social symptoms** show the society's condition to leaders. Like a good physician, a leader must discern these symptoms, interpret them, and be guided by them. These symptoms point to society's main parameter; that is, they indicate the degree of its cohesion.

3.   A leader must know the **properties of society** and how to "apply brakes or accelerate," depending on the symptoms. He must foresee the consequences of his actions to be able to "apply brakes or accelerate" **in time or beforehand;** in other words, the leader must work toward lesser or greater cohesion. A leader must know how to regulate cohesion.

4.   **Cohesion of society** is the main and only parameter, which a leader controls and uses to find his bearings.

Chapter 2

War as an Element of Evolution of Society

Wars are one of the worst calamities mankind is exposed to (they may be particularly destructive in our nuclear age). Nevertheless wars occur, claim millions of lives, squander enormous resources that could have been used to improve the lot of the disadvantaged sections of the population. It is common knowledge. Still, why do wars occur?

In the not too distant past historians and political scientists viewed wars as the outcome of the decisions taken by heads of state and their close advisors and even by the entire population. The present level of society science (sociology) renders such views naïve, which they really are.

Timashev N.S. Kak voznikayut voiny?
(What Gives Rise to Wars?)
by Novy zhurnal
1968, No. 90, pp. 205–211.

Many people cannot understand that the history of mankind is filled with conquests and wars. Progress cannot put an end to wars. Moreover, munitions is the first field to make progress. In many cases, it is the manufacture of weapons that serves to advance science and technology.

If mankind cannot get rid of war, we must try to understand the phenomenon of war and get to its root causes.

Before getting down to the crux of the matter, I would like to touch upon the generally accepted notion that some wars are "good" and some are "bad" ("just" and "unjust"). I would like to focus the reader's attention on the criterion for placing wars in these two categories, since it is the run-of-the-mill moral criterion. But morals and ethics depend on the degree of society's cohesion. Societies with different degrees of cohesion have different morals and ethics. In the process of degradation, however, even in the same society, morals and ethics are discarded in times of peace just as they are in time of war.

Evolution and Its Laws

Evolution, according to Darwin, is a statistical selection of rare events. In the animal world, the selection is done by other species. Wolves weed out deer by attacking the "bad"—the sick and the old. The "good" ones can run fast enough to leave the wolves behind.

People have no enemies among the animals. Who is it then that does the selection, categorizing people into "good" and "bad"? In my work, *Civil War, Terrorism, and Brigandage,* a chapter is devoted to *amphigony,* which is common to all mammals and is caused by the need to adapt to the environment. Man is also a mammal and has to adapt to the environment, and here is where "natural selection" comes into play.

The next stage of the evolution takes place on a higher level—on the pack or society level. It is a life or death fight for territory among animal packs of the same species. Today, this fight for territory is typical of rats or monkeys.

Let's assume that there are two societies. Which of them is "good" and which is "bad"? We have no criteria or any way to examine them to answer this question. Human evolution has been going on for at least thirty thousand years, and in this relatively short period, a Neanderthal man evolved into a man of the atomic and computer civilization of today. The landmarks along the way were the Stone, Bronze, and Iron ages, the ages of steam engines and electricity. What is the criterion for selection?

The selection system is as simple as the elimination system to select participants in the Olympic Games. Of the two societies or countries locked in an armed conflict, the defeated one is "eliminated." This system is cruel but fast and reliable. What remains of the defeated combatant may be dug out thousands of years later, as was the case with what remained of Carthage. It may happen that even a good team is defeated and "eliminated." This is the course the evolution of humankind takes and the way a hierarchy of societies is formed, with some on top and others below them. In some cases, the victors adopt the culture of the defeated.

A struggle, or rather a war, ensues, like that among rats or monkeys, for territory, wealth, and power over others.

Sociology does not regard war as an indispensable element of natural selection and evolution. However, war is the yardstick to assess whether the changes (mutations) that take place in the course of one cycle are "good" or "bad." It is clear that the victor had "good" changes and in sufficient amounts.

Bifurcation

"Each historian knows that studying an exceptional role in history of some personalities presupposes an analysis of

social and historical mechanisms that made this role possible. The historian also knows that if such personalities had not existed, the same mechanisms could have shaped a different history." Prigozhin I., Stengers M. Vremya, khaoc kvant (Time, Chaos, Quantum). Moscow, 1994, pp. 54–55

Bifurcation is the term derived from *bifurcus* (Latin) meaning "split into two." It is used in a broad sense to denote various qualitative changes or metamorphoses of various objects caused by changes in their basic parameters. Mathematician Yakobi first used the term in 1834. Below are some examples of the usage of the word "bifurcation."

Bifurcation in medicine: a tubulous organ—a vessel or bronchus—branching out into two vessels or bronchi of equal caliber and at equal angles. In mathematics: bifurcation changes the number and stability of equation solutions.

Bifurcation is a change in the character of a dynamic system movement over a long period of time, if one or several parameters are changed. The parameter values that change the movement's qualitative or topological properties are called critical or bifurcation values. For instance, compression of a core causes its bulging, with a certain state of equilibrium to lose its stability, and to be replaced by new stable states of equilibrium.

Imagine a column with rectangular cross section exposed to downward pressure P (see fig. 1).

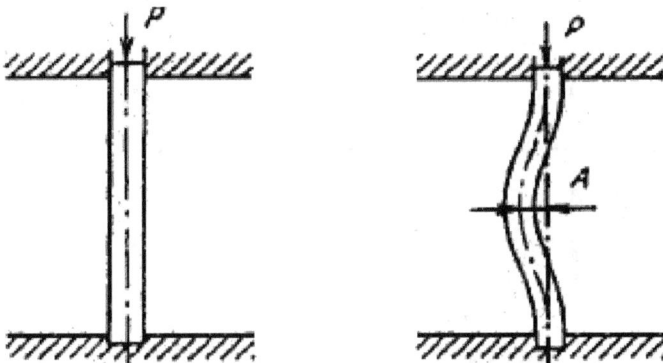

Fig. 1.

As the pressure increases, the column grows shorter and thicker, but its axis remains straight as is shown in the left-hand drawing. When Pc reaches some critical value, a qualitative change occurs: the column loses its rectangular form and bulges rightward or leftward (right-hand drawing). With $P<P_c$, the column has one form of equilibrium only. With $P>P_c$ there are three forms of equilibrium— the rectangular form, which has become unstable, and two stable forms (one with a rightward bulge, the other with a leftward bulge). Column axis bulge A plotted against pressure **P** produces the picture shown in fig. 2.

In fig. 2, below, the stable states of equilibrium are on the solid line, and the unstable states are on the broken line. With **P=Pc** the number of equilibrium states and their stability change.

Point

(Force)
Fig. 2. Pitchfork.

Bifurcation point is a critical value reached by the "dominant" variable (force), which upsets the system's equilibrium. At the **P=Pc** bifurcation point, the system acquires a "choice" with a share of randomness, which makes it impossible to forecast further development of the system.

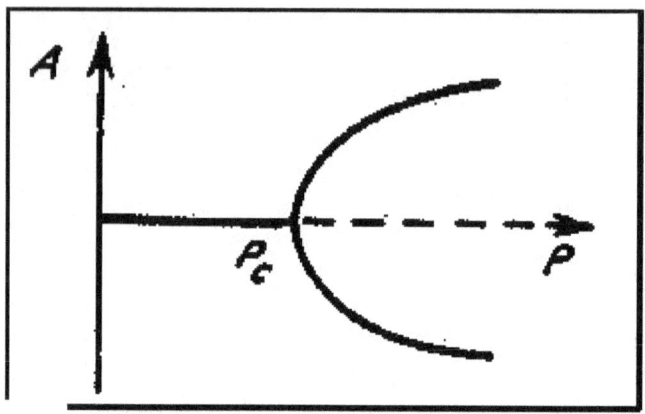

In physics, the meaning of this phenomenon is clear, because the force may be described by means of *potential* energy. When **P>Pc**, which is a one-well potential, is replaced by a two-well potential, the system dynamics undergo a qualitative change. That is why **P=Pc** is a critical bifurcation value.

Bifurcation allows many solutions of a problem, and we do not know which of them is the best. As the example of the column shows, we have two stable solutions—leftward or rightward bulge. No matter how many times the experiment with the column is repeated, the column will bulge leftward or rightward, but *the result will be always unpredictable.*

War Is Bifurcation

War can be described as a column with two forces acting on its abutting ends in opposite directions: P_l—leftward and P_r—rightward. Irrespective of the compression forces ratio, there are only three random outcomes of this process. (1.) The broken line—war has not changed the position of the belligerents, which means that the equilibrium is unstable. (2.) The upper branch of the parabolic curve—there will be a winner and a loser. (3.) The lower branch of the parabolic curve—as in the previous case with the opposite results for the belligerents.

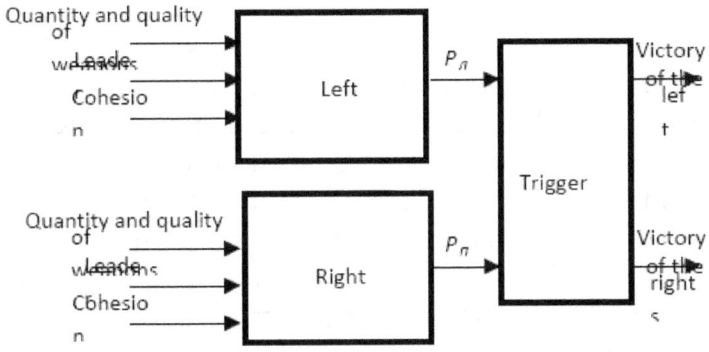

Fig. 3. War as the transformer of initial data into victory

The diagram shows war as a process of transforming initial values, first into acting force P and then into victory.

The protracted and bloody Iran-Iraq war (1980–1988) was an instance of unstable equilibrium. Iraq used chemical agents, and Iran used its teenagers and elderly people as cannon fodder. There were no winners. The relations between the two countries were hostile for a long time, but none of them had the capability of restarting hostilities.

The cold war can be seen as a kind of unstable equilibrium. A wild occurrence, however, may put an end to instability and a turn cold war into a hot one.

Bifurcation is uncertainty. We do not know which way the column will bulge, nor do we know the outcome of war. There are too many unknown quantities; therefore, as Machiavelli said, it is easy to begin war but difficult to end it.

A gifted leader is as important for victory as the weaponry. It may happen that the leader is mediocre or impotent or even that there is no leader. The German Emperor Wilhelm II did not expect that the war he had begun in August 1914 would become a world war, last long, and end by his abdication.

Today, the chances of victory in a war are evaluated in terms of the quantity and quality of the belligerents' armed forces. There is no sense in counting them as they are evident, but there is no doubt that the counting detracts from uncertainty. Social factors, however, which are not evident and are incomprehensible for many leaders, are completely ignored. This is the main reason for the US defeat in Vietnam, the USSR's defeat in Afghanistan, or Israel's setbacks in its war with Arabs.

This work is an attempt to draw attention to these factors and highlight their significance.

Rules of War

Pereat mundus et fiat justitia
While recognizing the right of Israel to self-defense, I censure the disproportionate and excessive use of force, as a result of which many civilians, including children, were killed.
Statement by the UN Secretary-General Ban Ki-moon at a session of the Security Council

There are two kinds of rules (sometimes referred to as "laws") of war: one kind is called strategy and tactics. Would-be generals study them at military academies to learn strategies to defeat the enemy. These rules ignore morals, humaneness, and other "idle talk." The main thing is to defeat and do away with the enemy.

The other kind of rules, devised by politicians, are laid down in various international agreements and conventions, which forbid the military to do certain things—for instance, to use weapons of mass destruction, including toxic gases, biological, and nuclear weapons. When formulating such rules, politicians are guided by public opinion, morals, and all other issues of "idle talk."

One can see that in the first case, the rules, though ignoring morals and humaneness, are aimed at attaining rapid victory with minimal casualties, while in the second case, the rules provide for some restrictions that protract the war and work to bring defeat.

In the first case, the rules are learned with the help of military role games and exercises. In the second case, politicians, philosophers, lawyers, and journalists formulate them as a warning to the military that they could be declared war criminals and brought to the International Court of Justice in The Hague.

This work will deal with the second kind of rules, as they have a closer relation to sociology. The first kind is the realm of gifted military commanders.

In this work, "rules of war" will refer to the second kind of rules only.

The History of the "Rules of War"

Some philanthropists may think that it is possible in some artificial way to disarm and rout without much bloodshed and that it is what military art should strive for. Tempting as this idea is, it is a delusion that must be dispelled. War is a dangerous thing and delusions stemming from ingrained optimism are the most calamitous to it.

Von Clausewitz

According to the current international law, wars cannot be prevented, but they can be made more "humane" and less cruel.

The rules of treating people whom a stroke of fate placed in the hands of the enemy were drafted in various periods and in different parts of the world. They differed in many respects. People in primitive tribes used to eat their prisoners. In ancient times, prisoners were used as slaves. In those times, war was bifurcation pure and simple. There were no problems like those that the world faces today.

Today, international law is based on the right to war (*jus ad bellum* in Latin). Naïve politicians and philosophers contend that these rules rest on theoretical and historical foundations. Theory is supposed to have philosophic and ethical substantiations for the rules of war, namely, "traditions of waging war that have been formed in the course of centuries." For instance, the rules of war specify the circumstances that give a state the right to use military force.

In his book, *War Crimes and Laws of Wars,* Donald Wells (http://www.washprofile.org/ru/node/4896) says that laws of war are subject to change in different periods. The first suggestion that rules of war should be set came as far back as the sixth century BCE from Sunzi, a Chinese warrior and philosopher, the author of the book, *Art of War.* In approximately 200 BCE, introducing the notion of "war criminal" appeared in India. Cicero, the great Roman orator, philosopher, and politician, held that that the only justified reasons for war were defense of a state's honor or security.

Rules of war are also defined in the Jewish Torah. They can hardly be called "humane," rather they are "expedient."

The spread of Christianity imparted a new meaning of war. Initially, Christians advocated pacifism. Later, however, their "Christian principles" were combined with cruelty. St. Augustine pointed out that fighting the forces of evil by waging a religious war was permissible. And Thomas Aquinas, a Middle Ages scholastic, formulated the reasons for starting war (a state must have a legitimate power).

Maurice Keen—a historian and author of the book, *The Law of War in the Late Middle Ages*—considers it significant that the first trial connected with cruel treatment of the civilian population was held in Western Europe in 1305. In that year, the English court sentenced to death William Wallace, Scotland's national leader, for killing noncombatants. Actually, however, there were other reasons behind this sentence.

In 1625, the Dutch lawyer Hugo Grotius, "the father of international law," published his *De jure belli ac pacis libri tres (On the Law of War and Peace)*, in which he formulated the rules of humane treatment of the civilian population. This work is regarded as the basis of the

concept of war in modern international law. Judging by the records of wars, his rules were never observed.

Jean-Jacques Rousseau's *The Social Contract, Or Principles of Political Right* was published in 1762. In this work, he wrote: "War is the relationships between states, not between people, and people become enemies by chance and the enmity is not between human beings, not even between citizens, but between soldiers, not between residents of their country, but because of being its defenders. If the purpose of war is to destroy the enemy state, the other side shall have the right to wipe out its defenders, as long as they carry arms, but the moment they throw down their arms and surrender, they stop being enemies or tools in the hands of the enemies and, again, become ordinary people, and nobody has the right to claim their lives." He was very sparing of humaneness, however, toward his children born by his cook.

International codes of war were revised and supplemented many times, and numerous new protocols were added to them. There are, for example, four Geneva Conventions and four additional protocols to them. Work in this field never abates, since the nature of war keeps changing. The first attempts to formulate the rules of war suitable for the present-day situation are already being made. In 2004, the US Department of Defense published its *Final Report of the Independent Panel to Review Detention Operations*, on detaining foreigners suspected of terrorist activities. The report suggested that the principle of reciprocity be introduced; that is, the actions of the persons suspected of terrorism should be evaluated proceeding from the actual harm the suspect inflicted or attempted to inflict.

David P. Cavaleri, the author of *The Law of War: Can 20th-Century Standards Apply to the Global War on Terror-*

ism? published by the Combat Studies Institute, came to the conclusion that additional legal research was necessary to answer this question. But what legal research can help fight instincts?

In 1859, Jean Henri Dunant, a Swiss banker (commonly known as Henri Dunant), chanced to witness the battle of Solferino (Austro-Hungarian Empire against France and Piedmont-Sardinia kingdom). Thousands of wounded were lying on the battlefield, and the medics were unable to take care of all of them. Dunant managed to organize the locals who tried to take the wounded from the battlefield and help them as best as they could. He published a book about this experience, which became a bestseller in Switzerland and drew the attention of the authorities. In 1863, Dunant and other like-minded people founded the Geneva-based International Committee for Relief to the Wounded and initiated the signing of the Geneva Convention that laid down the rules for the conduct of armies during hostilities (it entered into force in 1865), as well as the rules for obligatory protection of the sick, wounded, medics, and hospitals. The convention stipulated that they be given humane treatment and all possible relief. In 1901, Dunant was awarded the first ever Nobel Peace Prize.

After this Geneva Convention appeared, many of the world's armies (including the US army) issued manuals for officers and men on rules of waging war. In 1865, a Confederate Army officer was found guilty of killing prisoners of war and was executed.

The Second International Red Cross Congress meeting in 1868 added new rules, in particular rules concerning war action at sea. Among them was the following provision: if a ship flying the flag of an enemy country is under threat of shipwreck, this ship (its crew and passengers) are granted temporary neutral status, effective until the ship is brought to a safe port.

In 1896, Tsar Nicholas II, emperor of Russia, proposed to convene an international conference on the reduction of armed forces and the peaceful settlement of international conflicts. One of the results of his peace-making effort was a congress in The Hague (Netherlands) that approved some conventions, one of them on laws and customs of hostilities on land. It provided for the treatment of the wounded and sick, "unlawful participants in the conflict," according to the rules laid down in the Geneva Convention while it strictly forbade shooting down wounded enemy soldiers. Immoral Bolsheviks shot down the humane tsar and his family.

Stephen Neff, the author of *War and the Law of Nations: A General History*, notes that international law rests on two pillars—the Hague Convention that sets the rules for hostilities based on the principles of military need and proportionality (for instance, it lists the types of weapons allowed and not allowed), while the Geneva Convention puts stresses the humanitarian provisions.

A regular Geneva Congress took place in 1929, after the First World War, which claimed dozens of millions of lives, with radically new types of weapons, such as poisonous gases, aviation weaponry, and tanks, used for the first time. The Congress was called upon to set new rules of war required under the new conditions. The "constitution of war" was further extended by new provisions, namely, war prisoners should be given humane treatment and removed from places where there is a threat to their lives and health (for instance, if the frontline comes too close to POW camps), they must not be put into prison, and their rations must be identical to those received by the soldiers of the army that captured them.

The Second World War (1939–1945) was notorious for inhuman treatment of war prisoners and the civilian population. After the war, the victorious countries for the first ever time in history held two tribunals—in Nuremberg and Tokyo—at which German and Japanese high-placed statesmen and military commanders guilty of "war crimes and crimes against humanity" (prisoners of war included) were convicted.

Earlier efforts did not go beyond attempts to convict people for breach of war rules. In 1919, Great Britain tried to take the German Kaiser Wilhelm II to international court, since it blamed him for causing the First World War and for the war crimes committed by the German armed forces. At approximately that same time, Yugoslavia tried to bring action against Bulgarians who committed acts of mass violence against the civilian Serbian population. An attempt was made in 1918 to set up a tribunal for the investigation of mass killings of Armenians by Turks. India was out to sue the Pakistani military for their crimes in Bangladesh. (In 1972, some experts characterized some actions by Pakistanis as genocide.)

The USA urged the establishment of an international tribunal for the examination of the crimes committed by Iraqis against Kuwait civilians (1990–1991) and Kurds.

In 1997, Pol Pot, the leader of the "Red Khmers," guilty of genocide against his own people, was captured. At that time, the possibility of setting up a special tribunal for Cambodia was mooted in the United Nations. Today, international tribunals function in the UN framework and try people suspected of committing war crimes in the former Yugoslavia, Rwanda, and elsewhere.

Nineteen forty-nine saw the appearance of a new edition of the Geneva Convention. Many provisions were extended and better formulated. For instance, the expression "humane treatment of war prisoners" was deciphered as prohibiting killing, torture, threats to life and health, discrimination on the grounds of race, ethnic origin, and religious beliefs, extrajudicial executions, etc. The status of war prisoners was accorded to civilians fighting in resistance groups, crews of civilian ships, journalists, and local residents, who volunteered to take up arms and offer resistance to the invading enemy troops (provided they carried arms openly). Civilians in occupied territories could not be made to work without decent remuneration. In 1977, two more protocols protecting victims of war, civilian populations, and war prisoners were added to the Geneva Convention.

In subsequent years, international organizations and judicial authorities based their decisions on the articles of the Geneva and Hague conventions. The UN supported these rules on many occasions.

Michael Byers, the author of *War Law: Understanding International Law and Armed Conflict*, writes that inherent contradictions in these rules surface during almost every armed conflict.

The Hague Convention prohibited the use of percussion (dumdum) bullets; nevertheless, they were used against armies of the countries that had not signed this convention. Simultaneously, shooting wounded soldiers was prohibited, but nothing was said about the crews of disabled planes and tanks.

In 1981, after Israel bombed out the Iraqi atomic reactor that could be used to produce nuclear weapons, the USA declared that preventive strikes were not acceptable. In 2003, Washington held an entirely different view.

Today, the armed forces of many countries have weapons (bombs, missiles) capable of hitting people indiscriminately—not only combatants, who are seen as legitimate targets during hostilities, but civilian populations as well.

Discussion of the Rules

Let us begin with sea piracy, which is a breach of all rules and agreements. Today, we see its revival and growth. A salient feature of modern sea piracy is that it is rarely an object of countermeasures or complaints. Modern piracy is a commercial problem, only, whose impact does not spread beyond the interests of some shipping or insurance companies.

The rules of war are vague and are changed often. The changes depend on the mentality of the belligerents. It took a relatively short time for the United States to go from condemning the Israeli preventive attacks on the Iraqi nuclear facilities in 1981 to gratitude to Israel for rendering the Middle East free from nuclear threat by the time they were fighting in Iraq. What were the "new conditions" that were the subject of discussion at the Geneva Congress in 1929? The rules of war being drafted had to take into account these "conditions." These rules were completely ignored just ten years later, after the outbreak of the Second World War. The attitude toward war and, consequently, its rules depend on religion and its role in society. A religious sect just born is weak and champions peace. As its strength grows, such religion generates both ascetics and fanatics capable of mercilessly killing their adversaries and heretics. None of the rules of war ever mentioned this. Asceticism was not prohibited. Altruistic suicide of the type of Japanese kamikaze or Arab shahids, who explode buses with passengers in them, arouses admiration instead of censure.

There is no reciprocity in any of the "humane" rules. The strong hits the weak. In the case of Kosovo, the USA did not wait for Russia's veto in the Security Council and invoked a provision from the NATO Charter on protection of human rights (Sic) to bomb Yugoslavia. What has NATO to do with Kosovo and Yugoslavia? When the USA recently expressed its displeasure to Russia and Belarus with the violation of human rights in these countries, the response was "mind your own business." What is the US yardstick for measuring human rights to empower it to rectify the situation? Perhaps NATO should start bombing Russia to protect "human rights" there?

The victors tried to use the rules to dodge responsibility for the harm done to the adversary, avoid vengeance, and impose their domination.

The United States shows every support for the International Court of Justice in the Hague, but it does not even occur to it that this court can also be used to try the USA's military, which is now found throughout the world. A closer look at all cases of punishment for "war crimes" will reveal that all "war criminals" were the defeated. Victors are not judged.

In his book, *Three Cheers for Conscientious Objector Working for Civil Loyalty,* Professor Leon Shelef of Tel Aviv University extols those whose "conscience" urges them to refuse to observe laws and obey orders. The professor is an undercover pacifist, and his book is an undisguised call for trampling underfoot laws, morals, and traditions, a call for disobedience and anarchy. This is how "prisoners of conscience" appear. No wonder terrorists and traitors use this book as a manual—the book by Leon Shelef, published at the expense of the Israeli taxpayer. Thus, there are those who write rules and those who write how to ignore them. I would like to stress that incitement to disobedience and the justification of crimes does not come from such sophomores as Ben Gurion or Lev Trotsky but from professors, and even judges, which gives rise to a paradoxical dilemma—who is to be heeded?

The Meaning of the Rules of War

Despite the Holy Alliance, the Triple, and Quadruple alliances, Great Power Balance, the Entente, Pan-Asian, and Pan-American alliance wars have not been relegated to oblivion, and their number has not been reduced. Despite the League of Nations, the International Court of Justice in the Hague, and the numerous international conferences and treaties designed to put an end to wars, they are still waged. Actually, the League of Nations, conferences, and treaties were followed by the bloodiest war in the history of mankind. If the Leviathan states remain sovereign and their governments remain free to make decisions on the issues of war and peace, new similar attempts will not bring lasting peace to mankind.
Pitirim Sorokin, Prichiny voiny i usloviya mira
(The Causes of War and the Terms of Peace).
Sotsiologicheskiye issledovaniya
(Sociological Research). 1993, No. 12, pp.140–148

At the beginning of this chapter, I mentioned that the rules of war were designed to mitigate wars and make them less cruel and bloody. Declarations vs. realities, however, may be far apart.

Some countries and organizations, such as the International Red Cross, are out to use the rules of war to enhance their influence and authority. The same International Red Cross did not do anything to exercise its authority during the Second World War when Germany made short shrift of anyone who did not fit into the Fuehrer's race theory. Today, this organization is trying to worm its way into any place where it hopes to be tolerated.

Rules of war can be compared to pacifism—they are taken out when they are needed and are hidden when they are obstacles. They are sometimes used to intimidate, and at other times, they are trampled underfoot. What are the criteria used by the International Red Cross and other "humanistic" organizations to determine whether or not some reprisals or war are "adequate" or "excessive" responses? To demand an adequate response is an attempt at equal treatment of the aggressor and the victim of aggression. This demand may lead to a longer conflict involving more bloodshed.

As I already wrote in my book, *Civil War, Terrorism, and Brigandage,* in time of war, there are neither authorities nor forces capable of monitoring the observance of the rules of war and of compelling nations to observe them. That is the main hitch. Even if such authorities and forces were established, they would not be able to function normally in time of war. Cases in point are the impotence of the United Nations, paralyzed by the rivalry between the great powers, and the International Court of Justice, which is a pawn in the hands of NATO and the USA.

The rules of war have proved to be a bag, which the coalition that may be referred to as the "Democratic West" has put on its head. Today, it is trying to get rid of the bag without realizing that it has a bag on its head.

The problem is that the leaders of the "Democratic West" are nonentities who are unable to grasp the situation they have created and then get out of it. They keep talking about freedom, democracy, and humanism, without realizing that these comprise the bag they put on their heads. They do not understand that any over-united society—from a terrorist gang to a country like Iran—does not care a fig for any agreements or "Rules of War" and is aggressive to boot.

What are the criteria the judges of the International Court of Justice are guided by when they pass a judgment? Such criteria do not exist. I introduced the notion of morality in my work, *Civil War, Terrorism, and Brigandage,* in which I showed that morals depend on the degree of society's cohesion. Modern, "civilized" society has no morals left, just as it has no criteria to distinguish the good from the bad.

New Times—New Rules

In the past, the belligerents were neighbors who differed, but little, as far as their culture and morals were concerned, which made some rules possible. Today, the situation is different. In the past, colonizers fought primitive tribes without any rules. Today, these tribes have spilled over into former metropolitan countries in great multitudes, using the colonizers' humaneness to their advantage. Although they have not yet adopted the culture of the ex-colonizers, they already want to have all the boons civilization can bring.

Today, the Western world with its democracy is suffering from terrorism and guerilla wars "for independence." It is unaware of the social causes. Instead of fighting evil, the Western world is engaged in talk about humanism, morality, ethics, etc. It is high time it realizes that morality is a relative notion and that morals depend on the degree of society's cohesion.

Tony Blair, as prime minister of Great Britain, declared that modern antiterrorist strategy should be revised. He said that radicals should be fought, not only by military means but also by addressing such worldwide issues as climate change and poverty, as well as by drafting uniform trade rules.

Tony Blair as *former* prime minister made a really sweeping move, going even farther than myself. In my work, I have kept repeating that radicalism is a social problem to be dealt with by social means, by reprisals. But what does it have to do with world problems and uniform trade rules? Tony Blair is trying to put the cart before the horse when he says that poverty must be done away with to prevent extremism. First, radicalism and extremism must be done away with, and then poverty will disappear of itself.

Tony Blair's pronouncements show once again that politicians do not know anything and do not know how to do anything. Nevertheless, Tony Blair was appointed "peacemaker" in the Middle East. He promised to do everything he could to put an end to the conflict. He believes that great harm has been done to "moderate forces" that slow down the termination of the crisis. What are these "moderate forces"?

War against terrorism is the main war of our times. All rules and conventions, which took the Western world so much time to formalize, militate against victory in this war. These rules have united the Western world and put it in one bag, but fighting terrorism takes more than a coalition in a bag. The USA as the leader of the fight against terrorism should persuade the coalition members that the new military actions are justified, both from moral and legal points of view; in other words, they should persuade coalition members that war against terrorism protects law and order, which are the terrorists' targets.

Differences in the "coalition bag" do not derive just from the unwillingness of its members to pull the chestnuts out of the fire. There is no clear-cut line between the fight against terrorism and the wish of some coalition members to make use of this fight for plundering some country. This is exactly what the USA is doing. Having "protected human rights" in Kosovo by air attacks on Serbia, the USA established a major military base in Kosovo without any consent of Serbia or Yugoslavia.

There is little credence to what the US president says. It is this US policy that arouses wariness and distrust on the part of Russia and China.

On the other hand, the rules of war are no obstacle to the terrorist gangs and "freedom fighters" of all hues. The thing is that people in these gangs have no morals, nor do they crave money. They crave power, not money. They ignore all "humane" agreements and conventions. They do not invoke the rules of war unless they can pursue their objectives by taking advantage of them.

Terrorists will stop at nothing to attain their objectives. They will bend over backward to get weapons of mass destruction. Once they have them, there is nothing to prevent them from using them as a means of blackmail or as a means of warfare.

In my work, *Civil War, Terrorism, and Brigandage,* I wrote how and why terrorism appears, how gangs are formed, and how they grow.

Israel and Terrorism

Israel is one of the countries with its "head in the bag." At the same time, Israel suffers from Arab terrorism infinitely more than any other country. Israeli society is in a state of far-gone degradation and is split into two antagonistic camps. One of these camps, the nationalists, is ready to get out of the bag and start fighting terrorism. The other camp, the internationalists, actually regards terrorists as its allies in their confrontation with the rightists and invokes humaneness and rules of war as a smokescreen to paralyze the fight against terrorism. A concomitant of the over-united society is the disappearance of morals. "The end justifies the means" becomes the guiding principle of Arabs who are ready to go to all lengths for the sake of victory; they even do not hesitate to send their children to fight. Israel's response is "pinpoint strikes," lest the innocent should be injured. War is a clash of two societies, not of house neighbors. If the Arabs want to fight the Jews, the response of the Jews should be of the same kind, not according to the rules of war and without categorizing the enemies into "good" and "bad."

Israel is a showcase of the roots of humaneness and pacifism and of who benefits from them and how.

Rules of War and Bifurcation

The bifurcation examined above has an indestructible symmetry. The "rules of war" impose certain restrictions on the way war is waged. They are supposed to apply to both warring sides and be symmetrical. Yet the side that ignores them gets a free hand and military advantages. Naturally, the other side also begins to ignore the rules of war because, otherwise, it may be defeated.

Rules of war should be cut to a minimum. In time of war, moral norms shrink. This holds true for one's own society and for the enemy society. The rules of war are talked about much but hardly ever observed. And those who do observe them find their heads in a bag.

Machiavelli Is Exonerated

Although Machiavelli was a genius, his works are usually censured, and they have not been appreciated in the five hundred years since they appeared. Why? After five hundred years, some of his assertions have had to be updated and specified, but this does not mean that his work as a whole is worthless and harmful.

I do not know of any leader or monarch who had admitted taking his cue from Machiavelli. Instinct prompted Hitler and Stalin to act according to Machiavelli's recommendations, but they were completely unaware whose ideas they were implementing. Those who "heeded" Machiavelli rank among charismatic leaders; those who did not rank among impotents.

Rules of War and Machiavelli

Machiavelli is accused of immorality. Society's morals are a function of its cohesion, and morality is a relative notion. What is moral in one society may be considered immoral in another. What is moral today may become immoral tomorrow and vice versa. The French eat frogs, while Jews have an aversion to pork. It is quite possible that something that is reprehensible according to Bertrand Russell's moral code is commendable according to my moral code and vice versa. Now let us assume that Bertrand Russell and myself are warring sides. While he is restricted by his moral code and thinking of a moral way to finish me off, I will finish him off using the means he considers immoral.

Wars were, are, and will be fought without any restrictions, let alone "moral" restrictions or "pangs of conscience." All means are good if they serve to defeat the enemy—"the end justifies the means."

When the United States dropped two atomic bombs on Japan, its mortal enemy, it virtually acted as I acted vis-à-vis Bertrand Russell. True, fifty years later, there were those who took the side of the Japanese and condemned the United States' actions, but during the war, there were no such sentiments—there was only delight. Moreover, instead of condemning the US administration, the Communists hastened to smuggle the atomic bomb secrets into the USSR.

Today, use of weapons of mass destruction, atomic weapons included, is considered immoral. Let us go back to "immoral Machiavelli." It is no secret that many people want to acquire weapons of mass destruction and use them against their enemies. Such people are now called "terrorists." Who are their enemies? Their idea of an enemy is *he that is not with us is against us!*

The cold war between the "free West" and the Communist East was a war of two ideologies and of "morality" against "immorality." It ended by various agreements that restricted the amount of weapons and their proliferation. Strange as it may seem, the collapse of the *Iron Curtain* between the West and the East made these agreements worthless. Today, nothing stands in the way of using nuclear weapons. And they certainly will be used when somebody's urge to do so becomes irresistible.

Professor Asa Kasher's Codes

There are local rules of war apart from the international rules. The Japanese had the Bushido Code of the Warrior, applicable to the samurai only. Samurai were a privileged caste of warriors, who were entitled to carry two swords at a time and boasted the name of *bushi* (warrior), that is, a man who defied death and lived by special laws of *bushido* (the Warrior Way). The life of every samurai was dedicated to serving his master, from whom he took orders and whom he had to obey. An austere ascetic, highly disciplined life was considered an ideal. Martial skills polished to perfection were an art and a way of life. Translated into modern notions, the samurai are a special task force, and an individual samurai is a golem, an ascetic without any wish for anything for himself personally, infinitely loyal to his master and fulfilling his orders. A samurai army is a formidable force; it is not for nothing that all the world's languages borrowed the Japanese word "kamikaze."

Asa Kasher, professor of philosophy, is far from trying to bring together the officers and men of the Israeli Defense Army by means of a Bushido-like code. He is a leftist, an internationalist, and an anarchist. His code, like the rules of war, is a straitjacket put on the soldier to render him defenseless. Asa Kasher's code and ethics are designed to demoralize the Israeli armed forces.

The powerful US armed forces, stuffed by electronics to overflowing, also have a host of lawyers watching the fighting men to prevent them from breaking sundry rules and codes. A look at Prof. Kasher will tell you where the half-witted authors of rules and codes come from.

Apart from written codes, there are oral codes that take the form of talk about the "arms' purity," "refraining from coming down to the enemy's level," "innocent victims," and so on in the same vein. Lawyers do not accompany Israeli soldiers sent to do the fighting, but instead of bulletproof vests, they are clothed in the straitjackets of rules and moral codes. Violation of these rules and codes is a punishable offense.

In addition to a soldier's straightjacket, Asa Kasher has devised a university chair and professorial jobs for himself and his wife and lives off this ethics. He writes the ethical rules for the Knesset members and soccer players, and the mass media give him good advertising. The *Wikipedia* in the Hebrew language gives some details about Professor Asa Kasher. One gets the impression that he is the main Israeli authority on ethics—author and editor of books on ethics, chairman, or member of all centers and committees on ethics, and so on and so forth. In the past several years, he took part in scores of international congresses on the fight against terrorism, "arms' purity," and morality. He is much sought after and seems to have hardly any time for sitting on committees, writing, and eating—a veritable jack-of-all-trades. He has been teaching ethics in the National Military Academy and in the Academy of the Israeli Armed Forces General Staff for twenty-five years now. No wonder that these academies have graduates like Dan Khaluts and that the Israeli armed forces are degrading.

What makes Asa Kasher special is that he is a leftist, even an extreme leftist, which for him seems to be the door opener to all newspapers and magazines, committees, and academies. This does not mean that he is very bright, rather the contrary. He is a golem guided by his own instincts. When talking of morality and democracy, he reveals his ignorance and complete lack of understanding of either one or the other. Yet he writes instructions to Israeli soldiers and holds forth on "democratic values."

War Criminals

Criminals in general are supposed to have broken some laws or at least some moral norms. This cannot be applied to the so-called war criminals, as they are nonexistent by definition. There can be no laws of war, as all means are good if they serve to attain victory and crush the enemy. There are conventions that prohibit one thing or another. But how do other countries make the USA, for instance, honor a convention if it does not want to? There was a time when the Soviet Union refused to sign the convention on war prisoners; today, the USA does not want to sign the Kyoto agreements on the protection of the environment.

The issue of punishing war criminals first arose at the beginning of World War II. On December 4, 1941, the Soviet government published a declaration that, for the first time in history, pointed out that punishment of war criminals was inseparably linked with ensuring lasting and just peace. "After the victorious war and the punishment of war criminals," the declaration said, "the allied states should address the task of ensuring lasting and just peace." Similar demands were voiced in other countries that had fought against Germany, in particular, in the USA. An International Military Tribunal for the trial of war criminals was established on the basis of the agreement between the USSR, the USA, Great Britain, and France, signed on August 8, 1945. In October 1946, in Nuremberg, this tribunal convicted the main German war criminals for the crimes against peace, war crimes, and crimes against humanity. The Nuremberg trial started on November 20, 1945, and lasted ten and a half months. Twelve war criminals were sentenced to death by hanging; seven were sentenced to serve various prison terms. The tribunal also declared the Nazi Party leadership, the SS, SD, and the Gestapo criminal organizations.

For the first time ever, statesmen guilty of preparing, unleashing, and waging a war were punished like ordinary criminals.

The International Military Tribunal for the Far East followed the pattern of the Nuremberg Tribunal. The Tokyo trial of the Japanese war criminals lasted for two and a half years and was the most massive and protracted in the history of justice.

In its resolution of December 11, 1946, the UN General Assembly approved the principles of international law laid down in the Charter of the Nuremberg Tribunal that had been embodied in its sentence. Thus, the UN recognized that aggressive war, war crimes, and crimes against humanity were grave international crimes.

After the collapse of the USSR, NATO was happy to assume world dominance, with this bloc and the USA determining what is good and what is bad for peace. NATO's war against Yugoslavia offered a glaring example of what that meant. First, NATO incited Albanians in Kosovo to guerrilla actions, and then accused the Yugoslav government of reprisals against Albanians and began carpet bombing the country. The outcome was two hundred thousand Serbian refugees against the initial twenty-five thousand Albanian refugees. The world mass media took to heart the fate of the Albanians, but remained—and remains—indifferent to the fate of the Serbians. Yugoslavia's President Slobodan Milosevic was declared a war criminal and put on trial in The Hague for reprisals against the Albanians. As for US President Clinton and NATO leaders, it has never occurred to anyone that they could be accused of wrongdoing. Might makes right. Milosevic was brought before the International Court of Justice, not because he had committed a crime, but because he acted like a weakling. First he allowed the Kosovo Albanians to launch guerilla actions, and then he handed the country to NATO on a silver platter.

The USA and Great Britain punished Iraq for the crime it had not committed. What is this? A lapse of justice? There was no trial.

As a summary of the above, I can rightly say that VICTORS ARE NEVER JUDGED—even if victory comes as a result of mass reprisals.

Causes of War

One hundred years ago, Leo Tolstoy in his novel, War and Peace, *offered the following explanation of the causes of the Patriotic War of 1812 and its continuation: peoples of the West had to start their thrust eastward followed by movement in the opposite direction. This reduces the causes of war to fatality and belongs in the realm of philosophy or even theology.*
Timashev N.S. Kak voznikayut voiny?
(What Gives Rise to Wars?)
Novy zhurnal. 1968, No. 90, pp.205–211.

So far all attempts to achieve lasting peace have been futile. There are two reasons for this: first, objective unfavorable circumstances and, second, the nature of the proposed steps which did not do away with the causes of war.
Pitirim Sorokin, Prichiny voiny i usloviya mira
(The Causesof War and the Terms of Peace).
Sotsiologicheskiye issledovaniya
(Sociological Research). 1993, No. 12, pp.
140–148.

For the explanation of the causes of war, I might refer the reader to Pitirim Sorokin's works mentioned above. But in this case, I would have to dovetail our explanations. Sorokin characterizes society by means of "an integral system of main values reliably entrenched in life." My opinion is that the conduct of society is determined by its main parameter, that is, by the degree of its cohesion. It is precisely on the degree of cohesion that Sorokin's vague "system of main values" depends. Below, I would like to remind the reader of what I said above and to show how the degree of society's cohesion influences its readiness to start a war.

First, war is a natural phenomenon stemming from the laws of evolution.

Second, *the cause of civil war* is the full degradation, split, and disintegration of society. There is no doubt that, at this stage, the leader has an important role to play, because only he, alone, can reunite society.

The record of history shows, however, that at this stage, society's leaders tend to make themselves scarce and leave the reuniting to the military.

Third, the *cause of international wars* is the aggressive nature of over-united societies. The world wars occurred because there was a bellicose dictator at the helm of some state.

Classification of Wars
An All-Out War

A system, when the outcome of a war depended on a few battles between the armies of the adversaries, was gone as Napoleon left the world arena.

Having left the remnants of his army in Russia, Napoleon hastened to France to recruit a new army, which warrants the question of what his resources were. It turned out that France's soldier resources had been exhausted in the numerous wars. Napoleon desperately needed loyal soldiers. There were no soldiers. There were only juveniles.

During the First World War, Germany had a similar problem. The long, drawn-out war exhausted its manpower resources, and it was powerless against the Entente. At that time, the USA joined the Entente, and the Entente got the US expeditionary army as the fresh cannon fodder that Germany lacked so badly.

The wars in Europe after Napoleon, which subsequently became world wars, acquired the nature of all-out wars, when the entire population of the belligerents was directly or indirectly involved in war.

This sudden and cardinal change can be traced to the following factors:

First, the armed forces were better equipped with a growing amount of better technical equipment.

Second, the conflicts became protracted. In wartime, total mobilization was ordered. The entire country was working to meet the requirement of the army in equipment and munitions.

Third, there were stronger links between the population inside the country and the population and the army. After total mobilization, hardly any family was without a relation in the army. The fighting men had full moral support of the population. The main thing, however, was the imposed or voluntary cohesion of a country at war.

After the First World War, the world split into two military alliances. The same happened after the Second World War. After the war, the world split into two antagonistic camps.

Blitzkrieg

The German word "blitzkrieg" describes a warfare theory that originated in Germany. While "all-out" describes the scope of war, "blitzkrieg" describes the time it was supposed to last. Blitzkrieg is waged according to a strict plan, with strict interaction among all service arms of the attacking army. The objective is to win with minimal casualties and as quickly as possible. If the enemy manages to foil the plan of such a war, *blitzkrieg* can become a protracted war and result in defeat.

Lightning wars occurred when it only took one army several days to rout another army and win the war, which gave rise to the delusion that everything was back to what it was in the Middle Ages when war could be won by routing the enemy army. Germany harbored these delusions when it started World War I and World War II. At the beginning of World War II, Germany, assisted by the USSR, smashed Poland, and then occupied Belgium, Holland, Denmark, and Norway. The going was smooth. France was invaded and surrendered. For all that, the intended blitzkrieg turned into a protracted war and—like in the First World War—Germany was totally defeated. Contrary to German expectations, the German attack against the USSR fell short of a blitzkrieg. The USSR was actually a replica of Nazi Germany—its people were united by Stalin's dictatorship and communist ideology. German military successes in the first months of the war did not result in victory. They were followed by retreat up to Berlin and capitulation.

There is a recent instance similar to the expected and failed blitzkrieg of World War Two. It took the US-British coalition just a few days to rout Iraq and occupy the country with minimal casualties. On May 1, 2003, US President Bush declared that the war was over. Counting from that date, after four months of "postwar peace," US casualties exceeded the casualties sustained during the war. Terrorist attacks on the occupation forces are so numerous that they are likely to grow into a long guerilla war.

Israel acted contrary to its needs. It pursued the policy of Defense Minister Moshe Dayan and saved Egyptian soldiers in the Sinai Desert. After the Israeli troops occupied the West Bank of the Jordan River, Arabs left this territory en masse. Israel (Moshe Dayan) arrested their flight. He blocked bridges across the Jordan and ordered buses to take Arabs home. Twenty years later, these "refugees" became Israel's mortal enemies. When does blitzkrieg work, and when does it fail?

Blitzkrieg of the Twenty-first Century

Perfecting weaponry has always been the leading world trend. The ideal is to reduce everything to a war of buttons—like the golden cockerel in a fairy tale by Pushkin, which is perched on a tall spire to keep watch on the country's borders, and the tsar can destroy the enemy by pushing a few buttons.

Lessons of history are mostly of no avail. Blitzkrieg's failures are usually ignored, and it gradually grows into a regular war. However, people are impressed if an enemy army is smashed in a matter of days, and for politicians, a blitzkrieg has become something akin to obsession. Below is how the US President George Bush and his loyal military commanders visualize a future blitzkrieg.

Five years from now, the US military budget will exceed 360 billion dollars compared to 244 billion in 1996. At the peak of its confrontation with the heavily armed Soviet Union in 1985, the USA earmarked only 305 billion dollars for defense. The USA is about to cardinally change its army, air force, and navy. Nuclear warheads will be about as useless as the abstract of some US Defense Department's reports to President Clinton for 1999 and 2000, which shows that the United States was embarking on an ambitious rearmament program to be implemented by 2010. The authors of the reports say that it is a revolution in the art of war. The German blitzkrieg theory was also considered a revolution. In the 1930s, a breakthrough was accomplished by dive bombers, which precision bombed everything in the way of the fast-moving, attacking German tanks.

Today, things are different—the weapons of twenty-first-century blitzkrieg are high-precision weapons; air force and satellite communications battle management systems. By 2010, the Bush administration planned that there would be an all-embracing intelligence network to make the USA unequaled in battlefield-control capability. It would be supplemented by a communications network for passing intelligence to the troops and commanders without a moment's delay. The intelligence obtained nationwide would be coordinated with the intelligence received by commanders of the joint armed forces. US pilots, navy captains, and land forces officers would see the pictures captured by the host of satellites and scout planes in real time rather than hours or even days later.

Simultaneously, the Americans would build a more flexible management system to ensure perfect coordination of the actions of all service arms—the air force, navy, and land forces units. New combat control devices would connect intelligence data with the fire systems, complete with dynamic target indication, homing high-precision weapons in a heavy battle, fast evaluation of the fire results, and issuing the data necessary for finishing off the enemy that survived the previous attacks. The United States would also get the know-how for penetrating the information networks of the victim countries, and their work would be blocked.

The ACEUs—aero-cosmic expeditionary units, which were first used to rout Yugoslavia in 1999—are a combination of a strong air force unit with intelligence and communications satellites and scout and pilotless aircraft. ACEUs comprise various types of delivery aircraft, carrying high-precision bombs and missiles. Each follows a strict assignment; some suppress the enemy air defense forces; others take out command posts; and still others suppress life support systems. The ACEUs are highly mobile; they can be rapidly deployed and are capable of effective interaction with naval cruise missile carriers and carrier-borne attack groups.

An ACEU strike is a strike from a single aero-cosmic space, as powerful satellite groups scan the territory of the victim country in all possible ranges, capturing the slightest movement on its surface to guide aircraft attacks. And the main capability is that the satellites transfer the enormous amount of data to their processing centers with lightning speed. They connect these centers with the striking aircraft forces and indicate the target with the same speed. The ACEUs are always ready for attack. By 2003, the United States had ten ACEUs capable of hitting targets everywhere in the world.

The Americans realized that after its battering of Yugoslavia in 1999, any country attacked in this way was likely to use every kind of weapon it has—from short-range missiles to weapons of mass destruction—not only chemical, but also nuclear. In response, the US Air Force intends to act according to the concept of continuous fire, that is, to destroy short-range and ballistic missiles of the victim country on the ground before they take off.

The United States also focuses on building robot planes, intelligence pilotless planes, and target drones designed to disorient the enemy and blind its radars. The objective is nonstop intelligence and precision bombing guidance, with the prospect of using these pilotless aircraft for attack and hitting ballistic missiles at their take-off climb.

The US power of the twenty-first century will be mounted on space devices. Some will indicate the targets to US aircraft, ships, bombs, and cruise missiles. Some will ensure communication; some will listen to the Earth. Some will release a landslide of television and radio broadcasts on the victim to suppress its will to resist. Some will help US soldiers, tanks, ships and aircraft, cruise missiles, and bombs that are homing in to find their bearings any place of the globe. Some space devices monitor the launching of missiles; some process the results of the performance of thousands of computer "brains" and databases scattered throughout the globe. Any satellite system, with a few exceptions, is also a commercial entity having a profitable civilian application.

In its report for 1999, the Pentagon wrote: "We must move forward toward a fully intellectual cosmic battle-field, on which the belligerents would not view C4ISR as a support system but as an instrument of battle management. Any nation planning actions that militate against US national security will have to deal with the American space forces. These forces are an earnest need of the timely detection by the United States of hostile actions. Besides, the significance of outer space as the main way to achieve unhindered flow of information is growing as a factor, ensuring both economic prosperity and national security. Information operations are a force multiplier in all aspects of peace, crisis, war, and a return to peace. Information operations are used to attain specific objectives against the enemy information networks, its decision-making systems."

The NATO forces will be left the simple task of occupying a country paralyzed by such strikes. The Pentagon reports on the new military doctrine paint an impressive picture of the future of the US Navy, Marines, the armored forces, the cruise missiles stock, the so-called "nonlethal" weapons, and laser-beam guns in heavy Boeings capable of hitting "ground-to-ground" missiles at take-off from a distance of 300 km. Emphasized in all such reports is the tremendous increase in US combat power by linking all forces into a single computerized network.

It is for preparation of this kind of blitzkrieg that Bush, Jr., planned to spend billions of dollars. The outcome would have been a powerful system for waging world non-nuclear wars. The former fear of possible death from nuclear explosions is no longer a deterrent. But whom is the USA going to fight after 2010?

After reading all this, it is difficult to understand why a *shahid* can bring havoc to this reliable and beautiful system, despite its blitzkrieg and ACEU capabilities. Five years have passed since the end of a blitzkrieg in Iraq. The occupation forces are locked in their bases there, the country is rent by civil war, and its economy is in ruins.

Chapter 3

The Cohesion and Degradation of the Armed Forces

The process of the creation (cohesion) and collapse (degradation and split) of society is described in the chapter "Social Dynamics and Degradation of Society." Although the armed forces are a kind of over-united society (OUS) and, like any OUS, it has a membrane dividing it from the rest of the world and from its own society, the processes common to any society take place in the armed forces as well. Immediately after the armed forces are created, they have a high degree of cohesion, and then degradation sets in and they are broken up. At the end of the degradation process in society, at the stage of dual power, the existence of at least two antagonistic armed forces ready to start a civil war in the country can be clearly seen.

The infiltration of "sedition" through the military membrane is done in two ways, which can be described as physical and spiritual. The physical way is infiltration into the armed forces of officers holding "appropriate" political views via the defense ministry or its equivalent. The spiritual way is akin to ideological indoctrination: various "codes of honor," "rules of war," and the like are devised.

Private Armed Detachments

The hired private armed detachments (HPAD) stand somewhat apart. They are usually called mercenaries. Like any armed forces, they are highly disciplined and have a high degree of cohesion but no ideology or religion to unite them. These are substituted by a desire for enrichment of the type pirates or criminals have. Absence of any ideology is both an advantage and a drawback of the HPADs. The advantage is that up to a certain point, they are stable and immune to agitation and ideological influences. For as has been shown above, the degradation of ideology and its decline may lead to the decline of society and its armed forces. The desire for enrichment is stable, and only ascetics are not enticed by the promise of enrichment. For all that, ideology in a wider sense is a much stronger factor for cohesion than a desire for enrichment. An army of ascetics may prove to be more stout hearted and battle worthy than a HPAD.

My task in this work is to analyze the processes that unite and later degrade the army as functions of the processes in society.

The Armed Forces Are an OUS

A typical example of a voluntary army of ascetics united in an OUS was monastic orders in the Middle Ages. During the time of the Crusades, several of them operated in the Holy Land—the Order of Knights Templar, the Carmelite Order, the Teutonic Order, and many more. Christianity was the religion that united them. They had all OUS qualities: strict discipline, asceticism, aggressiveness, and the like.

Such orders did not have political instructors or commissars like those found in modern armed forces, but there was an abundant number of priests. The presence of priests shows that these orders of friars were "political organizations" out to occupy territory and spread Christianity.

In our times, the orders of friars may be compared with the Red Army in the Soviet Union. Apart from rigorous discipline, the Red Army was united by the communist ideology. The communist commissar was responsible for the loyalty of the officers and men in his unit. The commissar had powers equal to those of the unit commander, but he was not responsible for fulfilling combat missions.

The fundamental difference between the religious orders of the Middle Ages and modern armed forces is their numerical strength. In our times, with wars assuming mostly an all-out character and all national resources—first and foremost manpower—mobilized, there must be something in addition to ideology to unite the populace. This is clearly seen during hostilities when life hangs in the balance. It is impossible to compel people to fight by persuasion, calls, and promises of decorations, privileges, or food. There will always be those who would rather have life without boons and much esteem than heroic death. The higher the chances of being killed in action, the more numerous are the former and the less numerous are the latter. Hence, there is a need for political instructors to brainwash and coerce the modern armed forces.

Information War and Ideological Indoctrination

For all the different names given to psychological pressure in different periods—ideological struggle, psychological indoctrination, information war (recent vogue)—essentially a single objective is pursued, that of uniting a society and its armed forces in wartime and demoralizing the enemy. "Demoralizing" hereinafter is referred to as disintegration and split, that is, to what is contrary to cohesion. The notion of "demoralizing the enemy" is used in a general sense, because if society is split into antagonistic camps, members of one family may be found in different camps. It is only natural that the government should wage this kind of war and that the population and the military of both sides of the conflict should be exposed to brainwashing and indoctrination.

It is unreasonable, to put it mildly, to disclose in the mass media the true size of one's own casualties, the condition of its troops, the quality of its armaments or equipment, or to disclose the territories captured or left, stocks of foodstuffs still extant, and the state of industry still left in an enemy state. The enemy would scan this information and get the true idea of the effectiveness of its actions, of the condition of the troops, and the industrial and agricultural capabilities of the adversary.

To release verified information about the enemy casualties is just as unreasonable. They are usually understated. If the true information of one's own casualties (the exact figure is known) is released simultaneously, the comparison will not be in one's own favor. In this case, the population and the military may infer that the situation at the front is bad and that defeat is inevitable. And this dampens the spirits of one's own people who have to rough it in wartime as it is.

During the Six-Day War and the Yom Kippur War, the Israeli armed forces kept silent about the situation on the battlefields. Gradually, over the years, the silence was broken. The job of the armed forces press secretary was taken over by journalists who, guided by their ideology and out for sensation, did not hesitate to disclose military secrets. The second Lebanon war revealed the unseemly role of Israeli TV reporters who, by shooting pictures of the landing places of rockets fired by the Hesbollah from Lebanon, helped it to adjust fire.

In times of war, mass propaganda must unite the population and the armed forces, lift their spirits, and make them sure of victory. There appear reports of feats of valor, tremendous successes, unrivaled skill of tankmen and airmen. In wartime, the truth may not be the best thing to feed to the population. It may be harmful. The truth and analyses should not come until the war is over.

In the light of the above, it is clear that full freedom of reporting given to journalists, for instance, during the US war in Vietnam, was sheer folly.

Psychology of Writers and Journalists

The following experiment is known to have been carried out on monkeys. An electrode was planted in their heads to irritate them. If a monkey on top in the herd hierarchy was irritated, it became aggressive and attacked and bit everyone. If a monkey on the bottom of the hierarchy was irritated, it covered its head with its hands and cried, evidently meaning, "it hurts, stop biting me!" To make the experiment more conclusive, the researchers changed the positions of the monkeys in the hierarchy. The result was the same: any monkey on top became aggressive.

Something of this kind is also common to people, particularly to writers and journalists. The Soviet writer Andrei Sinyavsky proved it by analyzing the works of the best poets of the Soviet period. He pointed out that these golem poets extolled their henchmen and sang paeans to them. In this work, I pointed out that golem poets extolled the children who attacked the enemy with drums or arms in their hands. Another instance is "Liberty Leading the People," a picture by Delacroix in which the hero is a juvenile treading on dead bodies with pistols in both hands. But let's *return to our muttons*, as the French say. Journalists and writers can be patriotic, extol, and sing praises to their armed forces and their country. However, they need strict censorship to retain their team spirit. In the conditions of a disintegrating society, when power and censorship have vanished, these professionals turn into inveterate enemies of their country and their people.

From Whom Is Information Concealed?

Much has already been written about the role of the mass media in war or in the fight against terrorism, as well as about the psychology of journalists. In many of these writings, the Israeli nationalists (rightists) are labeled "hawks" while the "doves," that is, peacemakers and pacifists, surely are identified as the leftists. I must say that I haven't met a single "hawk" in Israel that would like to have war. Craving war is typical of OUS and their members. Israel has no OUS. Israel has "democracy." In this case, what's the big idea of labeling them "hawks"? The answer is to cast aspersions. Casting aspersions on one's own brethren? What for?

During the first intifada, Israeli soldiers used tear gas to disperse Arab protest marches. At the same time, news of Arabs dying of tear gas appeared. The news came from the "champions of human rights" who were members of the Israeli Betselem organization and who cited some mysterious Palestinian sources. All Israeli and European newspapers cited the Betselem news item. The UN Human Rights Committee and an Israel Shamir, a kibbutz man, asserted that Israel had created gas chambers and strangled infants. The number of the dead was growing at the rate of one to two per day and had come close to a hundred.

Inasmuch as tear gas is not toxic, I asked Betselem to produce medical documents confirming death from tear gas. Something evidently was amiss as the number of the dead stopped growing. No documents were produced, but I was told that a commission of inquiry had been set up.

I was invited to sit on this commission. I refused, as there already was a "head of a hospital ward" among the Betselem top men. Finally, no more dead bodies of the poisoned were found.

I sent the results of my investigation to all Israeli mass media. The letter was never published, nor was there any disclaimer of the false reports. I then learned that I was not the only one who had been looking for the "dead bodies of infants." The Israeli Ministry of Justice was also interested in the issue and carried out its own investigation. It did not find any dead bodies, either, but it soft-pedaled the investigation and its results, as it probably was indifferent to the image of Israel and its armed forces.

There is another instance.

In September 2000, the name of the Arab boy Muhammad ad-Dur made headlines in all major mass media throughout the world. The death of the twelve-year-old boy close to the Netsarim interchange in the Gaza Strip was filmed by the Palestinian cameraman Talal Abu-Rahma. The twenty-seven-minute footage was sold to a France-2 Channel reporter, Charles Enderlin, who made it into a fifty-five second story.

The succession of frames in this item depicts ad-Dur's "death" from the moment the crying boy and his frightened father were hiding behind an empty barrel close to the brick wall at the highway shoulder to the moment he stopped a bullet fired by an Israeli soldier. The collage leaves no doubt that the Israelis killed the boy.

The France-2 Channel did more than air the item; it provided the footage free to all mass media that asked for it. The item was viewed throughout the world and made ad-Dur the symbol of the second wave of intifada. A few days later, on October 12, 2000, Palestinians avenged the death of the boy by lynching two Israeli servicemen. The short video reportage shook the Arab world. An aggressive recruitment campaign for joining terrorist groups was launched under the banner of the "martyr Muhammed ad-Dur." The stance of the Israeli Arabs also changed. The death of the boy was the pretext for holding an anti-Israel conference in Durban (a South-African Republic). Modern anti-Semitism reared its head against the background of the "ad-Dur" myth. At that time, Premier Ehud Barak, Chief of General Staff Shaul Mofaz, and the Defense Army press secretary Ron Katari believed that it was the doing of the "cruel Israeli military." They admitted that the Israeli army should be blamed for the boy's death.

Nevertheless, an expert evaluation was made. The map of the locality and the positions of the Arabs and the Israelis at the moment of the fire exchange proved that the boy could not have been killed by an Israeli bullet, as he and his father were out of the area swept by the Israeli fire. Immediately after the accident, Yom-Tov Samaya, then commander of the Southern Military Area, assigned a team of experts headed by physicist Nahum Shahaf to investigate. These experts saw glaring discrepancies in the "reportage." In one frame, the dead boy's hand covered his face while, a few seconds later, in another frame, it was moving to his belly. At this early stage of the investigation, Shahaf noticed an amazing activity of the dead body—in the course of one minute, the lifeless frame changed its position four times. It looked like the tape was not authentic. There was a dramatic follow-up. Another experiment was carried out at some unit's shooting ground, where the situation at the moment of the boy's "death" was fully reconstructed. A brick wall was built, and a barrel with two mannequins behind it was placed near this wall. They were fired at from the weapons used during the operation in the Gaza Strip at that time. The experiment was filmed. The result was the same—not a single bullet could find these targets.

The Israeli physicist got in touch with the French reporter who had made and aired the item and asked him to submit to the commission the full raw footage shot by the Palestinian cameraman. The French reporter refused. But the commission could do without it. There were other reporters at Netsarim, and everything was faithfully documented in detail. Professor Shahaf's final report was also based on the conclusions of other experts. In particular, he was assisted by Maurice Rogev, head of the Institute of Forensic Medicine. It is worth noting that all experts agreed with Professor Shahaf's conclusions.

While the "death" of the Arab boy was widely publicized, the expert opinion on the Hollywood-style trick was carefully concealed. Why? The reasons given are strange indeed—"the armed forces command was too shocked," "the Israeli mass media did not dare tell the truth." They were ashamed. They were concealing the truth. Liars were encouraged by bonuses. The Israeli Defense Ministry must also be held responsible for distorting and concealing the true information. It awarded a literary prize to two Israeli journalists—Amos Harel of *Ha'aretz* and Avi Yisacharov of the "Voice of Israel" radio—for their book *The Seventh War* in which the authors say that the intifada was triggered by the killing of ad-Dur. Not a word is said in the book about the other version of the chain of events.

So the Israeli mass media "did not dare" to tell the truth. *Ha'aretz* journalists even questioned the experts' professionalism. There are certainly ample reasons for questioning the professionalism of such journalists. The Israeli mass media shirked its main obligation—to provide the public with true information about the developments. Paradoxical as it may seem, foreign journalists evinced keen interest in the conclusions of the Shahaf Commission. James Fellows, a US military analyst, visited Israel for the sole purpose of meeting the experts and verifying their evaluations. He wrote in the *Atlantic Monthly* magazine that speculations on the death of Muhammed ad-Dur totally disregarded the laws of physics and ballistics and had plunged politics into the world of fantasy, paranoia, and hatred.

This opinion of a US journalist did not bend the Israeli government toward recognizing the conclusions of the Shahaf Commission. There is another fact that makes the guilt of the Israeli government even more serious. Philippe Karsenty, a French Jew, sent out to all mass media a press release in which he accused the France-2 Channel of falsifying the footage it aired about the "death of ad-Dur." He published all the material he had on this matter at his Web site *Media Ratings*. Summing up his investigation, he accused the France-2 Channel of disseminating anti-Semitic invective and demanded that the reporter, who concocted this item subsequently aired throughout the world, be sacked.

The top management of the France-2 Channel and Charles Enderlin, head of this channel's Middle East Bureau, accused Karsenty of slander. Karsenty sought assistance from Israel. The Jewish state ignored his request. Jerusalem did not even back the initiative of France's Jewish community, which tried to help him. Israel had left a man trying to save its image to fend for himself. Karsenty lost the court case. But this story may have a happy end yet. Karsenty appealed the case, and the court demanded that France-2 submit the complete raw film footage from which the one-minute item was compiled. Karsenty believes that even without Israel's help, he will be able to prove in court that he and Israel were in the right.

Israel's society is split into nationalists and internationalists. The latter's hatred for their own country makes them capable of the basest actions: hence, their desire to tarnish Israel and its armed forces. The Israeli mass media are their loyal associates.

When Censorship Is Absent

On April 12, 1984, four Arab terrorists got on a bus going from Tel Aviv to Ashkelon. The cleaner at the Tel Aviv bus station thought they looked suspicious and notified the police. The pursuit began. The driver was ordered to stop, but the bus continued its southward course. At the turn to Ashkelon, army units blocked its way. The terrorists did not have firearms. Had they had Tommy-guns or pistols in their pockets, they would have been detained when they were getting on the bus. They had an axe and knives in their rucksacks. One of the terrorists leaned out of the window and yelled that all Jews would be killed if the bus was not let into Gaza. The police did not dare fire at the terrorists, as they could injure the passengers.

At sunrise, when the bus was three kilometers from the entrance to the Gaza Strip, the order to storm the bus came. The area around it was declared a battle zone. Everybody was ordered out of the bus. Those in the area were mostly journalists and cameramen. The terrorists were told to surrender and were promised that they would remain alive. They answered by swearing and hitting the passengers. One Palestinian hit a female soldier with an axe. Their leader declared that the passengers were hostages to be freed in exchange for the arrested terrorists, whose names would be given to the Israeli government after the bus got to Gaza.

Some journalists took advantage of the commotion to remain in the zone. The security forces (SHABAK) were ordered to burst into the bus. Shortly after that, the Israeli radio announced that the four terrorists had been killed in the operation. This was not true. A cameraman of the newspaper *Hadashot* of the Ha'aretz corporate group sent a picture to the editorial office showing two Palestinians being taken out of the bus. The *Hadashot* published the picture. A scandal erupted, for in the Israeli mass media the two surviving Palestinians were referred to as "prisoners" and ranked as soldiers, although no war had been declared by any side. With the Geneva Convention about prisoners in force, this was fraught with far-reaching consequences. Had the government's legal advisor Prof. Zamir instituted court proceedings, the results would have been disastrous. The Arabs would have learned SHABAK's methods and the names of its higher officers and agents.

Shimon Peres, then head of the Israeli government, and Yitzhak Shamir, his deputy, tried to talk Zamir out of taking the matter to court, but Zamir was adamant, and he was dismissed from all his positions. The president of Israel, Chaim Herzog, put an end to this story by granting amnesty—before the trial opened—to all who had taken part in this operation. Those guilty of killing the terrorists were dismissed from the SHABAK, but its secrets remained safe. Years later, after Chaim Herzog's death (on April 14, 1997), a participant in this operation said during a TV round table: "We burst into the bus and saw the hacked female soldier. The villains were wielding a blood-stained axe and laughing. They thought that our court would deal with them as it had with other terrorists, that they would be put into prison where their wives and the Red Cross would visit them and then they would be exchanged for another batch of Jewish hostages. We dragged them out onto the road. I could stand it no longer. I took a stone and smashed the head of one of them." He did not say who killed the other one.

An analysis of this event highlights among other things the great influence the mass media have in Israel. Anything published in a newspaper is taken on trust and is never refuted. Men from the police and the SHABAK want to see their names in the mass media. The questions that arise are who leaked the capture of the bus to journalists, who was in a rush to broadcast over the radio about the end of the operation, why did the mass media publish the information about the operation without censorship and rank the terrorists as soldiers, and who said it was immoral to kill the killer on the spot?

"Innocent Victims"

Why is it that the Israeli mass media and army lawyers keep demoralizing soldiers instead of defending them? Stories of "innocent victims" of Israeli soldiers are always present in the mass media. The sword of Damocles in the form of investigation hangs above the heads of the Israeli soldiers. No one appears to take any interest in how the "innocent victim" found himself or herself under Israeli fire.

Below is one of the many instances of an "innocent victim."

Great Britain may demand the extradition of the Israeli soldiers involved in the killing of a British TV cameraman in Rafiah in May 2003. In his letter to the family of thirty-four-year-old James Miller killed in the Gaza Strip, Attorney General Peter Goldsmith wrote that he had requested

Attorney General Menahem Mazuz of Israel to reply within six weeks.

An English expert holds that Israeli army men killed Miller. According to Lord Goldsmith, the doctor suggested that Israeli soldiers should be brought to trial on charges of premeditated murder in violation of the 1957 Geneva Convention.

Initially, the IDF believed that Palestinians had killed Miller, but a ballistics test conducted at the request of the cameraman's family showed that Israeli troops had killed him. After a lengthy investigation, in March 2005, charges were dropped against the soldiers involved, due to lack of evidence.

The entire case is proof positive of the impotence of Israeli politicians and the armed forces higher officers, who are incapable of protecting the Israeli soldiers from unfounded accusations, just as they are incapable of protecting Israeli citizens from Arab terrorism. What "lack of evidence" can there be if the cameraman was so incautious as to be in the fire-swept area?

Those who sent him to a crisis area should be held responsible for the cameraman's death and answerable to his family. Inasmuch as he was killed at his place of work, his family should be entitled to compensation and the insurance from his employers. Israeli soldiers cannot be blamed for the fact that a British stringer was present in the battle zone without notifying the Israeli military.

Who said that the letters "TV" was a cameraman's reliable protection from bullets? Terrorists are known to have used these letters as a disguise. In this way, the terrorists got at Ahmad Shah Masud, the commander in chief of the Northern Alliance in Afghanistan, and killed him. Such "cameramen" should be shot before they get at somebody.

A soldier on the battlefield who sees strangers approaching him cannot take them for peaceful civilians.

Lord Goldsmith's letter does not even question the extradition of the guilty. According to British law, a person suspected of killing a British national must be kept in a British prison until the investigation is over. Israel and Great Britain have an extradition agreement, and Israel's refusal to extradite the army men involved may lead to a diplomatic crisis.

What does it matter? This was just another crisis in addition to many. Great Britain is known to be keeping criminals without extraditing them to any country, neither the USA nor Russia.

Generals, journalists, and mass media reporters are enemies of the society. Their desire to show off is overriding, and they are ready to divulge secrets and disgrace people. Stay clear of them or keep them on a short leash. Follow the example of Lawrence of Arabia or Ehud Barak—they knew how to make themselves famous.

Barrier Detachments

The traditional system of disciplinary punishment in the armed forces—such as reprimand, extra duty, cancelled leave, or military detention—are insufficient in wartime. If one does not go into battle of his own free will, he may be motivated by fear of strict punishment and even of death. Lev Trotsky, the first commander in chief of the Red Army, gave an accurate definition of the repressive measures to keep the embattled army disciplined: "…a Red Army man must be given the only alternative to a possible glorious death in action if he goes forward. This alternative is the inevitable, disgraceful death by facing the firing squad if he deserts his position and runs back…"

Under the circumstances, a penal unit looks like a more humane alternative than being shot down for some offense, disobedience, cowardice, or defection, because a penal unit just presents a greater probability of being killed than in any other unit. The only punishment that can be imagined for the officers and men of a fighting army is a greater threat of death.

The ideological indoctrination mentioned above is no longer considered very important. During WWII, however, by mid-October 1942, the barrier detachments detained over fifteen thousand defectors at the Stalingrad Front alone. The total number of defectors detained along the entire Soviet-German frontline came to over 140,000, the numerical strength of more than ten divisions. Of course, all defectors could not be captured; perhaps only half of them were. Out of the 140,755 detained servicemen, only 3,980 were arrested, 1,189 shot; 2,776 privates and sergeants and 185 officers were dispatched to penal battalions, and 131,094 were sent back to their units or to distribution points. The authorities were surely very lenient to defectors—out of 141,000 only 9,500 were punished.

One wonders why such barrier detachments were not set up in 1941, at the beginning of the war. The Red Army could have followed the example of the Wehrmacht, which had field police (Feldgendarmerie), whose specially trained officers and men traced defectors, identified malingerers and those with self-inflicted wounds, maintained order in the rear, and purged rear units of unnecessary servicemen. The barrier detachments were indispensable, even if they were a somewhat belated step in the control of the defectors. Stalin and his party associates had put the emphasis on ideological indoctrination and persuasion, which was supposed to be ensured by an inflated and inefficient political service in the armed forces, instead of strict disciplinary measures that were justified when a war was on. When the worst came to the worst, barrier detachments joined the regular units and, in some cases, saved the day. It must be noted that shortly after barrier detachments were established, the institute of military commissars in the Red Army was abolished. Barrier detachments did their job better than commissars.

Prisoners of War

The Soviet leadership's prewar policy, with respect to its army men in case they were taken prisoner, largely determined the plight of the Soviet prisoners of war in German concentration camps during WWII.

On December 22, 1918, the VTsIK (All-Russia Central Executive Committee) approved the Field Service Regulations of the Worker and Peasant Red Army, with its professed aim of "bringing up the troops in the spirit of indomitable staunchness," as a condition of military service. The regulations said *inter alia*: "Each Red Army man…must bear in mind that holding on against all odds, even when encircled from all sides, he is working for the common cause, facilitating the counterattack that will rescue him. He must fight on until he can no longer wield his weapon." There was also an article forbidding servicemen to abandon their positions without the relevant orders from their superiors.

An analysis of these instructions and prohibitions makes it clear that they are in line with OUS psychology. They are reminiscent of admonitions to a Spartan warrior who had to fight exactly on the spot he had been ordered to.

The new service regulations issued in 1924–29 and 1937 were based on the first ones. They urged servicemen to fight to whatever end and made surrendering to the enemy a punishable offense. Such a serviceman was considered a criminal, inasmuch as he had broken the regulations.

Josef Stalin gave succinct "characteristics" of the Soviet war prisoners: "They are not war prisoners, they are traitors to the Motherland." The Soviet Union officially refused to recognize the Red Army fighting men taken as war prisoners and regarded them as criminals. This stance explains why, in 1929, the Soviet Union refused to ratify the international Geneva Convention on the status and rights of prisoners of war. According to this convention, the principles of treating prisoners of war were based on international law and therefore binding. In 1934, this convention was made a law in Germany and obligated all German soldiers to protect war prisoners from violence, show consideration and esteem for them (Art. 3), and take care of them (Art. 4). Prisoners of war had to be quartered in solid houses or barracks, with immaculate sanitary conditions and provided with sufficient amounts of food (Art. 10–11). All prisoners of war fell under the German Military Criminal Code, and if any of them committed an offense, he would be punished exactly like a German serviceman would be for such an offense (Art. 45–67). The authorities of a war prisoner camp had to ensure written correspondence with the war prisoner family (the 1929 Geneva Convention).

None of these provisions were applied to the Soviet prisoners of war. In justification of its actions, the German leadership referred to the fact that the Soviet Union had not signed the 1929 agreement, which made Soviet war prisoners outlaws not covered by the Geneva Convention. It is for the same reason that the International Red Cross could not monitor the conditions of life of Soviet war prisoners and render them assistance.

Stalin's stance determined the policy of other Soviet leaders vis-à-vis Red Army men who had been taken prisoner. On August 16, 1941, came the General Headquarters Order No. 270, which put the final touch on their status as that of "weak-spirited, fainthearted, cowardly elements." The order said *inter alia*: "Can the Red Army tolerate cowards defecting to the enemy and surrendering to it or fainthearted commanders who, at the very first hitch at the front, would tear off their rank insignia and defect to the rear? No, it cannot! If such cowards and defectors remain at large, the army will disintegrate in no time, and our Motherland will be ruined. Cowards and defectors should be eliminated." According to this order, any private or commander attempting to surrender would be "dismissed from his position, stripped of rank, and demoted to private or shot down on the spot if necessary." Those who became prisoners of the enemy should, the order said further, be eliminated "by all available means, using both ground and air forces." Stalin's words matched his deeds. After the end of World War II, the war prisoners released from the German camps were subjected to severe reprisals at home, in Soviet concentration camps.

For the sake of comparison, it should be noted that in the allied US and British armies, their servicemen taken prisoner were never victimized; they were viewed as their own people, and the attitude to them did not change after they became prisoners. There were even attempts to rescue and save them.

For all their menacing purport, the orders of the supreme commander in chief did little if anything to reduce the number of Soviet war prisoners. What could a soldier do if his regiment was surrounded, wiped out, and all those who had not run away were killed? The rumors of the inhuman treatment of Soviet war prisoners by the Germans, which reached the Red Army trenches, were a more effective deterrent to surrendering than the orders of the supreme commander in chief.

Chapter 4

The Israel Defense Forces

*Any theory becomes infinitely more complicated the
moment it enters the sphere of moral values. The objectives
of architecture and painting are clear as long as they deal
with material things—their mechanical and optical structures do not elicit conflicting opinions. But when it comes to
their spiritual impact and the feelings they evoke, the entire
code of effective laws gets blurred in vague ideas.*
Karl von Clausewitz

Above, I examined in this work the process of founding the
armed forces and making them cohesive. Below their degradation will come under scrutiny. The rise and degradation of society and its armed forces make up an integral
cycle of social dynamics. In this work, the degradation of
the Israel Defense Forces (*TSAHAL* in Hebrew) have been
taken as an example, as it was this unthinkable degradation of a once superb army that prompted me to show the
roots of this phenomenon.

It does not mean that the armed forces of other countries are immune to the degradation process. This applies
primarily to the US armed forces. I would recommend that
generals learn the bitter lesson of the IDF.

When examining the IDF actions, it is necessary to take
into account the specific features of the Middle East region,
which are constant and unchangeable.

First and foremost, Islam is the faith of the Arab
countries; Islam cements them into OUSs, and they act

accordingly; that is, they threaten Israel with aggression or even perpetrate aggression. Second, Israel's confrontation with Arab countries is aggravated by its lack of resources. A war of the Six-Day War type requires total mobilization, which paralyzes the country. Israel has no territory within which to maneuver. This situation makes a protracted war of attrition preferable to the Arabs, and they are trying to force Israel to get bogged down in such a war. Contrary to that, it is only natural that Israel should prefer a blitzkrieg.

During the Six-Day War, it took Israel six days to rout the combined forces of three Arab countries—Egypt, Syria, and Jordan, which were backed by all the other Arab and Muslim countries. All communist block countries headed by the USSR assumed a pro-Arab stance. The enemy air force, armor, and infantry were put out of action in these six days. This spectacular victory was marveled at in the West, but it did not bring anything to Israel, not even peace.

Intoxicated by the brilliant military victory, the Israeli politicians failed to grasp the new realities and turn the victory to Israel's advantage. This victory was taken advantage of by the USA and the USSR to get a stronger foothold in the Middle East. To attain this end, the USA kept Israel's appetite in check while the USSR gave all-round political support to the Arab countries and delivered arms to them. A mere six months after the war, the strength of the Arab armed forces was restored, and they had better arms than before the war—all with the assistance of the USSR. The next war was the war of attrition with Egypt. Having suffered defeat, Egypt applied for help to the United States. The ceasefire agreement concluded between Israel and Egypt, with US mediation, was violated by Egypt on many occasions, and in the autumn of 1973, the Yom Kippur War broke out.

It is important to note that in all its wars, Israel ignored the circumstances I mentioned above and did not pursue the enemy until its unconditional surrender.

None of Israel's victories, except the War of Independence, brought any tangible results to Israel. This war of independence was waged both by the Arabs and the Jews contrary to any rules and culminated in mass Arab exodus from the territories captured by Israel. The exodus was the result of the Arab propaganda that exaggerated Jewish atrocities beyond any reasonable measure and played into Israel's hands. After the war, the Arabs were still being ousted from their land to give way to new kibbutzes. Until Menahem Begin came to power in 1977, wartime laws were applied with respect to the Arab population of Israel.

Israel's error in the Six-Day War was its failure to seal its victory over the enemy. The enemy did not surrender; it was not demoralized by heavy losses. Why? Is Israel incapable of inflicting a blow bringing the enemy's unconditional surrender? To my mind, it is a matter of policy, rather than military capability. Israeli politicians would not take such a step.

The Arabs did not care how many lives the war claimed. Their state hierarchy did not change after the war and continued to function.

Israel acted contrary to its needs. It pursued the "humane" policy of Defense Minister Moshe Dayan and saved Egyptian soldiers scattered in the Sinai Desert. After the Israeli troops occupied the West Bank of the Jordan River, Arabs left that territory en masse. Unlike what was done during the War of Independence, Israel took efforts to arrest their flight. It blocked bridges across the Jordan and ordered buses to take Arabs home. Twenty years later, these "refugees" became Israel's mortal enemies.

Are the Armed Forces Outside Politics?

The first essential element in the armed forces degradation is their separation from "politics." "Politics" in this sense is the religion or ideology that cements the armed forces. The demand to put the armed forces outside politics comes in the wake of the collapse of religion or ideology, which society used to embrace. Society loses its cohesion and develops a rift. It corresponds to "democracy" in the circle diagram of the society dynamics.

The armed forces outside politics! In this way, the armed forces are actually deprived of the ties between their servicemen and between their servicemen and society. Considering that the armed forces are a structure that plays an important part in ensuring society's stability, the demand that the armed forces be apolitical is of dubious merit. Nevertheless, this demand is heeded in many democratic countries, including the USA and Israel.

To meet this demand, a civilian person who is often a mediocre politician is appointed to head the Defense Ministry. As distinct from democracy, under dictatorship there is always a general at the head of this ministry.

Saying that the armed forces are apolitical implies that their command is completely aloof from politics. This, however, does not rule out the opposite, namely, that a country's political leaders should appoint generals who share their ideology and political views to higher positions in the armed forces. As the split of society into antagonistic camps becomes ever more glaring, and the rift between the political views of these camps keeps widening, a "politician" in the capacity of defense minister means a lot.

It would be naïve to believe that introducing new ties could politicize "apolitical" armed forces. Quite the opposite: such a process would lead to their full disintegration. It is only natural that the disintegration of society should be accompanied by the disintegration of its armed forces, the judicial system, and all of society's structures. An example of the opposite process is bringing the armed forces together under a dictatorship.

Israel's Ministry of Defense

To what extent can Israel's Defense Ministry be considered a civil agency in control of the armed forces? Almost all of Israel's defense ministers were retired higher-ranking generals. Ben Gurion, who was not a career officer, thought it necessary to wear a field jacket and reserved the post of defense minister for himself. To avoid rivalry, he had a law passed in the Knesset that prohibited officers from being nominated for Knesset membership, who were doing compulsory military service or remaining in the armed forces for continuous service.

For twenty-five years, the post of defense minister was held by Itzhak Rabin and Ehud Barak, former Chiefs of the General Staff, and by Generals Ezer Weizmann, Ariel Sharon, Itzhak Mordehai, and Binyamin Ben-Eliezer. During the same period, there were only two defense ministers who were not career officers—Shimon Peres, a leftist, and Professor Moshe Arens, a rightist.

What were the political views of these six generals who made it to the position of defense minister? All of them, with the exception of Itzhak Mordechai, were leftists, internationalists. Even those who, like General Ariel Sharon, were for some time in the right-wing camp, shifted to the left camp guided by ulterior motives.

Getting a position in higher military echelons did not depend on military talent but on certain political views and loyalty to the leader. A kibbutz origin was an asset. In the sixty years of Israel's statehood, General Rafael Eitan was the only one who was appointed Chief of the General Staff because of his outstanding merits. According to Yitzhak Rabin, after the difficult Yom Kippur War, they were looking for a "fighter" for the position of commander in chief and decided that Rafael Eitan was the most suitable person. He held this post for seven years and was hated by the leftists for his pronouncements about the Arabs, for destroying the Iraqi nuclear reactor, and heading the armed forces during the first Lebanon war.

A similar phenomenon, that is, infiltration of leftist ideology alien to Judaism into the Israeli armed forces, could be observed in the higher echelons of the Defense Ministry. Retired higher officers would get a position in this ministry and become supervisors of their former friends and co-workers. This was a sure way to control the armed forces. To conceal this control, it was dished out as lobbying the interests of the armed forces by the generals working in the Defense Ministry. The 1976 Basic Law on Israel Defense Forces empowered the Defense Ministry to control them. The supposed lobbying was just a pretext. But what were the results of this control?

It should also be noted that the institute of rabbis in the IDF is of no appreciable significance. Their upkeep is paid by the IDF—and he who pays the piper calls the tune. The role of the rabbis is confined to meeting the needs of observant officers and men without meddling in politics. It has nothing to do with the role of commissars or political instructors. The leftist socialists do not go to synagogue, nor do they socialize with rabbis.

The above shows that ever since its inception, the Israeli armed forces have been in the hands of the leftists, and their antinational and pacifist ideology has been steadily

implanted in them, gradually eroding them to degradation. Yet the military is blamed for the setbacks in any war.
The politicians, even the defense minister, always come off
unscathed.

IDF Degradation

Below are some manifestations of the degradation
process.

In the late 1970s, Aviad Visoli, now a lawyer, was an
army officer. He was on night duty together with Sergeant
David Grossman, a future writer. They were processing the
information coming to their base. A piece of information
came to them, which was at variance with the sergeant's
internationalist views, and he refused to obey the order.
Aviad Visoli removed him from duty, reported him, and the
sergeant faced court-martial. Visoli pointed out that special attention should be paid to the incident and the work
of the sergeant carefully checked. The sergeant's political
views made him a threat to the national defense potential
if he was engaged in collecting and processing confidential information.

It was going from bad to worse. During the First Lebanon War of 1982, also known by the name of Operation
Peace for the Galilee, the degradation assumed alarming
proportions. The Israeli left camp came out against this
war in its first days. Almost every day, the leftists arranged
antiwar meetings and marches. During the war, Amram
Mitsna, then brigadier general, wrote a letter in which he
criticized the Defense Minister Ariel Sharon and said he
did not trust him. Amram Mitsna refused to go back to
Lebanon until Ariel Sharon resigned. His letter reached the
press via some "unknown channels." At a military meeting,
he demanded that Sharon resign. The defector was not

dismissed from the armed forces, due to the intercession of Prime Minister Menahem Begin. Mitsna was not even punished. After Begin's term of office expired, Mitsna was promoted and appointed commander of a military area. While he was commander, intifada was rife in the area. Later, he would boast that his letter was instrumental in creating a commission of inquiry to investigate the massacre of Palestinian refugees by Christian phalanges. This investigation led to Sharon's resignation. In 1991, Sharon sued the left-wing *Ha'aretz* for slander (the newspaper held him responsible for the massacre), and Mitsna testified in the newspaper's favor.

Another officer, Colonel Eli Gheva refused to obey the order to march on Beirut since it was against his political views. Rafael Eitan, then Chief of the General Staff, immediately discharged him from military service and cancelled all agreements between him and the IDF. He was stricken from the army personnel lists and was not even allowed to say good-bye to his soldiers.

Afterward, he was never called up, even for reservist training. The leftists were very considerate toward him and gave him some job.

Thus, at first, officers of the Mitsna or Gheva type are infiltrated in the IDF and then they are treated as "heroes."

It should be stressed that the above incidents took place when a war was on and soldiers were on the battlefield. Refusal to fulfill army orders did not come from pampered and frightened girls; it came from senior army officers. A comparison with the orders issued in the USSR during World War II suggests itself. Stalin would have put Eli Gheva in front of the firing squad made up of the soldiers to whom he wanted to say good-bye, and these soldiers would have shot him down without any compunction. As to Mitsna, he would have at best been dispatched to a penal battalion to be a company commander.

The course the Arab-Israeli conflict took in the1980s–1990s made the armed forces unable to attain the objectives the country's leadership set to them. Operation Peace for the Galilee launched on June 5, 1982, was planned as a blitzkrieg, following the pattern of the 1956 Sinai campaign or the 1967 Six-Day War, but it turned into a protracted and difficult four-month war. Israel got stuck in the Lebanese territory for eighteen years. Lebanon became the Israeli Vietnam. Israel's standing in the world community was dealt a blow as heavy as the blow to the Israelis' trust in the country's government.

The Lebanon war claimed 654 lives. As many as 3,859 Israeli officers and men were wounded; among the dead was General Yekutiel Adam, Deputy Chief of the General Staff. The protracted military operation that had been designed to ensure peace and tranquility on Israel's northern borders actually aggravated the situation. Officially, the operation ended on September 1, 1982, by the evacuation of the Palestinian terrorists and Syrian troops from Beirut, but the withdrawal of the Israeli troops from Lebanon did not take place until seventeen years later. Bashir Gemayel, who favored an agreement with Israel, was elected Lebanon's president on August 23 and assassinated on September 14. His elder brother, Amin Gemayel, the next president of Lebanon, signed a peace treaty with Israel on May 17, 1983. This treaty has never been ratified by the Lebanese parliament.

On September 29, 1982, the Israeli troops pulled out of Beirut. They retained control over a sizeable part of the Lebanese territory, intending to complete the withdrawal after a peace treaty was signed between the two countries. The refusal of Lebanon's leaders to sign a treaty with Israel put Israel in a tough predicament. The troops' pullout became a unilateral act not backed by any obligations by Lebanon and looked more like Israel's capitulation.

Later, by early June 1985, a great part of the Israeli troops left Lebanon, but an 18-km wide security zone remained under the control of Israel and the South Lebanese Army (TSADAL) supported by Israel.

Eighteen years later, on May 24, 2000, acting in conformity with the decision of Ehud Barak's government, all Israeli troops left Lebanon in a rush, close to panic, leaving the South Lebanon Army to shift for itself.

What prevented Israel from imposing a "peace agreement" on Lebanon by force?

While, before the first Lebanon war, the IDF was believed to be aloof from politics, its hasty retreat from Lebanon was proof positive that this view was erroneous and that the army, like the entire country, was in a state of degradation. This, however, passed unnoticed, and no conclusions were drawn. The country and its armed forces continued to disintegrate.

Any country is out to display its flag, be it in the Arctic or the Antarctic. Sports and military marches are organized for the sole purpose of hoisting a flag. The panicky retreat of the US troops from North Vietnam was an impressive achievement of North Vietnam and the USSR. Helping Afghanistan's mujahidin to oust USSR from Afghanistan and compelling it to pull out its troops from this country was the vengeance relished by the USA.

The IDF lost its strength and its role. It could no longer display the Israeli flag in Lebanon. Who ousted the Israeli troops from Lebanon, what force? Just a small force of Israeli journalists accomplished the ouster.

How they did it is immaterial. What matters is what they achieved.

Despite Israel's military presence in Lebanon that lasted many years, there was no tranquility on the Lebanese border. Shiite fanatics of the Hezbollah terrorist organization, supported by Iran and Syria, replaced the terrorists from the Palestine Liberation Organization (PLO), which had moved to Tunisia, Syria, and other countries. Today, too, the terrorist sorties by Hezbollah militants make the Israel-Lebanon border a major hotbed of tension. Outstanding among Hezbollah's actions are the kidnapping of three Israeli frontier guards in September 2000 and the infiltration into the Israeli territory of two terrorists who killed seven civilians. Terrorist actions of this kind, perpetrated by militants of the Hezbollah, which enjoys the support of Iran and Syria, led to the outbreak of the second Lebanon war. Unlike the first Lebanon war, the second ended in unquestionable defeat for Israel. Having lost its soldiers, the IDF left the Lebanese territory without attaining any of the set objectives. The second Lebanon war was testimony to full degradation of Israel and its armed forces.

The country's political leadership gradually nullified the victory in the Six-Day War. In the same way, the achievements of the first Lebanon war were reduced to naught. Impotent Israeli leaders are responsible for the peace treaty with Lebanon remaining only on paper and for Syria's comeback to Lebanon.

The outcome of Israel's operation in Lebanon is, in all respects, a replica of the outcome of the US war in Vietnam. It is common knowledge that the USA suffered defeat, not in Vietnam, but at home, in the rear. The two factors contributing to the defeat were the split in US society and the US presidents' blind adherence to "democracy." Instead of working toward cohesion, they tried to implant "freedom and democracy" wherever they could and in the meaning they attached to these terms. The USA succeeded in tying the hands of South Vietnamese generals and untying the hands of their own journalists. Everything was done to invite defeat. One is expected to learn from past mistakes, which may be true, but not in the case of US presidents. Something of the kind was later repeated by President Carter in Iran, when he substituted the Shah friendly to the United States for the ayatollah, its inveterate enemy.

The "information war" has been mentioned above. In Vietnam, the USA lost this war—with its journalists contributing importantly to its defeat.

As head of government, Menahem Begin should have followed the example of Ben Gurion who used "extremely painful methods" to unite the people in the fight for the country's independence. Begin, a nationalist, did not want to use "painful methods," and in addition to golems' marches and meetings, Israel got defectors and traitors in the IDF.

IDF's Police Functions

Various security actions are taken in Israel every day. They include guarding the country's frontiers and preventing terrorist actions inside the country, which involves the exercise of police functions by the armed forces in Israel proper and in the territories under its control. This state of affairs poses some problems. The IDF and the police force have different training programs, and army men and policemen are motivated differently. In Israel, military service is compulsory, while service in the police is a matter of choice. The armed forces cannot be fully successful when performing police functions. The need for servicemen to act like policemen, whether among the Arabs or the Jews, adversely affects the motivation both of draftees and reservists.

Intifada

A further test of IDF efficiency was the intifada that broke out in December 1987, on the West Bank of the Jordan River and in the Gaza Strip. In the course of six years of the Arab uprising, the IDF could not suppress the resistance of Arab terrorist organizations: the PLO, Hamas, the Islamic Jihad, the Popular Front for the Liberation of Palestine (PFLP), the Democratic Front for the Liberation of Palestine (DFLP), and others. The number or casualties among soldiers and civilians grew as acts of terror continued.

Why was the IDF, which had scored a spectacular victory in the Six-Day War, defeated in the intifada? Because of the incompetence of the leadership of the country and its armed forces. The internationalist ideology acted like a carpenter vise on the brains of the Israeli leftists. As usual, poverty and lack of education among the Arabs were considered the main causes of the situation. Nobody realized that the Arabs, united as they were by Islam and asceticism, were golems, and mass reprisals were needed to make them an OUS. There were no reprisals, but there was Israel-style "freedom and democracy," its worth demonstrated if only by the number of terrorist organizations. Moreover, Hamas was founded with Israel's support as a counterweight to other terrorist organizations.

The first Lebanon war saw the first signs of erosion of the glorious Israeli armed forces. At that time, the pacifist Yitzhak Rabin still dared to issue an order to break the arms of the Arab children stoning Israeli soldiers. By fulfilling this order, Colonel Yehuda Meir made his way into history.

During the first intifada, only a few lower- and middle-ranking officers refused to serve in the armed forces, and there were only a few cases of refusal to fulfill orders. Only fanatics did this, who realized that they would be sentenced to a prison term. Traditional methods of bringing them to trial were used against them. When the number of such cases had grown, instead of a stricter discipline and tougher treatment of such people, the reprisals became less severe and the number of such cases mounted. The degradation continued. Intifadas became the landmarks in Israel's history.

The second intifada is noted, among other things, by massive refusals of the leftists to fight Arabs. In 2002, as many as fifty reserve officers refused to take part in punitive operations against Arabs. They declared that they did not want to fight "for getting supremacy over an entire people, depriving it of means of sustenance, humiliating it, or ousting it from its own land." It certainly sounds impressive. Nothing of the kind was said when, with the support of Ben Gurion, a socialist, Arabs were evicted from their villages to give way to kibbutzes.

The physical stone and stick war between the Arabs and the Jews was accompanied by the information war. The declarations of all Israeli left-wingers were permeated with the ideas of the struggle for peace and humanism. Yosi Beilin, ex-journalist from the *Davar*, the ex-paper of the Israeli trade unions, said that he was ready to tell a lie if it served the cause of peace. Telling lies is only acceptable in wartime and to the enemy. Beilin was telling lies both to the Jews and the Arabs and only because he was silly and naïve. He promised the Arabs in the Gaza that the area would become a "Middle East Hong Kong." To promote the cause of peace =J concluded the "Oslo Agreement" with

Yasser Arafat, Israel's main enemy at that time. Menahem Begin drove Arafat's gangs from Lebanon to Tunisia away from Israel, while Yosi Beilin and Shimon Peres invited them back and gave them land and weapons.

Twenty years later, we can definitely say that the achievements of the "peacemakers" are nil.

According to the society dynamics, Arab society, which is securely held together by Islam, is ossified and aggressive. What can you expect from it? Its name—the Palestine Autonomy or Palestine—makes no difference.

In 1989, before the beginning of the first intifada, the living standards in Gaza were twice and, in the West Bank, three times higher than those in Egypt, somewhat higher than in Lebanon, and slightly lower than in Jordan and Syria. Today, they are only 40 percent of Syria's living standards, about a third of Egypt's and Jordan's, and slightly more than a quarter of Lebanon's. Contemporary Palestine proved unviable if "shut off" from Israel. Arabs have lost about two hundred thousand jobs in Israel, which provided sustenance to almost two million residents of the Gaza Strip and the West Bank. For them, these jobs are lost forever, as they have been taken by workers from Thailand, the Philippines, Rumania, the Ukraine, and Moldavia.

The moment has come when Israel no longer wants to feed the paupers and tries to get rid of them by handing over Gaza to anyone willing to take it. There seems to be no fools around. Egypt has refused to take care of it.

The Arabs' struggle against Israeli occupation is attributed to their striving for freedom and for return of the Arab lands. There is no doubt that when this struggle is culminated, the ranks of the unemployed and poor who live today on the "freed land" will be swelled by many more thousands.

This impoverishment process is not new. Those familiar with history may recall the situation in Russia after the civil war there. At that time, the Bolsheviks promised a "radiant future" to workers and peasants, but actually they brought them severe reprisals and abject poverty. It took decades to restore the economy ruined by the civil war and communist ideology. In 1939, poverty and reprisals came to the Baltic countries in the wake of the Soviet occupation troops.

In the late 1980s, an Israeli political scientist Yoram Peri (ex-chief editor of *Davar*), focused on political predilections of career officers. The top command was increasingly drawn into public discussions. The IDF was becoming an active participant in a political dispute, contrary to the principle that the armed forces should be kept away from politics.

In the 1990s, a new aspect was added to the issue. Besides sympathizing with the Arabs, some generals were trying to prove that the intifada could not be suppressed by force alone and that the situation called for a political solution. Other generals were of the opinion that in this age of missiles, territories, particularly occupied territories, are of no importance. They demanded that we should "not lower ourselves to the enemy level but preserve high moral principles." Professor Asa Kasher even wrote the nonsensical IDF Code for soldiers. Yet the "code" was used as some service regulations and its violation was made a punishable offense.

As the intifada gained momentum, the voices expressing the view that it was an excessive luxury to use the IDF to protect the settlers were growing louder. One can only wonder why none of these pacifists said that to use the IDF to protect Israel is also an "excessive luxury" and that it should be disbanded and the country disarmed.

Ehud Olmert, head of Israel's government, revealed his gross ignorance by adding his voice to this chorus. He said that after withdrawal from Gush Katif, thirty thousand troops would no longer be needed to protect 1,200 settlers. It is a waste of effort trying to drive it home to such a blockhead that the army's function is to ensure the security of the country and of the settlers as part of the country. Degradation of the army is the degradation of security.

Ami Ayalon, former head of Israel's intelligence and, later, of the internal security service, approved of those who refused to serve in the Israeli Defense Forces. He said that he was concerned over the increasing number of unarmed Palestinian children hit by the bullets of the Israeli military. I devoted a chapter to these "unfortunate unarmed children" and showed the roots of this phenomenon.

The pitch of argumentation of this kind was growing. In an interview with the director of the Israeli Arab newspaper *Ma al-Ahdat,* Shulamit Aloni, ex-minister and ex-leader of the extreme left MERETS party, said that in her lecture at the National Security College she asked the officers, "Why do you raise such a hullabaloo about people with blood on their hands? Don't any of you have blood on your hands? They throw bombs and you throw bombs. You have planes, they haven't, and therefore, they blow up themselves."

Why do left-wingers Shulamit Aloni and Asa Kasher deliver lectures to army officers? Why don't they invite me? After all, I am twice as clever as these two taken together. I wrote to Professor Asa Kasher, but he did not reply. (Is it to show how clever he is?)

Why is the IDF, which routed Arab armies in the Six-Day War, suffering defeat in the intifada? I could have again compared Israel with the USA that got stuck in Iraq, but it is useless. *Sapienti sat.* My experience tells me that a golem, especially on the top of a hierarchy, is unable to learn.

Why the Israeli Rightists Have No Armed Forces of Their Own

A democratic regime is characterized by a split society and by the emergence of separate armed forces in each camp, which are ready to go from "imperialist" war, or a war of independence, to civil war. This situation obtained in 1948, shortly before Israel's independence. Toward the end of the British mandate, there were four Jewish armed organizations in Palestine. The Haganah detachments of the Jewish trade unions took their orders from Ben Gurion and his social-democratic Labor Party, the PALMAH detachments under Iosif Tabenkin united kibbutz members, ETZEL (commander Menahem Begin) was a right-wing nationalistic or a "revisionist movement," as it was called at that time. There was also LEHI, a small leftist organization that followed in the wake of larger organizations.

Immediately after Ben Gurion staged a surprise attack on the rightists and sank their ship Altalena with its cargo of weapons, Begin declared that "Jews would not fight Jews" and surrendered. All detachments under his command merged with the Haganah into the unified Israeli Defense Forces under a sole command. Unlike Begin, Tabenkin refused to follow Begin's example and ordered his officers to defect.

Actually, Ben Gurion usurped power and became a dictator. At that juncture, with war with Arabs on, this was a correct step.

Although in the Knesset, Begin, who was a right-winger, was in opposition to Ben Gurion, who was a left-winger,

Begin always supported Ben Gurion in defense issues. The leftists were in power from 1948 till 1977.

I am citing Menahem Begin because, later, the principle of "Jews would not fight Jews" demoralized the rightist camp.

The contemporary nationalists do not realize that, today, the internationalists are a far cry from what they were when they were their allies in the joint fight against the Arabs and the British for the establishment of a Jewish state. At that time, the leftists and the rightists had a single goal—that of creating Israel as a Jewish state. At that time, the leftists were obsessed with nationalism, bandied about the "Jewish labor!" slogan, and would pound those who were speaking Yiddish and not Hebrew. Today, this goal is gone; nobody is pounded for speaking Yiddish, and the "Jewish labor!" slogan has given way to "Arab labor."

There were and always will be leftists who are internationalists. They came to Palestine, not because they had an irresistible urge to create a Jewish state; rather, they fled the reprisals of the Russian tsar. It is hard to say why they embraced nationalist goals and slogans at that time. The racist-type "Jewish labor" slogan was probably prompted by the desire of the leftists to compel employers to employ them, the leftists—capable of "fighting" but not capable of working.

At all times, the internationalists have been anarchists and traitors to their people and country. Let me remind you of the "Cambridge Five" in Great Britain or the Rosenbergs, US communists. At all times, the Jews professing internationalism have been anti-Semites hating Jews, the Jewish religion, and tradition. Karl Marx, Lev Trotsky, Ber Borokhov, and Shulamit Aloni are just a few of them. The internationalists need Jewish blood to "grease the wheels of the world revolution." S. Dimanstein, a Bolshevik and chairman of the Jewish Commissariat, seconded Trotsky when he wrote in late December 1918, "we must make Jewish blood fit not only to pour over the wheels of the world revolution whether we want it or not, it must be turned into small screws and wheels, into a mechanism creating revolution and carrying it forward."

Today, the descendants of Ben Gurion are pacifists, declaring that they are not coming out against Israel and Zionist ideology but against the occupation of Arab lands. Why is it their stance today? Why was it different in the past?

Today, Arab revolution is substituted for world revolution.

The nationalists do not realize that the IDF no longer has the function it was created for, namely, it cannot defend the country any longer. Today, it is a tool of the leftists in their fight against the rightists.

Israeli society is again split into leftists and rightists, as was the case almost sixty years ago. Invoking the "Jews would not fight Jews" slogan, the rightists have abandoned the idea of building their own armed forces to replace the IDF.

It must be noted that the principle of "love thy brother" is absolutely alien to the leftists; they are ready to fight Jews and even kill them.

Establishment of Settlements and Eviction of Jews On Mixed States

Machiavelli was perhaps the first to recommend that nationals of the occupying state should populate the occupied territories. Below are some citations about "mixed states" from his works.

"Conquered or inherited possessions may belong either to one and the same country and have a common language or to different countries and have different languages. If a conquered country has a language, customs and ways of life differing from those in the inherited country, it would be difficult to retain power there.

"One of the best ways to deal with the situation is to live there. For instance, a Turkish Sultan moved his capital to Greece to remain in power.

"Another way is to establish colonies in one or two places which would tie the new lands to the conquering state. Colonies are cheap for the potentate to keep, they are loyal to him and dispossess just a small number of residents who cannot do any harm to him when they realize that they have been ruined and dispersed."

Obviously, what Machiavelli meant by "mixed states" is a state populated by people of different cultures—first and foremost of different religions—as, for instance, by Arabs and Jews.

The populating policy was widely used—thanks to Machiavelli's recommendations or not. The rulers of Poland and Turkey invited the Jews banished from Spain. Having occupied Poland, Russia got a greater part of these Jews as its citizens. They were allowed to settle on the outskirts of the Russian Empire and forbidden to take up residence in the central regions. This is how the Jewish Pale appeared.

There were also uninvited settlers. The aborigines were evicted and confined to reservations. This is how the newly discovered continents were populated.

The Knights Templar first came to Palestine in the mid-nineteenth century. They were Germans who inherited their religion from their forefathers from the Middle Ages. Their quarters appeared in Jerusalem, Haifa, and Beit Lehem near Haifa. The knights wanted to teach "these Jews" how to restore the country. There are still neighborhoods in Israel that bear the name "German." Their houses were sturdy; near each was a stable and premises for domestics. Above the entrance was a citation from the Bible. For Palestine, which was a poor country at that time, the coming of the Germans signified economic progress.

The well-being of the Germans in the Holy Land ended when Hitler came to power. The Knights Templar accepted Nazi ideas during the Second World War, and all of them were interned and placed in a British concentration camp. Later, the Jews, mindful of their past deeds, drove them out of the country along with the Britons. When the German Chancellor Willy Brandt visited Israel, he was shown a "relic"—an old woman who was the daughter of the architect that had designed and built the German Quarter in Haifa.

Whether the Jews took Machiavelli's advice or used their own judgment is immaterial, but the policy of populating the land was practiced in prestate Israel. According to law, a roofed house cannot be pulled down unless there is a court ruling to that effect. This law provided the legal grounds for the *Homa ve Migdal* (Wall and Tower) policy. In an out-of-the-way place, a tower would be assembled and materials gathered. One fine morning, tractors and a host of volunteers would bring the tower and the materials to the spot of a future settlement. In the evening of the same day, the tower, complete with a spotlight and guards,

would stand in the center of a new fenced-off Jewish settlement. This was how many kibbutzes in Israel appeared.

I happened to visit the Hanita Kibbutz situated close to
the Lebanon border eight hundred meters above sea level.
It marked the northernmost point of the Jewish settlement effort in the country. Many kibbutzes have "memorial
rooms" in which materials relating to the kibbutz history
are kept. It was in such a room that the sightseers, including myself, were shown a film and told about the kibbutz
history. There is a well-tended forest path, kept to preserve
the memory of the time when it was used to hand carry
materials uphill under Arab fire. Ten people were killed
during this operation.

When the kibbutz member finished his touching story,
I mentioned the struggle the settlers were waging fifty
years later against the Israeli government. The man flew
into a rage:

"Do you want a political discussion?" he asked.

"Yes," was my firm answer.

To finish this section, I would ask this question: Why
does the Israeli government, contrary to Machiavelli's recommendations, use force to raze to the ground the settlements built twenty-odd years ago?

Benzi Liberman, Chairman of the Settlements Council

Means to disarm the rightists were devised that proved
as effective as Menahem Begin's dictum "Jews would not
fight Jews." Listening to Benzi Liberman's addresses at all
kinds of mass rallies, I could not help but notice his persis-
tent calls for disarmament. Those who come with arms, he
would say at each rally, are stool pigeons; they should be
expelled or disarmed. One day, after I had had my fill of

listening to speeches at a big rally outside the Knesset, I wrote an article to draw attention to this call of the settlers' leaders.

Benzi Liberman's role became clear later, after the settlers were evicted from their homes and Israel surrendered Gush Katif settlements to the Arabs.

Benzi Liberman admitted that he had "coordinated" his actions with the government, police, and the military throughout the entire campaign, which lasted about a year. In return for informing the police of their plans, the "protesters" as a sort of compensation received permission to hold their actions, even in places inconvenient for the police. It cannot be excluded that this "cooperation" was the reason why Benzi Liberman and other members of the Settlement Council were never persecuted for their activities. It was only once, just before the settlers were evicted from Gush Katif, that council members were detained for attempting to enter the Gaza Strip, which, by that time, had been declared a closed military zone. All of them were soon released.

The youngsters and teenagers were those who were punished and beaten up. They were paying for Benzi's "cooperation."

I have no doubt that if the settlers had had arms, their eviction would have not been so easy. Moreover, there could have been no eviction. I hope this blunder teaches the Israelis a lesson: the Amona events six months after the "disengagement" showed that the Olmert government, like the previous leadership of the country, intended to continue evicting settlers.

Why Did the IDF Prevail over Jewish Settlers?

Why did the IDF, which had failed in suppressing the intifada, prove so efficient in dealing with the Jewish settlers? I have already said that the IDF acts according to a "code," whose author demands that the Israeli military does "not lower themselves to the enemy level but preserve high moral principles." The enemy is the Arabs.

Is it necessary to "preserve high moral principles" when dealing with the settlers? fter all, they are only one's own countrymen.

Israeli soldiers and policemen are subjected to psychological brainwashing. In this case, the part of the enemy is assigned to the Israelis. Beating one's children is something not everyone would have the guts to do. This happens once in a blue moon, during a civil war. True, what we have is not manslaughter, just beatings. To blunt any compunction the military "educators" might feel, they were given a course of psychological brainwashing officially termed "mental preparation." Once they are through with this preparation, they are considered fit to beat up underage dissidents. Military psychologists taught soldiers to keep their natural human feelings in check in order to perform their "peace" mission, that is, eviction of Jews. The psychologists did their best to blunt emotions down to complete lack of sensibility and replace them with complete control of thoughts and feelings. Psychologists, working jointly with battalion and division commanders, invented a "new language" to help the Golani Division men and flying school cadets overcome their pangs of conscience. For instance, they kept repeating, "we have come to help, not to destroy," and the phrase, "we are part of the assistance force," was actually used for what should have been, "we are the enemy that has come to evict."

During World War II, mental preparation boiled down to a glass of vodka officers and men received before going into battle.

In What Case Is It Disgraceful to Be a SHABAK (KGB) Agent?

In a letter to me, journalist Barri Hamish wrote that he had been fined thirty thousand shekels for saying that a rightist activist was a "SHABAK agent." Is it now disgraceful to be a SHABAK agent? The Russian President Vladimir Putin began his career as a KGB agent. Perhaps the man thus described is already on his way to the presidency and should not feel offended.

I have no doubt that forty years ago, the "SHABAK agent" label was seen as an honor. I for one would have been proud to be so labeled. What has happened to the SHABAK that now cooperation with it is seen as a disgrace for an Israeli national?

Everything is very simple. In the past, we regarded the SHABAK as a defender of the interests of Israel and all Jews. It was an honorable occupation, and each Jew would have been only too happy to become a "SHABAK agent." Today the SHABAK defends the interests of such "Israeli leaders" as Olmert. It won't be far from the truth to say that today, almost all Jews hate Olmert, and at least 20 percent of them are ready to shoot him. Surely there is reason for him to be well guarded.

Today, the SHABAK is mostly engaged in hunting down Jews instead of defending them from the Arabs. No wonder being called a "SHABAK agent" is taken as an insult. Barri Hamish overlooked the changes in the SHABAK and has to pay for it.

I have no doubt that in a split society, when one camp hates the other camp, the leftists use the SHABAK to paralyze the actions of the rightists and plant their agents and provocateurs in the rightist camp. One such operation with an agent provocateur sent into the rightists' ranks was a success. The SHABAK provoked and organized the assassination of Prime Minister Yitzhak Rabin. The victim was responsible for the SHABAK work and knew about all preparations for the assassination. Barri Hamish collected documents and used them in his revealing book, *Who Killed Yitzhak Rabin?* Again Barri has to pay.

Judge Vinograd's Commission

Since the Yom Kippur War, it has been a tradition in Israel to set up a commission after the hostilities are over to investigate the mistakes made in waging the past war. The wars prior to the Yom Kippur War were waged well, and no commissions were established. The second Lebanon war also had to be investigated. The Israelis were frustrated by the defeat and the incompetent leadership and had many questions to which they expected answers. How could this come about? The failures should have taught the leadership a lesson, and the shortcomings should have been made good. These were allegedly the considerations that led to the establishment of a commission headed by Judge Eliyahu Vinograd.

On the very first day of its establishment, it became clear that its actual task was not to investigate but to conceal. All the blunders of the political and military leadership had to be swept under the carpet. The commission members were selected and appointed by Prime Minister Ehud Olmert himself. By that time, three criminal cases had been initiated against him. He had to fight back. If he had stepped down, the examination of these cases would have gone faster.

The conflict on the Lebanese border flared up in July 2006, after Hesbollah militants kidnapped two Israeli soldiers. In the thirty-four days the war lasted, over one thousand Lebanese and 160 Israelis, mostly servicemen, were killed. Israel suffered serious losses and setbacks.

It was already clear, at the initial stage of collecting information and hearing witnesses, that the commission was carefully selecting them. Only those expected to speak in favor of Olmert and help conceal his errors were invited. On the very first day of the commission's work, I applied to it, asking the commission to hear my testimony. To my request, I attached the list of issues I proposed to speak about. I stressed that I would only touch on social themes, on the demoralization of the Israeli armed forces. My request was ignored. I sent another request, but the result was the same.

In November 2006, Professor Asa Kasher, the author of the "Code of Honor" of the Israeli soldier, was invited to the commission session. In a letter I wrote and disseminated via the Internet before the commission was established, I pointed out that Kasher was doing harm to the IDF as his "code" had a demoralizing effect on the Israeli soldiers. I am not the only one who criticizes this "country's chief expert in ethics," and all to no avail. The reason suggests itself: Olmert, the Vinograd Commission, and their ilk need precisely this kind of ethics. Kasher was not asked the questions that I put to the commission. Here are some of the questions he *was* asked: Is it legitimate to fire at munitions depots located in high-rise residential buildings? Was it legitimate to start this war? The commission preferred to listen to the "chief expert in ethics" than to me. Had I been invited, I would have said, "esteemed commission members, yours is a case of truncated thinking. If it is necessary to destroy a residential building to attain your military objective, you should destroy it no matter how many stories it has."

The commission work proceeded in this way. When the work was finished and the commission submitted its report, everybody heaved a sigh of relief. Ehud Olmert's sigh also meant—thank God, the danger is over.

What were Olmert's blunders? Let us begin with the objectives of the war that literally, all mass media took such pains to conceal from Israel's society. It is averred that the war was started to save two captured IDF soldiers. Why, then, was there no response when, six years earlier, in September 2000, the Hesbollah captured three frontier guards? Why was there no response when in March 2002, two terrorists got into Israeli territory and shot seven civilians? What kind of impotence afflicted the IDF in those years? And what served as Viagra to stir them up?

The actual objective of the war was to bring laurels to the triumvirate of Prime Minister Ehud Olmert, Defense Minister Amir Peretz, and Chief of the General Staff Dan Halutz. All of them wished to be regarded as Israeli heroes. Wish and abilities, however, may be worlds apart. The "valiant triumvirate" overlooked the fact that in the forty years since the end of the Six-Day War, the IDF had been demoralized by such men as Asa Kasher and Dan Halutz and had degraded. This is precisely what I wrote to the commission.

The commission attributed the blunders to "systemic failures" with the obvious purpose of exonerating Olmert. Moreover, Judge Vinograd avoided mentioning names and accusing any definite persons. He stressed, "we believe that the prime minister and the minister of defense acted in the interests of the State of Israel." It is to be regretted that Judge Vinograd has never studied sociology. Had he studied it, he would have known that proceeding from the "Iron Law of Oligarchy" by the German sociologist Robert

Michels, for the oligarchy "the benefit of the people and the state" does not differ from personal benefit.

It goes without saying that if the true causes of the army's defeat are meant to be distorted, then there is no sense in setting up commissions and spending money on any analysis of any materials. In the second Lebanon war, the Israeli Army failed to attain any of its proclaimed objectives.

Inadequate as the Vinograd Commission's report was, it was the only way to demonstrate to the Israeli people that the country had no leaders and no leadership. Both in the government and the armed forces, as well as in the Knesset, the Israeli oligarchy is made up of impotents, whose main purpose is to lose no time in lining their pockets at the expense of the people and the country.

Vinograd stressed that alongside developments during the hostilities, the commission dealt with circumstances preceding this war. The activities of the Israeli government and the IDF command were investigated. It took four months to get the testimony of seventy-four witnesses.

He said that the commission's chief purpose was to inform Israeli society, which was disheartened by the results of the war and the government's actions, about the main reasons for Israel's setbacks and—what was even more important—to draw correct conclusions from these setbacks.

Israel launched a lengthy, broad-scale military operation, unprepared, and was defeated. Nevertheless, Judge Vinograd said the decision of the prime minister and the defense minister to start a land operation was necessary, and they both acted *in the interests of Israel.*

The Israelis must be very unlucky indeed to have such halfwits acting in their interests.

As an "achievement," Vinograd noted that the regular army servicemen and reservists showed bravery and a readiness to fight and sacrifice their lives. Whose achievement? Olmert's? Conscientious objectors'? Defectors'?

The interview with the *Maariv* newspaper by Professor Iehizkel Dror, a member of the Vinograd Commission, was a sensation that evoked the opposition's rage. He said, "would you rather have new elections and Netanyahu's victory than Olmert's government and Barak?" Netanyahu, the leader of the Likud party, from which Olmert had defected not long before, was regarded as rightist, which gave the creeps to the professor. This interview confirms that the Commission of Inquiry was set up, not to save the country, but to save the head of government only.

An aide of Olmert's summed up the results of the commission's work: "The Prime Minister and the government are assuming full responsibility and will make every effort to rectify the situation." The prime minister has remained in office, and there are no signs that he intends to step down. Doubtless, the commission has accomplished its mission and saved its creator, but once again it has made it clear that

Before the First Lebanon War, the IDF was regarded as being outside politics. However, its headlong flight from Lebanon has shown not only that it was an erroneous view but also that the country and its armed forces are in a state of degradation. However, nobody seemed to notice this, let alone draw any conclusions. The degradation of Israel and its armed forces goes on.

General Dan Halutz

The world has never seen an aircraft pilot and later commander of the air force becoming the supreme commander in chief. This miracle could happen only in Israel. The swift career of Dan Halutz was the result of his political views. Before Jewish settlers were to be ousted from Gush Katif, Ariel Sharon, the then head of government, was looking for an appropriate man to command the IDF. After all, not everyone can manhandle his own countrymen and evict them from their homes. He found such a man among pilots. It was immaterial to Ariel Sharon that the new IDF commander in chief did not know anything about land operations. The way to the top was hastily cleared for Dan Halutz. From commander of the air force, he was promoted to Deputy Chief of the General Staff in 2004 and Chief of the General Staff in 2005. Under him, the army fulfilled its mission of ousting the Jews from Gush Katif.

Ariel Sharon and Dan Halutz went on with the "politicization" of the armed forces. Proficiency in the sphere of responsibility of their subordinates took a back seat to the latter's acting in accordance with a definite policy. A retired general said in an interview, "the policy pursued by Ariel Sharon and Dan Halutz convinced higher-ranking officers that promotion would depend on the 'pull' a person had and his complete loyalty. This policy made many gifted officers tender their resignation, which certainly did not improve the IDF personnel." The degradation of the armed forces continued.

Shortly after Hesbollah militants kidnapped IDF reservists Ehud Goldwasser and Eldar Regev, Israel's Prime Minister Olmert declared the launch of a military operation, which later came to be known as the second Lebanon war. The over-all plan of the campaign was drawn up by Halutz, who renounced the existing plans of operations in response to the kidnapping of Israeli soldiers, according to which an air mass attack should have been followed by a broad-scale land operation. Halutz decided to do without a land operation and did not call out reservists. He held that Israel could win the war by destroying Lebanon's infrastructure from the air, which would make the Lebanese government assume responsibility for incidents on the Israel-Lebanon border and deal with Hesbollah's rocket launchers. This plan suffered a complete fiasco. In response to bombing Lebanon, Hesbollah subjected Israel's northern areas to mass rocket shelling. Under the circumstances, Halutz called out reservists and decided to start a land operation. But the troops lacked coordination and a single plan. Instead of bombs, the aircraft threw down leaflets.

Israel did not attain the set objectives (release of the kidnapped soldiers or destruction of the infrastructure and of Hesbollah's missile potential) and was defeated in the second Lebanon war.

The first operation carried out personally by the IDF commander on the first day of the war was of a commercial nature. He told his broker to sell all his shares. In the first two days of the Lebanon war, the stock index at the Tel Aviv Stock Exchange plummeted by 8.3 percent. Shares were going down, but Halutz had already saved his money.

General Doron Almog, who investigated the kidnapping of Israeli soldiers by Hesbollah men, in his report put the blame for this on General Gal Hirsh, commander of the Galilee Division. General Hirsh, in his turn, accused Halutz of procrastinating with launching a land operation in Lebanon. Money should be saved first; soldiers could be saved second.

In October 2006, Dan Halutz approved the decision of Brigadier General Mandelblit, the judge advocate general, who signed the order to investigate the actions of officers suspected of leaking confidential information to journalists during the second Lebanon war. When the war was still on, the IDF Information Security Department took steps to prevent passing confidential information to the mass media and started checking officers' telephone calls. The results of the checks were reported to the judge advocate general and the Chief of the General Staff. According to some sources, this investigation was a way for Halutz to square accounts with those high-ranking officers who criticized his actions during the war.

Thus, the only purpose of leaking information from the IDF General Staff to journalists was to do harm to one another.

How Was Dan Halutz Waging War, and What Was His Psychology?

The information given below was published in the Israeli mass media. I only collected it and commented on it.

Halutz: "When ministers asked me what could be considered victory in this war, my reply was: there will be no knockout, no complete defeat." These are the words of an impotent who, instead of routing the enemy, treats it as if it were a naughty boy.

Now about the strategy of impotents: Long before the second Lebanon war, government and IDF leaders adopted a strategy based on the concept that there could be no military solution to the conflict with the Arabs, who use guerilla and terror tactics. It means surrender even before a war. The purpose of this strategy is to justify impotence. Is this the right course in this age of Viagra and nanotechnologies?

In November 2006, after an internal investigation revealed that Israel had used cluster bombs, Halutz ordered the identity of the person who had decided to use the weapons prohibited by the Geneva conventions. Some experts also said that the IDF had used depleted uranium.

The Geneva conventions have been adopted to make life easier for terrorists, to impose a ban on the use of high technologies, equalizing the capability of a regular army with that of the terrorists. Terrorism can do without high technologies; it has no use for morals or the Geneva conventions. A clever general would follow the example of terrorists in disregarding the Geneva conventions. However, there are generals who never tire of insisting on "not lowering ourselves to the enemy level." The Israeli Air Force, on which the Chief of the General Staff relied for bringing him victory, dropped leaflets instead of bombs. The reason for this is also impotence.

The belief in well-nigh unlimited possibilities of the air force and high technologies on the battlefield resulted in negligence, with respect to training the troops for real war. For several years, the IDF had not held any exercises to train troops for an offensive on land or training to capture enemy facilities and territories, which could not but tell on the results of the second Lebanon war. The budget money was spent on erecting walls and disengagement.

In answer to the question of a Seventh Channel editor about the implications of the IDF troops' participation in disengagement, General Yaakov Amidor said, "the main thing is the time wasted during preparation for the 'disengagement,' when the troops were trained to evict unarmed people from their homes and were not trained to fight an armed enemy. Besides, this operation inculcated the idea that in the 21st century, armed forces must be used to deal with civilian affairs in addition to the military." The belief in almost unlimited possibilities of high technologies on the battlefield (bordering on conceit) led to negligence in the training of the troops other than the air force. The higher command was carried away by the fashionable concept that all problems could be resolved by superiority in high technologies, greatly overrating their role and underrating the abilities of the terrorists and guerillas.

As it transpired later, the appointment of Dan Halutz Chief of the General Staff was a mistake and was *not in the interests of Israel*. For the government, this became clear later, but for many Israelis and myself, it was obvious the moment the appointment was announced.

How to Seal the Victory over the Enemy

Up to this point, I described the process of demoralization and degradation of the armed forces, which is usually attendant on the degradation of society. In addition to this, I noted Israel's errors—the fact that it failed to seal any of its victories. I already stressed that the enemy had not been forced to surrender; it had not been demoralized by heavy loss of lives or destruction of the infrastructure, to the extent that restoration could take many years.

In this respect, the allies in World War II demonstrated an exemplary end of a war. Besides unconditional surrender and the tremendous loss of lives Germany had suffered, this country lay in ruins. But the allies were not satisfied. The persecution of "war criminals" began, alongside rivalry in trophy hunting—the objects being not so much armaments already not needed since the war was over, but German scientists and inventors and the fruits of their labor. These scientists had laid the foundations for modern rocket and tubeless weapons, both in the West and East. Besides, as a part of reparations, the USSR was taking trainloads of industrial equipment, in fact, complete plants, out of Germany to use in its own territory.

Japan, like Germany, was in ruins and paralyzed. Yet Japan had been chosen to test a nuclear bomb.

Both countries agreed to unconditional surrender, and since that time, there has been no talk of *revanche*. Even at the time of surrender, the Japanese were closely united, and their fighting spirit was high. The Japanese word "kamikaze" was borrowed by all the world's languages.

Why couldn't Israel emulate the allies, namely, inflict a demoralizing defeat on the Arabs, which would suppress their desire to wage another war? That would have been real victory.

I know people can say that it was the USA and the Soviet Union that prevented Israel from carrying the war to a victorious end. But then, after the Second World War, these two countries were no longer allies, and it is unlikely that in this particular instance, they would act as if they were. They *were* allies but up to a certain point.

The main obstacle to full victory was the Israeli leaders' psychology. They had no intention of making short shrift of the enemy.

Factors Militating against Victory

The main thing is to get rid of impotence both among the politicians and among the military. Having the nuke is important, but knowing how, where, and when to use it is just as important. The Moslems have it, and their morality would not deter them from using it.

Menahem Begin, for instance, had the will to destroy the Iraqi nuclear reactor, and he did it.

All weapons may be used to win, and my adversary will use them, even if I refrain from using some of them. Iran threatened Israel many times. It should be borne in mind that war is war.

No talk of morality and ethics of the kind "not to lower ourselves to the enemy level and preserve high moral principles" should be allowed in the armed forces. War obliterates morality and ethics. It is our shared duty "to lower ourselves" to the enemy level. Don't forget that victors are not judged.

This dictum is especially true when fighting terrorism. Mass reprisals, taking hostage close relatives of terrorists, threats, and blackmail—everything is permissible.

You can achieve everything by military force. But you must know where and how to use it.

"If We Have War Tomorrow, Russia has become a menace to Europe, America, and the world." These words adorn the wraparound of Edward Lucas's book *New Cold War* published by Bloomsbury Publishing.

Here is a question to the author: Do you think that controversies between Russia and the West may lead to armed conflicts?

Anton, Estonia

The gist of Edward Lucas's reply is as follows: I cannot exclude provocations especially if NATO falls apart (for instance if Americans pull out of Europe), but it is hardly likely. The Russian armed forces are just poor leftovers of what the Soviet Union had; the navy has only twenty surface vessels. As for the air force, it is short of everything from spares to airborne hours. The troops are in dire straits, with hazing rife and career officers lacking normal housing. I do not think that Russia may use serious military force in the near future. Something may happen in Georgia if the Georgian authorities do not see through provocations.

It is rather surprising that in spite of his scorn for the Russian armed forces, Lucas presents them as a menace to the West. As far as I can see in the mass media, it is Russia that is the object of provocations and not the other way round. NATO is expanding eastward. Golems accuse Russia of putting a stop to the liberalization process and embarking on the road to cold war.

It is immaterial who is provoked. Assuming that the war between Russia and NATO is to break out, let us weigh the chances of victory for both of them at this stage, proceeding from the principles of military sociology I laid down above.

Lucas's idea that the USA may leave Europe does not hold water. US presidents' psychology presupposes expansion rather than isolationism.

Yet in this case, NATO as a war alliance would immediately disintegrate, and more than half of its member countries would refrain from fighting Russia directly or indirectly There is no doubt that among them would be some Balkan countries, in which Orthodoxy is the predominant religion as, in days gone by, Russia liberated them from the Turkish yoke. The Baltic countries would declare their neutrality, although their feelings for Russia are anything but friendly. Only the USA and the United Kingdom would agree to fight, but they are already bogged down in Iraq and Afghanistan with no end to this situation in sight.

In its rear, Russia would have China, which would not enter the war but would be only too glad to make some of its manpower and industrial potential available to Russia.

Assuming that none of the sides would use weapons of mass destruction and that Edward Lucas's evaluation of the Russian armed forces as just leftovers of those of the USSR is correct, it should be borne in mind that it was the Soviet armed forces that made a decisive contribution to the Allied victory in Word War II.

Russia would be able to mobilize a great force to confront the USA. Russia's weapons would be less sophisticated than those of NATO. But the important thing is the degree of cohesion between the people and the army, for the battle worthiness of a belligerent's armed forces depends on that. There is no doubt that the degree of cohesion in NATO would be much lower than in Russia.

Chapter 5

The Regular Army and Guerillas

*Moishe: "Comrade Commander, take me
in your guerilla detachment."
Commander: "You must pass a test first. Here's a pack of leaf-
lets. If you manage to distribute them, I will take you."
Moishe returns in a week. He is tired and exhausted.
Commander: "How are you? What took you so long?"
Moishe (taking out a pack of bank notes from his pocket):
"Some goods you've foisted on me."*

Of Military History

If we go back to the earliest military history, we will find that guerilla detachments of primitive tribes were progenitors of a modern army. Primitive tribes had no regular army. A detachment of volunteers was formed in the tribe to plunder a neighboring tribe. They would steal up to the place of attack and, uttering their battle cries, would fall upon and kill everyone, children included, as children could later take revenge. The captured women would often be used as wives, which saved them from death. There were no moral or any other restrictions in wars.

Gradually leaders realized that well-trained and disciplined armed detachments of fighting men do a better job on the battlefield than guerillas. That spelled the end of anarchy in warfare and the emergence of a regular army. War became a clash of armies similar to the clash of teams on a football field. Bringing orderly practices to military activities led to the appearance of military uniforms and "rules of war."

Yet guerilla warfare did not disappear. Guerillas were particularly active in fighting Napoleon's army. In Spain, they were just a nuisance to his army, and in Russia, they defeated it. Napoleon had an army of six hundred thousand when he invaded Russia. Apart from the bloody battle at Borodino, there were no head-on clashes between the French and the Russian armies. Ultimately, however, the French army was routed in Russia, and Napoleon left its badly battered remains and hurried to France to recruit a new army.

The Russian troops did not engage the French army in serious battle while it was retreating, but they forced the French to retreat via the route they had come. Everything along this route had already been looted; the French faced famine and the severe Russian winter. Guerilla detachments headed either by Russian officers or composed of Russian army units and Cossacks attacked convoys, trains, which were separate units, to disrupt the supply of the Napoleon army. Russian detachments tried to prevent the French army from crossing the Berezina River. When nine thousand Frenchmen had already crossed it, Napoleon was told that Cossacks headed by Platov were approaching. Napoleon ordered his men to blow up the crossings. A tremendous baggage train with spoils pillaged in Russia and twenty-nine thousand French troops were abandoned.

No wonder R. Shumann arranged *Marseillaise* into the famous song with lyrics by Heinrich Heine starting with the words, "two grenadiers were plodding along to France from Russian captivity." From Russian captivity plodding along were the remnants of the Napoleon army routed in skirmishes with guerillas.

We will summarize the results of building a modern army out of individual terrorists. The hallmark of the process is better organization and precision, which, in terms of synergetics, can be presented as an ejection of entropy. The progress of the means of communication and management contributes to the process.

Terrorism and Guerilla Warfare

Terror, an extinguished volcano in the Antarctic on Ross Peninsula off Victoria Land, height up to 3262 m, basalt rock under glaciers. Discovered by James Clark Ross in 1841, named after a ship taking part in the expedition.

Today, after a brilliant victory in a war of buttons, the victors face the nightmare of its aftermath—terrorism and guerilla warfare.

In none of the defeated countries occupied by the Allies after World War II was there any resistance to them in any form. There were no guerilla groups or terrorist actions against them, either in Germany or Japan. Moreover, in Italy, it was the guerillas who lynched Mussolini and fought the German invaders, together with the Allies, to liberate their country. What were the reasons for alliance?

And why was resistance to foreign occupation so fierce in Iraq, Somalia, and especially in Vietnam?

The situation in Israel is unique in this respect. After the Six-Day War, the Arabs in the occupied territories thought they were the happiest Arabs in the world. After twenty years, they got tired of their happy life and began to fight for their freedom and independence and against Israel's occupation. The standard of living is now less important to them than "freedom and independence."

What are the special features of a victory or an occupation? What are the causes for the emergence of terrorism and guerilla movement in an occupied country? How should these problems be addressed?

The Americans believe that large guerilla armies are something to be relegated to the past—such armies as the Yugoslavs had under Tito in 1941–44 or the detachments headed by Soviet General Kovpak who fought the Nazis, not only in the Ukraine, but also made raids into Poland, Hungary, and Slovakia. Today, aerospace reconnaissance is capable of pinpointing large guerilla detachments by their camp fires during rest breaks, by the heat they emit, or they can be seen through powerful lenses and annihilated by cluster bombs. But guerillas entrenched deep underground ousted the Americans from Vietnam. The Americans now have bombs that can hit targets many meters underground, but this did not save them from the attacks of the Arab Al-Qaeda acting inside the USA.

Anarchy Is the Mother of Order

A guerilla's weapon is only what he can hold in his hands. Guerilla detachments have no artillery, tanks, or planes.

Going back to terrorism and guerilla warfare means going back to primitive warfare. In this case, a well-trained regular army and state-of-the-art weaponry are not employed. There is no general staff or centralized command. The fight is controlled by the elements and local initiative. If it turns out that there is general guidance, that means that terrorism and guerilla warfare have gone up to a higher level. The main thing in dealing with this regression to the primitive is to disregard any moral and international rules, norms, and laws of waging war. It is this disregard that makes terrorism and guerilla warfare advantageous.

The *gabbai* in the Haifa Technion synagogue was a guerilla fighter during the Second World War. He told me that the commander of his detachment was the arbiter of the fate of those who came to his detachment. If the commander had the slightest mistrust of them, they were shot. No prisoners were taken.

According to sociobiology, animals join in herds for hunting and ensuring greater security. There is a host of such herds, colonies, packs, etc. Every herd has a hierarchy to make it manageable. Each animal in the herd has its position in the hierarchy. In the herd, everything follows a stringent order. *Anomie* is disintegration of the herd, disintegration of society. Disintegration spells the end to the advantages derived from unity.

When hunting, beasts of prey always try to isolate their victim from the herd and deprive it of joint protection.

Terrorism can be compared to such hunting methods. Terrorists usually strike at innocent and unsuspecting victims at a random place. The main thing for them is the maximal number of casualties. Terrorism can cause anomie in the enemy camp, which is victory in itself. Under these conditions, the **advantages derived from order and cohesion, which the enemy of terrorism used to have, disappear, and each individual in a herd has to shift for himself. At this stage, morality, ethics, and the like vanish as they make it harder to defend oneself.**

However, the enemy cannot be defeated by terrorism alone. At a certain stage, terrorist gangs have to unite into an organization—first into guerilla detachments and then into an army.

How Terrorism and Guerillas Should Not Be Fought

Use of physical coercion to its full extent by no means excludes assistance by reason. Therefore the one using coercion without let or hindrance has a tremendous advantage over an adversary refraining from such methods. In this way one makes law for the other. Both adversaries are exerting every effort limited solely by the inner counteracting forces.

Karl von Clausewitz

The two musts in fighting terrorism:

1.   Not to cave in to it and not to do as the terrorists demand.

2.   Use collective punishment if the situation calls for it (mass reprisals, taking hostages).

The efficiency of such steps was demonstrated when a new regime was established after a revolution or civil war. A section below is devoted to mass reprisals.

Napoleon lost the war in Russia because Borodino was the only place where he fought against the Russian army. The rest of the campaign was fought on the occupied territory against the closely knit patriotic-minded Russian people. Moscow on fire was a manifestation of patriotism. Russians were setting their houses, their old capital, on fire to prevent the enemy from getting anything. *Patriotism of the Russian people at that time is proof of a high degree of its cohesion.* Napoleon could not resort to mass reprisals against Russians. Moreover, it was the Russians who made him retreat along the route he had already left ravaged.

After the war with Napoleon was over, the first Russian manual for waging a guerilla war appeared, entitled *Opyt teorii partizanskikh deistvii (An Attempt at Creating a Theory of Guerilla Actions)* (published in 1822) by Denis Vasilievich Davydov (1781–1839), a hussar hero of this war (later lieutenant general). During the war, he headed a guerilla detachment. This book is an account of his combat experiences and a summary.

I am not interested in the operational aspects of this and other manuals for waging a guerilla war. I will focus on the social aspect—the behavior of society.

V. I. Klembovsky (1860–1921), a Czarist Russian general executed by the Soviet power, in his work *Partizanskie deistviya. Opyt rukovodstva (Guerilla Actions. An Experience of Commander)* clearly shows that *a people's war has no rules and is waged as one sees fit without any connection with the actions of the army. They coexist side by side but never merge.*

Like the actions of a regular army, the actions of guerillas depend on the attitude of the local population. If the population is hostile, contacts with it should be minimal. Below is an instance showing what disregard of this rule may lead to.

The population of Byelorussia associated the fascist regime with Gauleiter Wilhelm von Kube. While he was in office, in Minsk and its environs alone, about four hundred thousand people were killed on his personal order. Standing on Minsk's Yubileinaya Square, he personally "saw off" several thousand Jews marching to death on the day of mass execution of Jews.

Nadezhda Troyan of the Artur Guerilla Detachment managed to make the acquaintance of Galina Mazanik (her true name was Elena), Kube's personal parlor maid. Terletsky, Mazanik's husband, was a driver at an NKVD base in Moscow and was there at that time. Troyan met Mazanik several times, and after she had made sure that Mazanik could come near the Gauleiter and—mainly—that she had remained loyal to the Soviet power, on August 18, 1943, she assigned Elena the mission of assassinating Kube.

The operation started on September 21, 1943, when the Gauleiter was out of Minsk. For three days, the resistance fighters involved waiting for him to return. The day before his arrival, at 2:00 a.m. sharp Elena turned on the time bomb mechanism—the bomb was to go off in twenty-four hours. In the morning, she brought this "surprise" to Kube's mansion in the bottom of her handbag. She managed to put it in Kube's bed. It was a mortal risk. A minute after she put the bomb in the bed, an officer on duty who was known for his particular hatred for Soviet people entered the room. He pushed her out of the room shouting abuse at her. She said she had a toothache and was allowed to leave the house.

At the appointed time, Nikolai Furts and Osipova from the reconnaissance squad waited for her in a lorry outside the Minsk Drama Theater. Nikolai took Mazanik and Osipova to a place 16 km from Minsk on the way to Lagoisk. From there they walked and, by midnight, came to the village of Yanushkovichi, where guerrillas were waiting for them. Kube returned home at 1:00 a.m. Twenty minutes later, the bomb detonated. The Gauleiter was blown to pieces. All of the Gestapo's force was assigned to apprehend the culprit. Local newspapers published Mazanik's distinctive marks, and a huge sum of money was promised for her head. But by that time, Maria Osipova, Nadezhda Troyan, and Elena Mazanik had already been flown out to Moscow.

What about the Situation in Israel?

Why did Palestinian Arabs, who had been happy to have their lands occupied after the Six-Day War, start the struggle "against the occupation" twenty years later? After the occupation, Israel gave substantial sops to these Arabs and—mainly—gave them work in its territory. Their standard of living soared instantly. And yet, acts of terror against the Israeli invaders became a common occurrence.

Why did Iraqi Arabs, who welcomed the overthrow of their dictator Saddam Hussein by the US and British invaders in 2003 and the freedom they got, unleash terror and guerilla actions against the invaders shortly afterward? These are questions for sociology to answer.

In chapter 1, we dealt with the hierarchy of man's needs. First in this hierarchy are man's physical needs. If the invaders satisfy them by ensuring the supply of food, water, and the like to the population under occupation, this population feels happy and grateful to the invaders.

Having quenched their hunger and thirst, however, this population enters the second stage—"cohesion in society." At this stage, it became clear that the invaders who had toppled Saddam Hussein had not taken the trouble to find somebody to be an adequate substitute for him. Obsessed with democracy, the Israelis and the Americans forced it on the Arabs, while the Arabs, fettered as they are by Islam, have yet a long way to go before they are ready to accept it. Their herd feeling, which I called "hevraav," remains unsatisfied. They are hungry and angry.

These are the roots of terrorism and guerilla actions.

There is a simple remedy for this situation: the use of reprisals to unite them in a society that would meet their needs. The example of V. V. Putin can be followed. He assigned the mission of uniting the Chechens to Akhmad Kadyrov, also a Chechen.

Demoralized Society

It is quite another thing when society is demoralized and disorganized. In this case, the state is unable to protect its citizens from terrorism, despite the armed forces, the police, and the security services it has at its disposal.

In addition to the centralized security service, there are local security officers, self-defense units, and security guards at every door, checking the bags with metal detectors of the people entering. The country becomes strewn with electronic detectors of weapons and explosives, dogs, fences, etc. For example, in Israel, there are one hundred thousand security guards at doors. An eight-meter-high fence separates Israel from the Arabs at the cost of $8,000,000. It reminds one of the "great building sites of communism" in the Soviet Union. A fence of this kind cannot be registered as a Guinness World Record, since it is much shorter than the Great Wall of China. Israel cannot put an end to terrorism. But then, since when has it been possible to *deal with social issues by technical means?* Is it possible in general?

The Israeli government has been acting against my recommendations. Why? The question is warranted.

Israeli society is split into two antagonistic camps: the leftists (internationalists) and the rightists (nationalists). The leftists support terrorism directly or indirectly; their instincts tell them that it is an ally in their struggle against the rightists. The paramount task for Israel is to unite its society.

Chapter 6

Joint and Individual Responsibility and Collective and Individual Punishment

When speaking of society's behavior, I have always stressed that it depends on the degree of its cohesion. Cohesion is the main parameter of society. Both society's responsibility and its punishment depend on cohesion.

As I said above, there are three types of society characterized by the degree of their cohesion:

1. Over-united society (OUS), with a very high degree of cohesion—close to 100 percent.
2. Optimal society, with the degree of cohesion around 50 percent.
3. *Anomie*, with cohesion close to zero.

This order follows the process of society's degradation from absolute dictatorship, that is, excessive cohesion, to full disintegration. We will examine society's responsibility and its punishment as functions of the degree of its cohesion. Let us start with OUS.

Joint Responsibility and Punishment

The OUS characteristics examined above warrant the conclusion that the "all for one and one for all" principle is widely practiced in such a society, and it is natural for it to practice joint responsibility and collective punishment.

It must be stressed that prior to the 1917 Bolshevist revolution in Russia, individual responsibility was practiced in that country. After the revolution, the new authorities introduced joint responsibility and the institute of hostages, the new ways reflected both in mass reprisals and in laws. The codes and laws adopted in the first decade of Soviet power leave no doubt about this. Some of them are mentioned and commented upon below.

I will not dwell in detail on the reprisals following the decree of the RSFSR government "On Red Terror" (*Compiled Decrees of the RSFSR*, 1918, No. 65), and other forms of judicial and extrajudicial punishment of real or imaginary enemies of the Soviet power. Of special interest in this context, however, is the addendum to the *Regulations Concerning Crimes against the State*, 1927 Art. 13 (Art. 581 of the Criminal Code of the RSFSR of 1926), of June 8, 1934. According to these regulations, if a serviceman was convicted of treason, a member of his family who was no accessory to said committed or planned treason and who did not even know anything about it was punished by exile to a remote Siberian region for a five-year term (*Compiled Laws of the USSR*, 1934, No. 33). This signified the introduction of the institute of hostages in the criminal law, later giving rise to such notions coined by the NKVD and OGPU as "wife of traitor to the Motherland" (WTM) and "member of the family of traitor to the Motherland" (MFTM).

The "Servicemen Case" of 1937 is an illustration of the persecution to which WTMs and MFTMs were subjected. In that year, sentenced to death and shot were higher Red Army commanders: Gamarnik (committed suicide before the arrest) and Tukhachevsky, Deputy people's commissars for the defense; Yakir and Uborevich, former commanders of military districts; Kork, head of a military academy; Primakov and Sangursky, deputy commanders of military districts; Feldman, head of the department for higher commanders; Putna, military attaché in Great Britain. Reprisals of the above-mentioned commanders were followed by reprisals against their wives, children, and relatives. The adults were confined to concentration camps, and the children were sent to special orphanages.

Another departure from the principle of individual responsibility was the following instance of joint responsibility. According to Art. 8, Para. "n" of the Regulation on Disciplinary Comrades Courts of 1921, blue- and white-collar workers were considered responsible for breaches of labor discipline and were guilty of the offense, but so were the blue- and white-collar workers who aided and abetted them. They could also be punished by up to a six-month term of corrective labor or confinement in a concentration camp (Compiled Decrees of the RSFSR. 1921, Nos. 23–24).

The Decree of the USSR Council of People's Commissars of February 16, 1933, also rejected the principle of individual responsibility. Pursuant to it, persecuted for stealing state property were not only the perpetrators of this crime but also heads or enterprises who failed to take steps to prevent it (Compiled Laws of the USSR. 1933. No. 13).

According to the Decree of the USSR Supreme Soviet Presidium "On Going Over to an Eight-Hour Working Day and Seven-Day Work Week and on Prohibiting Blue- and White-Collar Workers from Quitting Jobs of Their Own Accord," of June 6, 1940, failure on the part of head of enterprises to bring to trial persons who had quit their jobs of their own accord was a criminal offense (Journal of the USSR Supreme Soviet, 1940, No. 20).

Order 270, which was signed by J. Stalin on August 16, 1941, at an early stage of the patriotic war against Germany, says *inter alia*:

"Commanders and political commissars tearing off their insignias on the battlefield and defecting to the rear or yielding themselves prisoner to the enemy shall be considered inveterate defectors, and their families shall be taken into custody as families of defectors who have violated their oath and betrayed their Motherland."

And further in clause 2:

"…and the families of privates who have yielded themselves prisoner shall be deprived of the state allowance and assistance."

Thus, family was made a hostage as the first subject of reprisals by the authorities. Joint responsibility tightly bound parents and children.

"Can the Red Army tolerate cowards defecting to the enemy and surrendering to it or fainthearted commanders who at the very first hitch at the front would tear off their rank insignia and defect to the rear? No, it cannot! If such cowards and defectors remain at large, the army will disintegrate in no time and our Motherland will be ruined. Cowards and defectors should be eliminated." According to this order, any private or commander attempting to surrender should be "dismissed from his position, stripped of rank, and demoted to private or shot down on the spot if necessary." Those who became prisoners of the enemy should, the order said further, be eliminated "by all available means, using both ground and air forces."

Commanders and political commissars who would tear off their rank insignia on the battlefield and defect to the rear or are taken prisoner should be regarded as vicious defectors, and their families should be arrested as the families of defectors who violated the oath and betrayed their Motherland. And further on in Para. 2.

...and the families of privates taken prisoner should be deprived of the state allowance and assistance.

So the family is a hostage, the first to be subjected to reprisals. Parents and children were bound by joint responsibility.

In 1922–23, some thirty thousand students were expelled from higher schools for their social background. Those who refused to disavow their parents in newspapers were doomed to a life inappropriate to their abilities and upbringing.

The "all-Russia purge of state agencies of alien and improper elements" of 1929–30, which Ilf and Petrov described in their book *The Golden Calf* with such humor, was a tragedy for tens of thousands of people, mostly past their prime, who lost their jobs for one and the same reason—for "having the wrong kind of parents."

The codes, decrees, and other regulations cited above provide documentary evidence of the process of building cohesion and joint responsibility. But the process may take place without any documents.

I would like to add episodes from my own life to these ruthless orders and decrees. In the early 1950s, when anti-Semitism flourished in the USSR, I was an undergraduate of a naval academy to which I was assigned after I had been drafted. My immediate superior, a Russian guy, would complain: "You are like all the others, but I am always reprimanded because of you." And, indeed, why should my commander be punished because I was guilty of being

Jewish? After all, he was a purebred Russian. Finally, I was commissioned as an officer, expelled from the Komsomol, and—something I could only hope for—demobilized. I was a lucky Jew in this anti-Semitic drive launched by the Soviet power. I have a pleasant recollection of a Komsomol meeting at which my "comrades-in-arms" accused me, a rascal, of going to museums and the opera instead of drinking vodka.

The apprehension and conviction or execution of one member of a gang does not cut short the gang's activity, as the member would be immediately replaced, because the situation that led to the emergence of the gang persisted. Moreover, even the elimination of the entire gang was no cause for optimism. One gang would be replaced by another one. Thus, elimination of a gang was impossible without eliminating the situation that contributed to its emergence. As shown above, some laws and decrees by the authorities that provide for joint responsibility make people unite in a gang. But there is more to it.

It has been generally accepted that poverty is the breeding ground for terrorist and criminal gangs. This is an erroneous view that goes contrary to what I said about OUSs. Financial injections are powerless against asceticism. The money would be spent on weapons and pleasure. The Bolshevist ascetics who came to power in October 1917 wore coarse army greatcoats and high boots and quasi field jackets, but preferred to live in palatial mansions formerly belonging to aristocrats who had fled the country and to get their foodstuffs at special shops and canteens, entrance to which was barred to an ordinary citizen. A similar situation obtained with respect to medical services.

In order to get a better understanding of what I mean, let us go back to a bigger society like Sparta. Joint responsibility and collective punishment were clearly manifested not only in the heroism of the Spartan detachment led by King Leonidas, but also in the attitude of Spartans to the people who survived the battle by sheer chance. The Lycurgus laws were a powerful factor for cohesion. To erode cohesion, it would have been necessary to repeal the Lycurgus laws. Today, the countries of the "axis of evil" should be subjected to collective punishment to make them discontinue supporting terrorists in other countries. The Turkish government decided to make raids into neighboring Iraq to put an end to attacks of terrorist gangs from its territory.

☆ ☆ ☆

Who Is to Mete Out Collective Punishment?

It is clear that it does not make any sense to apply individual punishment to an OUS, because it will be unproductive of results: hence, the need for collective punishment and mass reprisals when dealing with an OUS.

But who is to mete out the punishment?

The Soviet power had no problem finding the right kind of people to do it. It had special, "uniting" agencies for the purpose, such as Cheka, VCheka, OGPU, NKVD, MGB, KGB, etc.

It becomes a problem when OUS aggressiveness spills over its boundaries. The conflict between two or more over-united societies may be called war. It may be war between street gangs or war between parties expounding different ideologies. For instance, before Hitler's takeover, there were armed hostilities between communists and Nazis in

Weimar Germany. Another example is internecine strife for power between Arabs in Algiers, Lebanon, or "Palestinian Autonomy." The 1941–45 war between Nazi Germany and communist USSR belongs in this category. It is immaterial who is the winner in this crucial clash.

It is quite different when an OUS clashes with democracy or even an anomie, the extreme form of democracy. Something of this kind is taking place today between Turkey and the Kurds in Iraq, and between Israel and the Arabs. It is typical of democracy to have society divided into two camps. In this situation, the internationalist camp usually includes those who would come out in defense of the enemy and who would justify any moral or other OUS crimes. An apposite example is the war in Vietnam. Some mass media in the USA pictured the Americans fighting in Vietnam as monsters killing defenseless civilians.

Now we come to a typical Israeli example. In an interview with Zuheira Andreus, director of the Israeli Arab newspaper *Ma al-Ahdat,* Shulamit Alony, former minister and leader of the extreme leftists, condemned Israeli Defense Minister Ehud Barak for his "punitive operations" in the Gaza Strip:

"Collective punishment is an inhuman step. Ehud Barak is the most dangerous man in the State of Israel owing to his nature—he is trigger-happy and conceited."

In her opinion, Barak should be brought to the Hague International Court of Justice for his "crimes against humanity." It should be noted that Ehud Barak is also a leftist, although he is a member of another party. Shulamit Alony, like Karl Marx, is an inveterate anti-Semite, but she would stress that she is Jewish if she could profit by this.

Thus, the internationalists see collective punishment as a "crime against humanity"—but only if this punishment is applied to themselves and their allies. They turn a blind eye to mass reprisals against the rightists and do not regard them as crimes. After her discourse on collective punishment, Shulamit Alony continued with her accusations of her own people and justification of the enemy. She has an ingrained hatred for her own people. She needs a united society, while Israeli society is split.

"One who uses cluster bombs in a neighborhood populated by civilians," she says, "to my mind is a criminal. He must be brought to court first here [in Israel] and if it is not done here, then to the Hague International Court." It means that terrorists and criminals are defended in the enemy camp and their actions are justified and "viewed with understanding."

Here is another example. It appears that justification and "understanding" may come from other quarters, too.

The EC is also against "collective punishment" in Gaza. This organization warned Israel against cutting fuel and electricity supplies to the Gaza Strip and called these steps "collective punishment of the Palestinians." The Israeli authorities declared that they had begun to put into practice their plans for putting an end to rocket shelling of their territory and that fuel supplies to Gaza would be cut by 14 percent, and in approximately 1 percent of the Gaza territory, electricity would be switched off for fifteen minutes a day.

Benita Ferrero-Waldner, EC commissioner for external relations, told a *Reuter* correspondent that the EC realized what Israel suffered due to the ongoing rocket attacks from the Gaza Strip. Yet, she added, the new sanctions of the Israeli government would have far-reaching adverse consequences for the local population and would only strengthen the positions of radical paramilitary groups like Hamas. Sanctions cannot be allowed to become collective punishment, she declared. This declaration betrays an EC commissioner's lack of knowledge of sociology and the fact that she is guided by instinct rather than by common sense. Why is it forbidden to apply collective punishment to an OUS? This example shows the extent to which ignorant and mediocre people can rule society and force their views on others.

Israeli Prime Minister Ehud Olmert promised that he would not allow a humanitarian crisis in Gaza to happen. The annual consumption of electrical energy in the Gaza Strip is 200 MW, of which 120 MW is supplied by Israel.

"The Enemy Territory"

Israel has declared the Gaza Strip an "enemy territory," which, it says, relieves it of compliance with international laws obligating it to provide the utilities to the civilian population in the occupied regions. The world community, however, holds that, according to law, Israel is responsible for the situation in the coastland, because it controls the Gaza Strip borders and its air and water space, even though it has withdrawn its settlements from the area.

Israel imposed an economic embargo against Gaza after the Islamic Hamas movement ousted representatives of the Fatah party from the government in June.

Meanwhile, three Palestinians and one Israeli soldier were killed in the skirmishes between the Palestinians and the Israelis in the towns of Khan Unis and Beit Khanun in the Gaza Strip. Rockets targeted at the Israeli territory are often fired from these towns.

The EC has a strange mind indeed. The joint USA and EC blockade of Cuba, Belarus, and the economic boycott of Iran are never referred to as collective punishment. At the same time, Israel's retaliation to continuous rocket shelling of its territory by cutting fuel and electricity supplies to its enemy brought about a spate of accusations. This approach practiced by the USA and the EC can only be described as "we may and you may not!"

Israel and the Arabs

The Jewish religion prohibits asceticism. During holidays, Jews make merry and become tipsy. They may engage in usury or charity. But stories about a rich man giving all he had to the poor and becoming a monk are alien to Jewish history. There can be just one reason for this—we don't need another pauper. Contrary to Judaism, Islam and Christianity, which the Arabs have embraced, encourage asceticism. This difference fuels the conflict between the Arabs and the Jews. What does an ascetic need? Nothing. Any relief he gets will be spent on weapons.

Optimal Society

Optimal society is positioned between anomie, with its excessive individualization, and OUS, with its excessive cohesion. It seems reasonable to expect that optimal society should derive some features from both anomie and OUS, that is, both from left and right.

The modern criminal code is based on complete negation of the principle of joint responsibility. All decrees and codes of the type mentioned above in this section have been abandoned. Today, in Israel, only the person who committed a crime can be held responsible for it. It would seem outrageous today, if in compliance with the decrees, codes, and ordinances quoted above, responsibility for a crime would be imposed on an uncle, a nephew, or cousin of the criminal. There is every reason to believe that complete rejection of collective punishment is a sign that Israel has skipped the stage of optimal cohesion and passed to the anomie stage.

Yet there are exceptions. If you apply for a bank loan, you will be asked to provide surety that the loan will be returned. Your relations and friends, who, in this case, assume the role of guarantors, may provide this surety. If you fail to pay back the loan, the bank will demand it from your guarantors. This is also a form of joint responsibility.

The Jewish religion allows punishment based on a principle akin to "clan responsibility." A child born out of wedlock (*mamzer* in Hebrew) is punished. Moreover, the child's descendants over ten generations are not recognized as Jewish, and they cannot marry a Jewish man or woman. Proselytes (Gentiles converted to Judaism) are an exception. So children are punished for their mother's sin. Women should surely think twice before sinning.

How should optimal society treat a criminal or terrorist gang, should it appear inside an OUS optimal society? Theoretically there are two options:

1. Capture and punish each gang member.
2. Act on the principle of joint responsibility like banks do and divide the punishment among relatives and friends of the gang members.

Actually, today, joint responsibility is taboo in democratic countries.

Public Emergency is an extraordinary legal regime governing the work of bodies of state power and management, as well as other establishments and organizations, which is introduced in the country or some of its regions to protect them from external or internal threat and to maintain public order.

The public emergency regime presupposes curbing some of the liberties of physical persons and legal entities and imposing some additional duties on them.

The 1976 US National Emergencies Act empowers the president to declare a state of emergency for a six-month term and to prolong it for an indefinite number of times.

In the Russian Federation, the president can declare a state of emergency under the circumstances specified in the federal constitutional law, "On the State of Emergency." He must immediately inform the Federation Council and the State Duma about it.

A state of emergency is only introduced under the circumstances divided into two categories:

1. An attempt at forcible overthrow of the constitutional regime, armed mutiny, regional conflict, etc.
2. Emergency situations caused by natural or man-made calamities.

The president of the Russian Federation can declare a state of emergency for the maximum term of thirty days and, in individual areas, for the maximum term of sixty days. A new presidential decree is needed to prolong it.

Inasmuch as a government may use a state of emergency as an excuse to curtail human rights, the International Covenant on Civil and Political Rights stipulates that a state of emergency should meet the following conditions:

It should be "to the extent strictly required by the exigencies of the situation, provided that such measures are not inconsistent with their [the states'] other obligations under international law and do not involve discrimination solely on the ground of race, color, sex, language, religion, or social origin." Some basic human rights cannot be impinged even under a state of emergency.

The above warrants the conclusion that introduction of a state of emergency, curtailing as it does "human rights," can unite society to the extent of making it an OUS with all its merits and demerits.

Anomie

Anomie is a disintegrated society. It is obvious that joint responsibility cannot be practiced in this kind of society. Besides being divided into two antagonistic camps— the nationalists and the internationalists, it has a plethora of competing and feuding sects, factions, parties, organizations, etc. Prominent among them are the Mafia and terrorist organizations. Such organizations are typical of OUS, yet they have their roots in anomie. The Mafia is a criminal organization held together by a common desire for enrichment. Terrorist organizations are united by some religion or ideology. Even sex can be a factor for uniting small groups of swingers, gays, and lesbians. Man is a social animal and needs socializing. Hence, this great number of various organizations people choose to join depends on the degree of cohesion they need.

The leftists are anarchist—pacifists. Their mottos are "Liberty, Equality, Fraternity!" or "Peace to the Peoples, Land to the Peasants, Bread to the Hungry!" They are very popular, no doubt about it. But they are unrealistic, because they lead to society's disintegration, the trampling down of its morals and culture and, ultimately, to anomie. Their implications, however, do not become obvious until after a revolution, when mass reprisals begin and the declarations about freedom and equality turn into their opposites. Most citizens do not know sociology and have hardly ever heard of the "Iron Law of Oligarchy" by Robert Michels. This law makes it abundantly clear what will happen after a revolution.

Language is the only thing that unites members of anomie, even though there can be exceptions. Indifference, lack of empathy, and in many cases, animosity are typical of the relationships prevalent among anomie members. Inasmuch as man is a social animal, society's decay makes some society members prone to frustration, developing into depression, which may end, according to the French sociologist Emil Durkheim, in "anom suicide." Aggression may come instead of depression, and in this case, terrorist organizations appear.

A society of this kind is ungovernable. One of the reasons for this is that it does not have any leader. A person who is society's official leader and is supposed to represent it is divorced from it and is neither trusted nor respected. Its leader is actually engrossed in his own affairs and, while in power, is out to rob the people and grab everything he can lay his hands on. He is impotent and worthless as a leader.

Punishment in Anomie

Inasmuch as anomie develops from optimal society, whose judicial system is based on individual punishment, anomie inherits this kind of punishment. In my work *Civil War, Terrorism and Gangs,* I showed that degradation and the split of society are accompanied by the collapse of its judicial system, armed forces, etc. This collapse is primarily manifested in their politicization, then in corruption, and so on. Degradation brings about the collapse of morals and ethics. Thus, even though individual punishment is practiced in anomie, its fairness and trustworthiness are very low.

In anomie, like in OUS, there is no judicial system or morality. Everything depends on the position in the eroded hierarchy—those on top are always right.

A judicial system practicing individual punishment exists in optimal society only.

Collective Punishment in Anomie

There seems to be no reason for collective punishment in a society that has no joint responsibility. Collective punishment affects every society member, although half of them are guilty only of hating the society, while others have committed no punishable offense. In this case, collective punishment—would call it "mass reprisals"—has a side effect, namely, enhanced cohesion, up to the disappearance of anomie. This is the reason for mass reprisals after revolutions and *coups d'etat*, because immediately before them, anomie conditions prevailed.

Anomie conditions in Russia before the 1917 Bolshevist revolution confirm this thesis. These conditions ended in a four-year civil war and Bolshevist dictatorship attained through mass reprisals.

Unfortunately, in anomie, the government is impotent and cannot protect its country and its citizens. The government should be held responsible for creating conditions conducive to terrorism. The government should be held responsible at every stage of a terrorist attack, from intelligence and timely warning, to neutralizing terrorists and setting the hostages free.

Mass Reprisals

Mass reprisals are sometimes identified with "collective punishment." The possibility and expediency of mass reprisals were already examined in the section about joint responsibility and collective punishment. In this section, I will continue the examination. The issue calls for special treatment because, usually, attention is focused on one of its aspects only. The substance of the punishment, rather than its name, is important. Any punishment is resented even if it is justified. The victims criticize and condemn dictators without giving thought to whether the dictators' and their own actions are justified. This gives rise to a clash of "justifications."

The discussions about the expediency of mass reprisals in which I take part and which are sometimes very heated always boil down to two questions. I am asked, "would you like to be punished?" I say, "no!"

The other question is the one I put to my opponents: "What would you suggest instead of mass reprisals as a means to end anarchy and restore order?" I have been waiting for an answer for a couple of decades already. I am telling about my discussions with sociologists, and I hope that opponents of reprisals would think twice before leveling accusations at me.

Those in power always resort to mass reprisals when the need to put an end to anarchy arises. Anarchy emerges as a result of slow degradation of society, or rather the government, after defeat in a war. Reprisals are a natural continuation of civil war or a means to prevent it. They are also used to suppress a putsch or put an end to terrorism—which are signs of anarchy in the country.

Reprisals become a problem, not because of their consequences, but because of society's leaders. A leader should not be an impotent—if reprisals are needed, they should be used. But this should not be overdone—as soon as the aim is attained and legitimate power and order are restored, reprisals should be discontinued. It should be borne in mind that the degree of cohesion in an optimal society is 50 percent.

Use of Reprisals

Reprisals can be compared to medication, which is prescribed when it is necessary. Medication is taken at a definite time and in a definite dosage. As has already been said, reprisals come automatically after a civil war. The winning side carries out mass reprisals against the vanquished side.

My task is to show that reprisals are necessary to seal victory after the first military success. In this case, reprisals have a dual objective: first, to fully demoralize the enemy, and second, to fully subjugate it.

World history abounds in stories of reprisals after the hostilities were over. England subjugated Scotland by means of reprisals. Even the traditional kilts were prohibited. The Scotch were ruined and had no alternative to being mercenaries in the British armed forces.

During World War II, Germany did not hesitate to carry out reprisals in all occupied countries. After this war was over, there was no need for reprisals against the Germans. They were utterly demoralized by the occupation, suffered heavy casualties at the fronts, pummeled by air raids in the rear, experienced economic dislocation, etc. The main thing was that the Iron Curtain appeared in Europe, and the West wanted to win over the defeated Germans to their side. The situation in vanquished Japan was basically the same.

It is no less interesting to examine the use of mass reprisals in our time, especially the cases when reprisals are not
used for ideological or other reasons. Modern psychology
of the US leadership, reflecting as it does also Western and
Israeli government's psychology, rejects collective punishment. Considering that the USA today aspires to world
domination and thinks it legitimate to send its troops to
the Balkans, Africa, or Iraq, this psychology merits attention. The American troops were already in Vietnam, Lebanon, and Somalia, with the best of intentions. In Somalia,
for instance, they had to see that the relief sent by international organizations was distributed among the population. In Lebanon, a single terrorist attack killing 250 people
sent them packing immediately. From Somalia, they were
driven out after some time, and in all these cases, the US
adversary was poorly armed.

According to the US administration psychology concept, it is essential to maintain friendly relations with the
conquered local population to use it for intelligence, additional manpower, etc. In the "Whip and Carrot" section, I
show that this policy is erroneous. It goes without saying
that coercion, reprisals, and other such steps against the
population are bound to arouse unfriendly feelings in the
population and, instead of cooperation and help, may lead
to the emergence of a guerilla movement. This recalls the
mistakes made by Israel after the Six-Day War. In all cases,
the USA had to deal with an OUS, the type of society that
needs dictatorship more than "friendly relations." I hope
it is clear why love for the occupying power in Somalia
and Iraq lasted just a few hours, despite the USA's best
intentions.

Let us examine the situation in Iraq during the reign of
Saddam Hussein, the dictator. His heavy reprisals broke the

resistance of the Kurds fighting for independence, of the Shiites whose religion did not suit Saddam's objectives, and all the others in the country. It should be noted that Shiites constituted the majority of Iraq's population.

Saddam Hussein's enemies rejoiced when the Americans toppled the dictator. They were grateful to the invaders. Today, however, the coalition of Saddam Hussein's enemies has fallen apart; moreover, power-hungry coalition members are taking actions against the occupiers. This is precisely the situation that arises after victory over OK colonizers. A similar situation obtained in Algeria. In Iraq, Saddam Hussein had to be hastily replaced by new organs of state power with all its attributes: a new hierarchy and oligarchy and new reprisals. I can remind the reader that the moment Saddam was toppled, anarchy set in, and there was universal pillage of everything—banks, museums, libraries, hospitals, with Arabs robbing one another.

Any attempt to stop the pillage leads to clashes with the population. This is the situation the Americans encountered in Somalia. Can it be called friendly contacts and good relations of the invaders with the local population? Relations of this kind existed only at the very beginning.

Thus, any victor faces the problem of mass reprisals after the hostilities are over.

After the Six-Day War, Israel missed the opportunity to sign a peace treaty and bring war to an end, only because it failed to demoralize the Arabs by heavy casualties and mass reprisals, thus letting victory slip away. The lesson Israel had been taught was wasted on the USA, because US leaders were guided by their instincts and ideology instead of sociology. In 2003, Iraq's army was routed by the US-British coalition, with the same lightning speed as the Arab armies in the Six-Day War. But unlike the situation after the

Six-Day War, Saddam Hussein was stripped of power, and he disappeared. The state hierarchy collapsed immediately, and the country was paralyzed by anarchy—as was only to be expected. Anarchy and pillaging were the first signs that the American President Bush and the British Prime Minister Blair were ignorant of the social processes and unable to foresee the consequences of their actions. Mass reprisals that should follow anarchy were not carried out in Iraq.

Mass reprisals are a natural tool of social dynamics, and this tool must be used every time the situation calls for it.

Stick and Carrot

This expression aptly describes the wise methods of rule, for either one or the other is employed depending on the situation. Doubtless, reprisals are the "stick." In what cases is the "carrot" used? Having established order, a wise leader would change over from "stick" to "carrot" in the form of economic relief, some benefits, and the like. But "democracy" should be practiced sparingly.

The order is very important—the "carrot" should always come after the "stick." The record of history confirms it if only by the conquests of Alexander the Great and of other successful conquerors. In all cases, after routing and punishing the enemy, the victor changes his wrath to kindness, which turns his former adversary into an ally. If the victor tries to start with the "carrot," he lets his victory slip away.

Crime and Punishment

The difference between ideology and sociology is most glaring on the issue of punishment for mass reprisals. Each interprets the existing norms and laws to suit its purposes, ignoring the other aspects of the issue. For instance, the Arabs demand that the terrorists arrested by Israelis be considered war prisoners. But war on Israel was not declared, so from whence did the prisoners of war come? Then, if a war, even an undeclared one, is being waged, wouldn't Israel be justified in acting accordingly? Can you imagine what would happen if Israel should intern (resort to mass reprisals) all its Arabs and put them in concentration camps as the USA did with one hundred thousand of their nationals of Japanese background during the Second World War? It should be noted that the US Supreme Court examined the issue and did not find these actions at variance with the Constitution. Britons interned all Germans in Palestine. There were no objections.

The attitude to reprisals greatly depends on the person's ideology. Reprisals are usually disapproved of by the leftists, but they usually come out against reprisals long after they have been carried out. The purpose of reprisals is to unite, and unity leads to like-mindedness. Protests against interning the Japanese in the USA did not come until twenty years after the war was over. General Pinochet of Chile subjected some three thousand people to reprisals. The world took the *coup d'état* staged by him as something in the order of the day. Twenty years later, when the general was a retired octogenarian, who had already transferred his powers to a government elected in a democratic procedure, his hounding began on a worldwide scale. Nobody thought of his merits, of the fact that he had returned stability to the country and made the economy flourish.

Why did it all happen twenty years later? Because this seems to be the time it takes society to split.

Lawmakers and judges are frequently guided by ideology in their decisions concerning reprisals. Decisions prompted by ideology are mostly silly and cause enormous losses to the country. The hounding of General Pinochet began in Spain, following complaints lodged by some Spanish nationals. Nobody evinced any interest in what they were doing in Chile and what they were punished for. When the ailing general came to England, he was "interned." His upkeep cost England a pretty penny, but adhering to ideology was considered more important. Eventually he was released.

Punished Without Guilt

Mass reprisals come when the judicial system collapses as an outcome of war, anarchy, or for any other reason. Reprisals produce the punished, both those who were guilty and those who were "punished without guilt." It is impossible to tell the former from the latter because there are no courts of law whose function is to determine guilt, nor are there any laws. In Israel, the expression "punished without guilt" is very popular among the leftists (internationalists). They use it in an attempt to prevent mass reprisals and demoralize those who resort to them. Amnesty International urges Israel to stop practicing "collective punishment." This organization accuses Israel of violating the Geneva Convention and flouting international norms of humaneness.

It is because of this expression (or the principle underlying it) that Israel has already been for three years unable to put an end to terrorism. For instance, Israel tried to kill the leader of the Hamas terrorist organization by a rocket fired from an aircraft and targeted at his window. The whole floor was destroyed, but the power of the rocket was not sufficient to kill the Hamas leader. The objective was not attained. A more powerful bomb capable of demolishing the entire building, together with their dwellers, was not used for fear of punishing those who were not guilty. But then, the Hamas leader was not guilty, either, as he had not been brought to trial or convicted. All Arab terrorists shot down from Israeli aircraft were punished without trial. Then, under the circumstances, why should not one more step be made and mass reprisals continued? After all, there are no courts of law and no laws.

In September 2003, a collective letter of twenty-seven Israeli aircraft pilots was published in the mass media. The pilots, seconded by some Israeli men of letters, protested against hunting down Arab terrorist leaders from the air. The pilots wanted to see the rule of law; that is, they wanted a terrorist to be tried after being caught red-handed.

What is the difference between the pilots and myself? The difference is not only in ideology, which made them hate their country and their people and commiserate with their enemies and terrorists, but the leftists can only see the disadvantaged on the other side of the trenches. I hold that anarchy and the absence of laws warrant a wider scope of reprisals, while the leftists demand that laws should be obeyed even if they are absent.

The record of history shows that the leftists resort to reprisals to establish their power after a revolution on a more extensive scale than any others. This was the case in France after its king was dethroned and, in Russia, after the Bolshevist revolution.

Chapter 7

Snotty Golems

Mercy should be practiced sparingly.
Machiavelli

I used to admonish my grandsons doing their terms of active service in the IDF:

"If a snotty Arab boy flings a stone at you, shoot him down."

"I would be brought to trial," came the reply.

"I would rather defend you in court," I rejoined, "than mourn you at the cemetery. Those to blame for the Arab boy's death from your bullet are first and foremost his parents, then his teachers, and last your superiors. There is no ethics in battle; there is military duty. If a boy is sent to fight against you, shoot him down so they do not send children to fight anymore."

I sent out my admonition to all Internet addresses I had. I will not dwell on the answers expressing approval. Far more important are those that expressed disapproval. Below is one such letter.

Everything you write is disgusting racism and fascism.
I am an IDF Major, fought in the Yom Kippur War, in the First Lebanon War, was awarded for combat operations near Beirut, been thirty-six years in Israel, my daughter was an army officer and my both grandsons have just finished their terms of active

service in the IDF. Your man-hating, openly Nazi harangues are revolting. "'Snotty Arab boy'—it's outrageous."

Have you served in our army? Have you been in Israel long enough to understand what's going on here? After I asked this "IDF Major" to add some arguments to his emotions, this humane ramrod kept silent. And people like this major are trusted to dispose of the lives of our soldiers! However, there *was* a discussion on using children in battle.

I was censured for "war against children," and they appealed to my "humaneness." However, if the parents of these children are inhuman and can send them to fight against me, why should I surrender to these children? I suggest that my scrupulous opponents first read my arguments and then make up their minds as to who should be censured.

Children on the battlefield: what are the roots of this phenomenon?

Plutarch wrote about ancient Sparta: "Lycurgus decided that children do not belong to their parents, but they belong to the entire state and, therefore, he wanted them to be born not of any parents but of the best fathers and mothers." This sentence, especially its first part, can be made an epigraph to this section. The second part dealing with the "natural selection" is fully in the spirit of our times. In Sparta, women were exhorted to give birth to excellent warriors, and they were looking for excellent mates. The husband could bring a young, strong mate to his wife, and it was not regarded as procuration. Everything was being done for the good of the party and the people.

State interests were above all other interests. Children were born to serve their country and the people and were sacrificed in the interests of the country and the people.

Below is a short item in the site of the *Novoye russkoye slovo (New Russian Word)* newspaper of Aug. 26, 2007. I am citing it in full.

Al Qaeda is training six-year-old terrorists

Servicemen fighting in Afghanistan are facing a new enemy—six-year-old children. Al Qaeda is recruiting boys just above preschool age for military operations. It is a cause for grave concern. These terrorist tactics may be a serious blow to our troops, Chris Dobson, British military expert, said. The fighting men cannot pull the trigger right off when they see that they are firing at a child. This can become a fatal mistake. Modern weapons are not heavy and children can handle them.

And these boys have been programmed to kill, says the *utro.ru* site.

A video recording on the Internet showed kid fighters. Experts believe it was taken at a training camp close to the Afghanistan-Uzbekistan border. The video is supplied with the text saying it is a new mojahed generation.

Citing a high-ranking officer of the Israeli military intelligence, the Israeli *Ediot Ahronot* newspaper writes that during an IDF anti-terrorist operation in the Gaza Strip, Palestinian terrorists used a new method to protect their facilities. They put children on house roofs to prevent Israeli aircraft from bombing them.

Before an attack on a weapons shop or warehouse, leaflets were thrown in the area in which the IDF asked the population to leave the dangerous zone. The leaflets usually had the opposite effect: instead of taking their families to a safe place, the terrorists used them as human shields.

The military officer says that Israeli aircraft pilots saw little children on house roofs and in several cases did not attack the target buildings.

Here is an item from the Israeli newspaper *Sedmoykanal.com,* September 4, 2007.

Citing Arab sources, the Yoav Yitzhak NFC site writes that on Tuesday evening (September 4) IDF men wounded eight-year-old Maruan Aklik in the head. He was flinging stones at the Israeli military. According to Arabs, the Israeli men used rubber bullets against a crowd of Arab schoolchildren standing outside a school and flinging stones at them.

The life story of the Arab terrorist Rabia Hamad, described by Ksenia Svetlova, an Israeli journalist, on the BBC Russian.com site on August 27, 2007, gives a still better idea of Arab practices.

Rabia Hamad was born in the Silvad Village in the West Bank and joined the Fatah movement when still a schoolboy. Membership in Fatah was considered part of growing to manhood for every Palestinian boy.

"When I joined this organization," Rabia Hamad said, "I did not know anything about the struggle of the Palestinian people. However, at the age of fifteen, when I first landed in an Israeli prison, I began to understand what Rais Arafat was talking about.

"Like all my peers, I took part in the first Palestinian intifadah often referred to as the 'intifadah of stones.' I was arrested for throwing stones at the soldiers and sentenced to a ten-month prison term even though I was underage. I was arrested many more times. No official charges were brought against me as they were "administrative arrests."

Thus, this snotty boy began fighting without understanding anything. Only in an Israeli prison did he begin to see the situation. He is by no means an exception; there are thousands of such "snotty Arab boys," because all Palestinian boys "grow to manhood." This "stone flinger" knows very well that he is a minor and therefore is not subject to punishment.

Once a boy threw a stone at me in the center of the Israeli city of Haifa. I phoned to the police and was promised that "a police cruiser would arrive immediately." It never came. I lodged a written complaint to the police. An Arab policeman came to my place. Nothing seemed to impress him, until I said I would organize a pogrom against Arabs. There was no stone flinging anymore.

In reply to my complaint, the Ministry of Internal Security wrote that they had received many complaints of this kind against Arabs and that they were powerless. "Good gracious!" I thought, "What are these good-for-nothings paid for?"

Here is another significant quote from the story told by Rabia Hamad: "Carrying weapons has always been something of an obligation for a Palestinian man. In the past several years youngsters and even children have taken to carrying weapons."

Just look at the men of primitive African tribes. In days gone by, they carried spears. Today, all of them go about with a multifiring rifle. Now look at the Arab men. In Yemen, they have a short dagger tucked into their belts. In Palestine, "in the past several years youngsters and even children have taken to carrying weapons." Are Arabs primitive people?

"Our common goal," Rabia Hamad says, "is the establishment of an independent Palestinian state." It is a rather strange goal for primitive tribes. Having won independence and put an end to colonialism, they leave their dearly loved motherland in an attempt at all costs to creep under the blanket of the hateful colonialist and invader. Today, both the Old and the New worlds see a dense network of mosques springing up in their territories, and it looks like the time of the colonialists having to fight for their independence is not far off.

I remember the period after the Six-Day War. The gates of civilization were thrown open to the Arabs in the occupied territories. Small trucks scurried about Israel, and the Arabs in them were shouting "alte zahen." They were buying everything. An old refrigerator was a token of civilization in an Arab village. Every Israeli town had a "slave market" where Arabs from the occupied territories patiently waited for a "damn Israeli" to offer them some work. Now that they have independence, Israel is closed to them, and they are waiting for handouts from the USA and European countries.

The Iran-Iraq War

During the protracted and bloody Iran-Iraq war (1980–88), the belligerents were accused of using children and youngsters, aged fourteen to fifteen, and even twelve, in operations on the battlefield. The protracted character of the war and heavy casualties compelled both countries to resort to these steps toward the end of the war.

The Iraqi army built a fortified defense line that made it possible to wipe out the attacking "live waves" by outfiring the enemy. The "live waves" were children, youngsters, and older people incapable of fighting. They were tied together in groups of twenty so that cowards could not run away. "Live waves" were also used as a shield in front of attacking soldiers.

At that time, due to the US and West European boycott, the Iranian armed forces were drastically short of armored vehicles and aircraft. The Iranians kept them out of action, to be able to press the success and consolidate the gains at an opportune moment. Meanwhile "the live waves" were used as a substitute for munitions. Iraqi television showed maimed teenagers taken prisoner. They had been driven through a minefield before an offensive.

Iran and Iraq were not the first to use children in an offensive. As far back as 1212, a "Crusade of Children" was launched during the Crusades to recover the Holy Sepulcher. More than twenty thousand children from Europe were sent to recapture the Holy Land. Theirs was a tragic fate: all of them were sold into slavery in Tunisia, Italy, and elsewhere.

The partition of Poland and its occupation by Russia swelled Russia's Jewish population. Nicholas I ruled that Jewish boys should be taken from their parents to become soldiers (they were known as cantonists). Nicholas I followed the example of the Sultan of Turkey, who had imposed a special tax on Christians. They had to give their boys to be trained for the elite Mameluke troops. Somewhat later, the Mamelukes established an empire of their own.

Left photo: An infant with an explosive belt of a shahid. Suicide-bomber-baby01.jpg *The photo was found when a terrorist home was searched on June 29, 2002.*

In addition to laying down the civil and economic rights of children, the Convention on the Rights of the Child makes it obligatory on the signatory countries to keep minors of under fifteen years of age away from hostilities. According to the convention, childhood ends at eighteen.

Left photo: Suicide bomber aged fourteen wearing an explosive belt. He was captured at the Israeli check point on March 24, 2004. He had been given one hundred shekels as payment and promised Paradise teaming with houris.

The journalist hates my grandchildren who are doing their terms of military service and blames them for the death of Arab boys. He is not concerned about the safety of my grandchildren or other Jewish children who have to be cooped up in bomb shelters instead of going to school because Arabs shell their towns. Yet this journalist dares to engage in moralizing. It should be borne in mind that moralizing comes from a lack of gray cells or argument. Below is an article by Gideon Levi, an Israeli journalist, who has a sensitive conscience and a weird love for children:

The Israeli Army Is Fighting Against Children
The IDF do not care that children may become victims of their operations. They admit that they know that the "suspicious figures in the launching zone (of missiles)" may be children. Nevertheless they order direct fire. One should bear this in mind before raising a hue and cry if children are hit by an Arab rocket fired at Sderot.

IDF spokesmen explain that the Palestinians send children to assemble rocket launchers. Even if this is true and children *are* used for this purpose (it is yet to be proved), Israel should immediately discontinue hitting the zones from which rockets are launched. The military do not care that children may become victims of their operations. They admit that they know that the 'suspicious figures' in the launching zone may be children, yet they order direct fire. This means that the Israeli Defense Forces are fighting against children. It is not a case of 'tragic errors.' It testifies to deliberate disregard for children's lives and to impermissible indifference to their fate on the part of the military.

A moral society would have at least questioned the permissibility of firing at figures approaching launchers if it is very likely that they may be children unaware of what they are doing. Or are we giving free rein to the military? Even if we accept that the army's optical devices are incapable of telling a ten-year-old child from a grown-up person, the military must be held responsible for their criminal actions.

Even if in accordance with the amoral but strictly followed instructions any person that approaches the launchers should be killed, this instruction should be ignored if there is the slightest likelihood that the approaching person may be a child.

The fact that such "counter-measures" do not stop or even reduce shelling warrants the accusation that the military kill children to take revenge and to punish. This makes not a single child in Sderot safe! Anyone following the developments in the past few months must have noticed a certain sequence of events—namely, that Qassam shellings follow the so-called "pin-point eliminations" carried out by the IDF. In this context the question of who was the first is not a child's question. The IDF widely practice such "pin-point eliminations" which are followed by a more intensive shelling. This is the truth and it is concealed from the public. The havoc began immediately after Gabi Ashkenazi and Ehud Barak assumed office. Had Barak been a rightist, a public outcry about our doings in Gaza would have been inevitable. But everything is permissible for Barak. Nether the Defense Minister nor the Israeli public care a straw for the children who are victims of the actions of the Israeli military.

It's true—children in the Gaza Strip keep loitering near Qassams. But what else should they do? Rocket launchers are their Luna Park. It is only those who have not been to Beit Khanum that can think of demanding that parents there should take better care of their children. Dirty passages between dilapidated houses are all children can see there.

This child lover teaches us:
Even if it had been proven that terrorists use these unfortunate children for their purposes, Israel should think of morality. It should practice restraint. Response

is not always necessary, especially if counteractions can cause casualties among children.

The IDF cannot stop the shelling by random fire. There is a sufficient number of rocket launchers in Gaza. The beginning of the school year does not bode well either for us or for them. Those who are interested in putting an end to the shellings in all earnestness must negotiate a ceasefire with the government in Gaza. This is the only way and the only real possibility. "Pin-point eliminations" and killing children will bring the opposite of what we want. Just think of what is happening to us and to our armed forces!

Is it my grandchildren and I or who have turned Beit Khanun into a dirty and stinking Luna Park with a "sufficient number of rocket launchers"? As for what is happening to us and our armed forces, it is ignorant journalists like Gideon Levi who have demoralized us and our military. It is time we stopped "pin-point eliminations" and killing children and started large-scale operations.

Professor Asa Kasher

When the Israeli newspapers were filled with news of innocent children killed by the Israeli military, Professor Asa Kasher came out with his authoritative opinion.

After stating that the government must protect its citizens, a statement ridden to death for the Israelis, he went over to the "innocent Arabs," who just watched on the sidelines how rockets were launched at Israel. Such Arabs, he opines, especially if they are just curious children, must not be hurt.

The problem with Professor Asa Kasher or other such child lovers is that they have perverted ideas on this issue and use only their own moral yardsticks to evaluate developments. They do not understand that morals are a function of society's cohesion. In one society, it is moral to sacrifice their children to G-d or send them to the battlefield, while in another society this is amoral. The attitude of society toward children is the touchstone of society's morals and cohesion. Professor Kasher does not seem to know or understand that in a society over-united by Islam, all its members are golems.

Other child lovers resemble the chief Cheka man, F. E. Dzerzhinsky. Some of them are united in the Human Rights Watch organization, which published a report about minors in the Burmese armed forces. It strongly disapproves of the Burmese military for forcefully drafting children starting with the age of ten. Below is the BBC item about this, published on October 31, 2007.

Human Rights Defenders: Children in the Burmese Armed Forces

The document says that paid military and civilian recruiters seize teenagers in the streets and take them to recruiting centers by force. The teenagers are beaten and intimidated, and their age is falsified in documents.

One of the victims says, the report points out, that he got a slap in the face when he said he was sixteen. He asked them to let him go home but was refused. Officially, a person must be eighteen to be recruited for service in the armed forces. The armed forces are built on a contract basis and are short of volunteers, which human rights defenders attribute to the fact that servicemen were used against Buddhist monks and unarmed marchers in late September.

According to the Human Rights Watch, the number of minors comes to several thousand in Burma. After an eighteen-week training, the new soldiers are dispatched to military units and to remote regions to fight the insurgents.

The Burma military regime admits that it is a problem and has even set up a committee to study it, but, according to the Human Rights Watch lawyer Jo Becker, it is just a feigned struggle against violations of law. The higher generals turn a blind eye to this barbarous treatment of children, and those guilty of it have been given a free hand. "The army recruiters can act with impunity," she said.

The UN Security Council is going to return to the issue of human rights in Burma, where thousands of September protesters remain imprisoned.

The Human Rights Watch demands that the Security Council should also focus on the issue of minors in the army and toughen the sanctions against the Burma regime.

Left photo: Burma, "People's Army"

✣ ✣ ✣

To amplify the above, I will dwell on how children are used in peacetime, after civil war, or in a struggle for freedom and independence that has long been over.

Eaglet, Eaglet

Those who grew up under communism must be familiar with revolutionary romantics and the words "I'm only sixteen, it's too early to die," from the song *Eaglet* (lyrics by Ya. Shvedov, music by V. Bely) appearing in 1936 (almost twenty years after the victory of the Bolshevist revolution). At that time, there was another popular song about a young drummer "marching in front of the attacking troops." The culmination of both songs is the death of the youngsters.

Night is for children to be asleep. Yet the famous Soviet poets Mikhail Svetlov, Eduard Bagritsky, Vladimir Mayakovsky, and others sang paeans, both to Cheka henchmen and to children going into attack.

Why should civil war or war for independence be waged with children's hands?

If my opponents think that the period after the Civil War (in Russia) saw a happy, peaceful life, they are mistaken. I must remind them that famine in the Volga area was rife, even in the years of the most bumper harvests in the Soviet Union. As a boy, I used to collect postage stamps. They bore the inscription: "Relief to victims of famine in the Volga area." The Soviet power dispossessed, ruined, and exiled to Siberia thousands of peasant families. There were millions of homeless children.

My mother told me that when she was a student of a teachers' college and a communist youth movement member, she was assigned to work with such children. The experience was worlds apart from A. Makarenko's *Pedagogical Poem*.

She had to go to places where they could be found—dumping grounds, basements, flophouses. While she was reading a book to them, one of them tried to take off her shoes on the sly. Lice, these typhoid carriers, crept from a homeless child to the neat student. She stole glances at a louse but didn't dare show that she saw it.

I learned "Abandoned When a Toddler," a song of an orphan, in a Moscow streetcar. I remember very well a boy of about eight getting on the streetcar and starting to sing in a thin voice as he moved along with his hand cupped to accept alms.

At a certain moment, the problem of homeless children was addressed by the Cheka and "personally by Comrade F. E. Dzerzhinsky." This ascetic and confirmed bachelor was very fond of children and hated their parents. He handled them accordingly—the parents were sent to Siberia, and the children to orphanages. It was at that time, when A. Makarenko, "a prominent Soviet educator," came to the fore.

After the Civil War, the war of children against spies and saboteurs burst out. Literature for children abounded in stories about children who captured spies and unmasked "enemies of the people."

The "happy years" of Soviet power saw the appearance of *pavlik morozovs*. A Soviet legend has it that Pavlik Morozov, a Young Pioneer, informed on his father. His father was arrested and sentenced to a term in prison. The irate grandfather killed his stoolpigeon grandson. The Soviet press extolled this stoolpigeon as a Young Pioneer hero and his action as worthy to be emulated. The heart of every child succumbed to this all-pervasive brainwashing campaign. Children informed on their parents to the Soviet authorities. Parents trembled with fear. The main thing for a child is to show off, but a child does not know the price of showing off. In the 1930s, mass reprisals in the USSR reached its peak, and any negative information on parents was fraught with capital punishment for them. It was the time when a boy who had stolen a loaf of bread was executed at the Butovo shooting range in Moscow.

Family had disintegrated! Children no longer belonged to their parents. As in Sparta, they belonged to the people, to the state. The leader knew how to use them. He could send them to fight against the enemy, the "enemy of the people," against their parents, or against whomever he thought best. What else are snotty children good for?

What Kind of Society Is It, After All?

The yardstick for evaluating any society is the extent of its cohesion. The extent of cohesion determines the behavior of society and its members, as well as the attitude toward children. An OUS is held together either by reprisals or by religion. In a society of this kind, people lose their individual traits and become identical; they become golems. Golems do not need anything (they are ascetics who are unable to work). Their lives are devoted to serving the society's interests, for which they are ready to give their lives. The French sociologist Emil Durkheim calls this phenomenon *altruistic suicide*. If golems would not spare their own lives, they would certainly not spare the lives of others, even of their children. They could sacrifice them to Moloch, but they prefer sending them to the battlefield. In such a society, *family* disappears.

In conclusion, it can be said that some, those like Soviet poets and writers, extol children's "heroic deeds" and altruistic suicide. Others, like the Israeli journalist Gideon Levi, condemn those who come out against such "heroic deeds."

Chapter 8

Volunteers, Mercenaries, or Draft

Russia is going to change over to an army of hired contract soldiers (mercenaries). The other "advanced" countries have already effected the changeover. Today, soldiers are no longer drafted in compliance with the law of compulsory draft, and the contract soldier becomes akin to the civil servant. Such soldiers are offered remuneration for serving in the army or paramilitary units. The deal is formalized by a contract. The conscripts used to swear an oath of loyalty to the leader, the party and the government, the people, and the country. Today this has been replaced by a contract.

Is it worthwhile to change the system of building a country's armed forces? The pronouncements of advocates of such a changeover make one wonder why it took so long if there is nothing better than an army of contract soldiers.

Volunteers, Mercenaries, or Draft

There are three systems of building the armed forces and three types of fighting men: volunteers, mercenaries (or contract soldiers), and draftees. Which of the three is the best and what army is preferable? Another important issue is the reasons for changeover to one or another system.

Let us examine each of the three types of fighting men and their motivation.

The Volunteer

The volunteer is not paid for his service in the armed forces or for the risk of being killed in battle; yet as the record or history shows, an army made up of volunteers is the best, the most staunch, and most reliable. As a rule, volunteers are united by ideology or faith.

A good illustration of this thesis is provided by ancient Greece. Leonidas, the king of Sparta, defended the Pass of Thermopylae against a large Persian army with his three hundred volunteers. Only three Greeks survived, but twenty thousand Persians lay on the battlefield after the engagement with a handful of Spartans. The exploit of the three hundred Greek warriors was a hard moral blow to the Persians and an uplifting experience to the Greeks in their fight against the enemy.

In the Middle Ages, orders of Christian knights were actually volunteer armies. The Teutonic Order is known in Russia only too well. It was out to capture the land in the Baltic area and spread its influence to the region and, farther, to Russia. Alexander Nevsky routed the Teutons in battle, and their drive eastward stopped.

The Teutons were ascetics. They lived on prayer and war.

In the last century, there were three international volunteer brigades fighting in Spain on the side of the republicans. Despite assistance from other countries, the republicans were defeated.

In all the above and other cases, an army of volunteers has a high degree of cohesion, so high that its men lose their personal traits and become golems ready to commit altruistic suicide, that is, to give their lives for the benefit of society. A society of this kind is highly patriotic and fanatically religious. Ancient Greeks were staunch patriots. In Sparta, boys were brought up to become patriots and warriors.

In many cases, soldiers were united by their faith, particularly a faith that required asceticism. Christianity united orders of knights. The volunteer international brigades during the civil war in Spain were held together by Marxism-socialism.

Today, Islam has emerged onto the international arena. At this juncture, Islam is at the terrorism stage and is trying to get hold of atomic weapons. The next stage is guerilla warfare, usually followed by creating a regular army. Today, it is hard to say what will "follow," because much depends on the policy of the Western countries. If they are passive…

During the Great Patriotic War, Soviet fighting men shouted, "for Motherland! For Stalin!" as they went into battle. In Spain, the international brigade volunteers also shouted, "for Stalin!" on the battlefield, says the writer Ilya Ehrenburg, who was in Spain at that time. Dictator Stalin was God for Marxists everywhere.

The Japanese word "kamikaze" is known the world over. Kamikaze is a warrior ready to die for his country and people. These warriors were held in great esteem in Japan, although such suicide was, in some cases, considered unnecessary. In our times, the Arab shahid who blows himself (or herself) up, not in battle but in a crowd of peaceful civilians, is more popular.

All volunteer qualities described above hold true for ascetic volunteers. Not all volunteers, however, are prone to asceticism, and an army of such volunteers differs very little from a criminal gang. Even before the revolution, the Bolsheviks built their own armed forces, which deposed the Provisional Government in Russia and then made the October Revolution. Russia was at war with Germany and Austria at that time, but these "armed forces," composed of deserters, remained in Petrograd, and nothing on earth could make them leave it for the front. In his poems, "Seaman" and "Red Army Man," Maximilian Voloshin gave an apt description of them.

My relative, an old Jew, told me the following story. He was a steward of a rich landowner who had fled from the country during the civil war, leaving my relative to manage his estate, which had a distillery. Once, Red Army commanders—Voroshilov, Budyonny, and Schadenko—appeared at the estate and demanded vodka. They got it, and after a day spent in the manor house with nurses, they left. What makes this run-of-the-mill wartime story interesting is the names of the commanders. Later, they rose to the top of the Soviet hierarchy and, for some time, stayed there even after Stalin's death. Such volunteers were power-hungry hoodlums and criminals, rather than ascetics loyal to their motherland and religion. Lev Trotsky used commissars and reprisals to reform these deserters and criminals into Red Army men.

The Bolshevist Red Army was initially recruited on a voluntary basis. Considering that any democratic society has 50 percent internationalists and 50 percent nationalists, there must have been Russian citizens who had no sympathy for the Bolsheviks and disapproved of their revolution. Consequently, the numerical strength of the volunteer Red Army did not meet the requirements of the Bolshevist regime, and compulsory draft was introduced. This principle of building the armed forces stood the test of time and was followed till recently. However, the time has come for a changeover to a contract army. What are the reasons for this?

The Contract Soldier

The "private armed detachment" (PAD) is a recent development. It is a unit made up of former career military men recruited on a contract basis. They are well paid, and their professional level is very high. They are often and effectively used against primitive gangs in African tribal wars. PAD's efficiency has attracted the attention of drug dealers, and they are forming similar units.

Yes, can you imagine a contract soldier shouting, "for Motherland! For Stalin!" when attacking the enemy? Hardly. This is precisely what makes a PAD contract soldier different from a volunteer or a draftee. The contract soldier may risk his life in a military operation, but he is incapable of "altruistic suicide" or any suicide, whatever the reward might be.

We'll begin with what is on the surface: contract soldiers are held together by their contract obligations. By signing the contract, a contract soldier assumes the obligations to observe military discipline and risk his life. For breach of contract, he will be dismissed and will forfeit his good pay.

The only difference between a draftee and a contract soldier is that the former does not receive a monthly pay sufficient for sustenance and upkeep of his family. He only gets a token sum to pay for his cigarettes and girls.

The Mercenary

Today the term "contract soldier" is a substitute for the former "mercenary" in contemporary Russian language. But they are not synonyms. A contract soldier serves under a contract in the army of his native country, while a mercenary is a national of some other country tempted by the money.

While effecting a changeover to a contract army, Russia pays no attention to the nationality of the contract soldiers. In the Ukraine, similar practices made a prosecutor general's office employee cite the Criminal Code. According to him, the Prosecutor General's Office of the Ukraine is empowered to bring action for "recruiting, financing, logistic support, and training of mercenaries to be used in armed conflicts between other states or in violent actions aimed at a *coup d'etat* or invasion, as well as in military conflicts or hostilities." A breach of this clause carries a prison term of from three to eight years. At the same time, "participation in armed conflicts of other countries for remuneration without permission of the respective state agencies," is punished by five- to ten-year confinement.

The linguistic difference between a contract soldier, a mercenary, or a volunteer is of little interest to us. We want to determine which army is better, the one made up of volunteers, contract soldiers, or draftees—we'll refer to the latter as the "people's army." This issue will be examined in general, not as applied to Russia or to any other country. Why isn't Israel, for instance, planning a contract-based army?

We know that paid warriors existed in ancient times. It is they who are held responsible for the collapse of the great Carthage state. Carthage had no army of its own and had to rely on "contract warriors." In the Middle Ages, the same fate befell Khazaria, which stretched from the Caspian Sea to what is today Hungarian borders. Itil, the capital of this powerful state, vanished like Carthage before it and left many riddles both for historians and archeologists to solve. Kiev, the capital of the Ukraine, was founded by Khazars. Another Khazar heritage is the word "hussar." All European languages have it, and it means a "daredevil horseman."

In addition to causing collapse, which happened in Khazaria, there were cases of contract soldiers or mercenaries, as they were called in the past, seizing power and turning from defenders to looters. Today, sculptured figures of *commodores* and *condotiers* (mercenaries) grace many Italian cities. They led the detachments of mercenaries that had been invited to ensure protection but, subsequently, stayed at these places as absolute rulers. Instead of remuneration, they were paid duties.

In spite of the fact that use of contract soldiers brings dubious results, the demand for them keeps growing, because they are regarded as well-trained armed forces.

They make up a category of fighting men motivated not by convictions but money. What kinds of people sign such contracts?

A man responsible for recruitment of soldiers at a Military Commissariat in Russia said, "there are three main reasons that make people serve in the army under a contract: beliefs, money, and despair—when there is no work, no sustenance. If an applicant has been detained by the police, let alone convicted, he is rejected. It is also necessary to have the place of residence, registration, and Russian Federation citizenship. The army is not for vagabonds. Admission requirements keep toughening. Sometime back, incomplete secondary education was sufficient. Today, a would-be contract soldier must have at least ten to eleven years of schooling. The age limit, however, has been raised from thirty-five to forty."

Below are the descriptions of three men planning to become contract soldiers.

Alexei, twenty, unemployed. "I'm just through my term of compulsory military service. I tried several places, but they don't need people like me, without higher education and work experience. This means I have to return to the army. There is nothing to keep me from it—no wife, no children."

Dmitry, twenty-six, used to work for a security firm. "I'm no fool and no weakling. I'll try to keep clear of bullets.

And, then I'll be getting normal money. Now they pay me two-thousand, five-hundred a month. What can you buy for it?"

Alexander, thirty-one, a worker at a plant. "Well, Motherland must be defended. You see what is going on in the Caucasus. I can't sit at home and see on the TV how they blow up our houses and kidnap our people. I'm sick and tired of it. Money considerations also play a part. They haven't paid me for six months."

Unpleasant incidents involving contract soldiers also occur.

Eight contract fighting men (seven sergeants and one private) of the Russian peace-keeping battalion in Southern Ossetia deserted their stations, taking along two Tommy-guns, one hand-held machine-gun, ten grenades, and five hundred cartridges. The incident caused a commotion in the headquarters of the peace-keeping forces in the area of the Georgia-Ossetia conflict. It was the first incident of this kind in the ten years the battalion had been in the area of the conflict.

The command could not understand what guided these men, whose average age was twenty to twenty-five. Their living conditions were not bad, and they were not bullied, owing to their position and age. The supreme commander of the land forces, however, had no difficulties in explaining their actions.

On the night of June 13, these men had too much booze and were at the center in a state of alcohol intoxication, he said. An officer rebuked them, and the sergeants began preparing the documents for terminating their contracts. On the night of June 16, they deserted their center and headed for Tskhinvali to lodge their complaint with the battalion commander. Judging by all the signs, they never got there. According to the Southern Ossetia minister of the interior, they had no martial fervor and were "drunkards and loafers."

What kind of people become contract soldiers?

Those who want to become career officers enter military academies. Those who are unable to study and want to make easy money become contract soldiers. They are trained and drilled, which does not improve their poor moral qualities.

Contract soldiers are good fighters, but they are only capable of heroic feats when defending themselves, not those who pay them.

In light of the above, it is clear that comparison with the other types of fighting men would not be in their favor. So, I repeat the question: Why, then, are they preferable in some cases?

Some conclusions can now be drawn from the above. Putting the army on a contract basis signals the degradation of society and the emergence of some elements of anomie in this society. In such cases, the degradation should be stopped and a people's army based on compulsory military service should be retained.

A volunteer army is cheaper to maintain than any other. Still, money appears to be no object when the quality of an army is at stake. Our examination of the contract soldier shows that if he does a good soldiering job, those who hire him are ready to pay him well. But what is it that cements fighting men into a reliable, battle-worthy force? Sociology will provide the answer.

Being a reliable battle-worthy force makes all the difference between the contract soldiers on the one hand and the drafted and volunteer soldiers on the other. This quality is of vital importance at crucial moments when the risk of death is very high. At such moments, contract soldiers may desert, surrender, or even defect to the enemy—something a volunteer would never do. Volunteers would rather die than surrender. I will cite a few instances to confirm this.

The Masada fortress built by King Herod in the Judean Desert was the last stronghold of the Maccabees, who fought against Roman domination in Judea. The fortress was located on a mountaintop, was well protected, and had an ample stock of water and food. The Romans had to remove part of the mountain rock to get close to the Masada walls. The numerical strength of the defenders of the fortress was patently inadequate to stand up to the overwhelming force of the Roman legion. When resistance was clearly coming to an end, the defenders chose death instead of surrender. First, all women and children were killed, and then the men killed themselves.

In our times, some sixty Chechen "people's volunteers" fighting in Afghanistan on the Taliban side in Kunduz refused to surrender to the troops of the Northern Alliance and committed collective suicide by drowning in the Amu Darya River. CNN reported this incident and referred to Kunduz sources. Northern Alliance spokesmen and other witnesses of the hostilities in Northern Afghanistan also spoke about stiff resistance mounted by the foreign volunteers who were fighting on the Taliban side. The Taliban militants also preferred death to surrender. An Alliance field commander reported that twenty-five Taliban men trapped near Kunduz shot each other so as to escape surrendering to the attacking forces of the opposition. Northern Alliance sources added that Taliban fanatics gunned down their own fighters, who intended to defect to the Alliance. These actions can account for the fact that despite negotiations lasting several days, there were just slightly more than one hundred defectors from the Taliban troops near Kunduz.

The cited instances of boundless loyalty of fighting men to their people, their faith, their Motherland, and their readiness to sacrifice their lives are typical of a society with a high level of cohesion. The USSR under the Stalin regime, Japan of the same period, and ancient Sparta were such societies. Patriotism is their salient feature.

Draft

In some sense, the draft can be compared to barrier detachments. Barrier detachments are used in exceptional cases during a war. A draft is conducted according to plan, irrespective of whether or not the country is at war. Before I was drafted, I was working and studying. The draft interrupted both. When, at the Military Commissariat, they learned that I was already a student, they started pressuring me into applying for admission to a military academy. My "komsomol conscience" succumbed to the pressure. But I still hoped that I would not pass some test and do my term as a private. I was unlucky and passed all commissions down to the party-political one.

Duty to their country, to society, is what keeps drafted soldiers in the army, even during a war. Duty made me complete my studies at the Naval Academy, and I was ready to do my duty on ships. Anti-Semitism flourishing in the Soviet Union saved me from this piece of bad luck.

Duty guided my grandsons to do their term of military service in IDF fighting units. In the course of my elder grandson's service, three of his commanders were killed. They were also young men. Who is to blame for their deaths?

Israeli politicians and politicized generals who sacrifice Israeli soldiers to their ideology should be censured. The Israeli soldiers are fighting handcuffed. Golems of the Asa Kasher type think up "codes" and slogans like "not to lower themselves to the enemy level." Israel's "fight for peace" has created a situation where fighting and missile and mine shelling are everyday occurrences, where "morality," supposed to be fought for, has long gone. Responsibility for hostilities is put on the soldiers.

Chapter 9

Genocide, Deportation, and Reprisals

As a rule, mass deportations and genocide mark the prelude of war or the culmination of a war and postwar revision of boundaries, which makes them an important element of military sociology. On the other hand, genocide, deportations, and reprisals provide a clue to the type of society in which such phenomena are practiced.

Defining genocide and deportation is necessary before discussing these phenomena. The Russian-language *Wikipedia* gives the following definition of genocide: "Genocide" (from the Greek "γένος"—"clan," "tribe," and the Latin "caedo"—"I am killing") are actions aimed at destruction in full or in part of a certain ethnic, racial, or religious group by killing members of the group:

Causing serious bodily or mental harm to members of the group;

Imposing measures intended to prevent births within the group;

Forcibly transferring children of the group to another group; and

Deliberately inflicting on the group conditions of life calculated to bring about its physical destruction in whole or in part.

Since 1948, genocide has been regarded by the UN as a crime against international law.

The definition of "deportation" (from Latin "deportatio") is taken from the Russian-language *Extensive Law Dictionary, Ed. A. Ya. Sukharev, V.E. Krutskikh, Moscow. 2002.* The word is defined as forced dispatch of a person or a category of persons to another country or another place, often under police escort.

According to the Criminal Law of the Russian Federation, the deportation of the civilian population is *one of the banned methods of warfare.*

In the Administrative Law of the Russian Federation, the use of "deportation" is synonymous with "expulsion."

The deportation ban appeared in Russia simultaneously with democracy. Below, I will show that deportation was widely used in Soviet times and under Stalin's dictatorial rule.

Refugees or Displaced Persons

In their new place of residence, the deportees get the status of refugees or displaced persons. At this stage, the subject of "human rights" emerges and "defenders of human rights" appear. They oppose deportation and advocate equal human rights for all people. This is how two sides to the problem appear—the *nationalists*, who are usually in favor of deportation and genocide of the outsiders and other "hostile elements," and the internationalists, who are usually opposed to any form of deportation and advocate "the rights of man and citizen." The nationalists frequently fail to foresee the consequences of deportation and genocide. The massacre of Huguenots on St. Bartholomew's Night in France was followed by a severe economic crisis.

The deportations and genocide carried out by Nazi Germany boomeranged in a most merciless way after its defeat in the war. Germans were ruthlessly banished from all East European countries and from Palestine, even though they had contributed to Palestine's economic development. As stated, the *internationalists* advocate "the rights of man and citizen," as is written in the Russian Criminal Law. They seem to ignore the interests of society and primarily its safety.

Cohesion of Society
Internal and External Deportation

Everything depends on the degree of society's cohesion. In an over-united society (OUS), all of whose citizens are golems, nationalists, and patriots, deportation and genocide do not pose a problem—people are deported or killed at the slightest suspicion. In the past, the deportation was internal, inside the country. People whose presence was undesirable were exiled to faraway regions. For Russia, these regions used to be Siberia and the Far East; for Great Britain, they were North America and Australia. In this way, sparsely populated areas were developed. Today, no more of such areas are left. Hence, there has been the emergence of external deportation, that is, banishment to another country. This kind of deportation may cause tension in relations between the two countries, because the presence of the banished people may also be undesirable in the other country or cause economic and social problems in it.

Degradation of Society and Deportations

With society gradually degrading, and its cohesion slackening, the opposition—that is, internationalists—appears. The attitude toward banished persons (refugees) is being revised. The degradation reaches a point where refugees are offered apologies and paid compensations. The reasons for their deportation are not taken into account. Deportation as a function of society's cohesion may be presented in a graph.

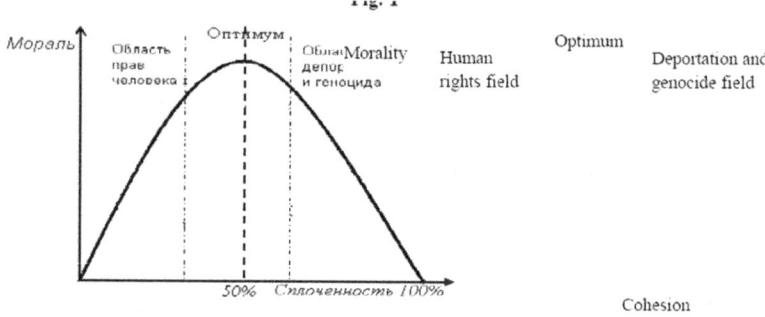

The left-hand side of the graph corresponds to a complete degradation of society, that is, anomie. A society of this type has no leader and is incapable of carrying out the deportation (even expulsion) of "hostile elements" to serve the interests of society.

Today, Israel fully meets this description. In Israel, the "hostile elements" are Arabs, both Israeli nationals and nationals of neighboring countries. Raised and brought up as demanded by Islam, they need an OUS, a strict dictatorship, which Israel with its "rotten democracy" cannot give them. These are the roots of Arab hostility toward Israel. It must be noted that this situation did not appear all of a sudden. In 1948, immediately after independence, Ben Gurion, a dictator, was at the helm. Despite his socialist leanings, he was a nationalist and did not hesitate to deport Arabs from their villages and their land plots. At that time, Israel was in the right-hand side of the graph where the degree of cohesion is very high. However, degradation, which had set in, shifted the country to the left-hand side. Under Ben Gurion's rule, the Arabs had the cohesion they needed (a curfew was imposed in Arab villages), which gradually petered out.

Deportation and Mass Reprisals

There is no essential difference between deportations and mass reprisals—both are unwelcome. Usually, deportations are done selectively; that is, persons to be deported have one or several features that place them in the category of those selected for deportation.

Mass reprisals affect everyone in a certain area or those in opposition to the government.

Reprisals are usually frowned at, which cannot be said about deportations. Below, I will show that there are many volunteers who wish to banish their neighbors. There are many reasons for this wish, but the main reason is in the realm of instinct. Man is a herd animal and needs society. As has already been said, society is characterized by its cohesion. There are people who need a homogeneous society with a very high degree of cohesion. We can call them "golem-nationalists." The appearance of people of other nationalities or confessions in such a society dilutes its homogeneity and galls the nationalists. Homogeneity dropping below a certain level may arouse frustration and aggressiveness, which lead to ethnic or religious clashes. It is not difficult to see that clashes of this type occur when the central power is weak, as was the case in Yugoslavia. While Josip Broz Tito ruled the country with an iron hand, there was ethnic peace. After his death, interethnic wars fueled by the USA and NATO burst out. The USSR is another example. The moment the communist rule collapsed and Boris Yeltsin, a drunkard, took over, the great empire disintegrated, and interethnic armed conflicts flared up. This instinct is frequently expressed in a burning wish to take vengeance or in actions prompted by pecuniary considerations—plundering, doing away with competitors, etc. Mass reprisals are undesirable, yet in many countries, they are lawful and are allowed in the form of curfew, a state of emergency, and the like. Deportation should also be stipulated in national laws. The extremes, that is, deportations carried out on a flimsy pretext, as is the case in OUSs should be excluded. On the other hand, in democratic countries—in Russia, for instance—deportations are banned and are a criminal offense. This approach does not meet the imperatives of the time, and deportations are in some cases carried out despite the ban imposed on them. Avoiding deportation may result in terrorism and war. The interethnic conflict in the Karelian town of Kondopoga described below could have been prevented by deportation. But first, we need a few words about the role of Caucasians in the conflicts in Russia. The peoples of Northern Caucasus were separated by mountains from each other and from civilization, which made all of them an OUS. Civilization and modern means of transportation have opened the way to the outside world to them. However, lack of certain abilities and proper education limited their endeavors to trade, a field in which a mediocre mind and modest education are no obstacles to earning money. OUSs combined with trade have produced criminal, Mafia-type groups that came to dominate markets and other retail outlets in Russia and established their rules at them. Discontent with the actions of the Caucasians had been brewing among the local population.

The Chechen Mafia in Kondopoga

According to the police, on the night of August 29–30, 2006, two patrons in the Chaika Restaurant belonging to a Caucasian argued with the barman, an illegal immigrant from Azerbaijan, and beat him up. The barman escaped from the patrons who pursued him, and he told about the incident to his Chechen acquaintances. Half an hour later, the restaurant's Chechen protection racketeers arrived in two cars. They were armed with knives, bats, and iron rods, but the people who had pounded the barman were gone. Eyewitnesses said that they had attacked everyone they could lay their hands on near the restaurant. Two people died of knife wounds on the spot; nine were taken to hospital, five of them to the intensive care unit, where one more person died the following day. None of the attackers was injured. The two people killed on the spot were buried on September 1. The local television broadcast a piece in which the incident was called a "family fight." This stirred the local population to action. On the night of September 1–2, several retail outlets, garages, and cafes belonging to Caucasians were set on fire. More clashes occurred in which another eight people were injured. About six hundred policemen and military men were concentrated in the town with a population of thirty-five thousand.

The DPNI[2] organized an ongoing news line based on eyewitness accounts from Kondopoga. DPNI representatives headed by Alexander Belov arrived in Kondopoga to take part in a rally of local residents scheduled for September 2 at 12:00. Some two thousand people gathered on the main square and demanded that the authorities banish all illegal immigrants within twenty-four hours. The rally adopted a resolution calling for the establishment of what they termed "people's militia squads to maintain law and order in the town, since the law-enforcement bodies cannot do it unaided," and they called for the expulsion of the Caucasian and Central Asian migrants from the town.

There were also calls for allowing "representatives of the people" to take part in the revision of the registration of the newcomers to Kondopoga. Part of the protesters— several hundred people—made for the Chaika Restaurant. First, they stoned it and then burst inside and set fire to the back rooms. After the police pushed them away from the restaurant and the firemen extinguished the fire, the crowd to smashed trade stalls. At 18:00, the Karelian Minister of Internal Affairs deployed forces from the ministry's crisis center in Kondopoga. The republic's prime minister, the minister of internal affairs, and deputy head of the Federal Security Service Directorate arrived in the town. Close to 22:00, Moscow Time, protesters returned to the restaurant and again set fire to it. A spokesman of the Ministry of the Internal Affairs said the protesters were mostly youngsters aged sixteen to twenty-two. The Karelian leader, Sergei Katanandov, put the blame for the Kondopoga events on Chechens. The Karelian authorities had to deport some sixty Caucasians in a rush. They were temporarily quartered in Petrozavodsk. Almost a week later, on September 5, a wildcat meeting was held in front of the town hall building. According to the Ekho Moskvy (Echo of Moscow) Radio Station, there was an undeclared curfew in the town— identity was checked in the streets at night. Those who could not present his or her ID were detained. Six murder suspects were arrested (among them four Chechens and one Dagestani.). Three of them were detained shortly after the fight at the Chaika Restaurant; three more reported at the prosecutor's office after the local law-enforcement men had a talk with the leaders of the Chechen Diaspora (protection racket) in Karelia. Four of the six arrested were accused of murder, two of hooliganism. On September 6, the conflict in Kondopoga flared up anew. Some unidentified persons set fire to a sports school building, which housed several families from Central Asia. More than thirty families fled Kondopoga to escape pogroms; they were given shelter in Aino, formerly a Young Pioneer Camp. As many as 109 people were arrested, twenty-five of them were served charges of hooliganism.

In the morning, Movladi Akhmatukaev, a representative of the president of Chechnya, arrived in Karelia, accompanied by officers of the republic's legislative and law enforcement agencies. They talked with members of the Chechen Diaspora, or more exactly, with the Chechen protection racketeers.

Kondopoga residents held that the police obstructed the actions of the local population, while the federal authorities were pursuing the policy of hushing up the actual situation in Kondopoga.

On September 8, some three hundred people rallied in Kondopoga to demand that the banished Caucasians should not be allowed to return. The authorities tried to prevent the rally. The people of Kondopoga were wearing white armbands as a sign of mourning.

The Movement against illegal Immigration (its Russian Abbreviation is DPNI) is a public movement that proclaimed struggle against illegal immigration in Russia as its objective. The objectives and ideological basis of the movement are similar to the current trends in European policy, expressed by such major legal political parties as the French National Front and the Austrian Freedom Party.

On September 9, Ramzan Kadyrov, the leader of Chechnya, came out with threats against Karelia, saying he would find a "legal way" to deal with the Kondopoga population if the Karelian authorities failed to do this.

On September 12, people from the Chechen Diaspora accused of murder and gang hooliganism did not plead guilty and refused to give evidence on the case. On November 2, the Chechens who had fled the town following the unrest came back. On November 14, the RTR Channel aired a running commentary titled "The Ringleaders Are Tried Earlier Than the Murderers." The commentary noted the remaining tension in Kondopoga. As of May 2008, none of the Caucasians suspected of murder was facing trial. The number of those detained on suspicion of committing murders dropped to one person. The murder remains unsolved.

The Chechen Mafia got off scot-free, but those who tried to fight it were punished. On November 2, 2007, after standing trial in the town court, twelve Kondopoga residents were found guilty of participation in mass unrest aggravated by pogroms, arsons, and destruction of property, and each was given a three-year suspended sentence. Three of these twelve appealed the sentence to the Supreme Court of Karelia, and on February 4, 2008, the Judicial Division for Criminal Cases of the Supreme Court of Karelia rejected the appeals. On November 16, the Prosecutor's Office of the Republic of Karelia opened a criminal case against Alexander Belov, the DPNI leader.

To consider the Kondopoga conflict over and the hatred of its residents for Chechens having given way to brotherly love is wishful thinking. Just another accidental scuffle and the hatred may spill over. Had there been a deportation law, the Chechen Mafia could have been deported to Chechnya, and the conflict would have been nipped in the bud.

My Prediction

The events in Kondopoga may serve as a model of what Western Europe is in for. The colonization of Europe by immigrants from Muslim countries will have dire consequences. I have already said that Islam is an ascetic religion uniting its followers into aggressive OUSs. It is clear that the new colonizers form communities whose place is on the right-hand side of the graph in fig. 9-1. The democratic rule in all European countries puts these countries in the center or the left-hand side of the graph. The cohesion they have is insufficient for the new colonizers. The newcomers will stage riots, create terrorist cells, and the like. There are two options to remedy the situation: either deport the colonizers to their native countries or substitute dictatorship for democracy.

I would like to explain why Jewish communities have never had any conflicts with the authorities of their countries of residence. First, Judaism prohibits asceticism, which makes it worlds apart from Islam, Catholicism, and other such religions. The place of Jewish community with its degree of cohesion is in the center of the graph. This religion is not aggressive. Second, Judaism complies with all the laws of the country in which a Jewish community exists.

For deportation to be acceptable and conducive to society's stability and safety, the society's place should be in the central part of the curve in Fig 9-1. The degree of cohesion should be optimal, that is, around 50 percent.

The defenders of human rights and their ilk would certainly assail me with the question: "Do you want to be banished?" The question is not new to me. I was asked that question with respect to reprisals. My answer was: "No, I don't." Today, I would act in a Jewish manner and reply with a question: "Do you want to be banished from your native country by the newcomers who envy your economic flourishing and hate your religion and culture?"

Below, I will show that some of the deportations carried out during the Second World War were justified. No belligerent would tolerate a hostile population in its rear, which was the reason for the deportation of the Chechens, Ingush, and other North Caucasian peoples.

Deportation of the Population

Let us take a close look at the historical record of a mass deportation of the population, the "deportation of peoples."

The Deportation of Peoples was the most typical form of reprisals in the USSR during Stalin's dictatorial rule, "an instrument of the nationalities policies" at that time. In plain language, it meant forced relocation of citizens of a certain ethnic background (or followers of a certain confession) to remote regions of the USSR, where they were kept in special settlements.

The Soviet Deportation Policy

The first deportations were carried out from 1918 to1925, immediately after the Bolsheviks came to power. The first victims of the nationalities policy of the Soviet power were the Terek Cossacks, who were evicted from their homes and exiled to other regions of Northern Caucasus, Donbass, and the Far North. Their land was given to Chechens and Ingush. In 1921, the victims were the Russians in the Semirechye, who were banished from the Turkestan Area.

Apart from these mass deportations, there were "minor" banishments of Soviet scholars in what was known as "Ships of Philosophers." They were indeed ships that carried away from Russia Pitirim Sorokin, the sociologist, Ber Brutskis, the economist, and many other prominent scholars. The deportation saved their lives. Toward the end of the 1920s, the borders were closed, and the scholars were "reformed" and exterminated.

A New Nationalities Policy in the 1930s

In 1933, there were 5,300 ethnic village councils and 250 ethnic areas. In the Leningrad Region alone, there were fifty-seven ethnic village councils and three ethnic areas (Karelian, Finnish, and Veps). Schools with instruction in national languages were opened. In the early 1930s, newspapers in forty languages, including Chinese, were published in Leningrad. There were radio programs in Finnish (at that time, some 130,000 Finns lived in Leningrad and Leningrad Region).

In the mid-1930s, a backsliding on this policy began— cultural (and in some cases political) autonomy of some peoples and ethnic groups was abolished. Jews were not deported, but all Jewish schools in the country were closed. All this took place against the background of the concentration of power in the country (building up an OUS). A shift from territorial to branch management followed. The processes were accompanied by reprisals against the real and potential opposition. The country's citizens were being turned into identical and obedient golems who had no nationality or confession, with communism serving as the only confession to be shared by all. The situation had a positive aspect: when people were getting married, the nationality or confession of the would-be spouse was immaterial to them.

In the mid-1930s, first many Estonians and later Finns were arrested in Leningrad. The deportation of local residents, mostly Finns, from the northwestern border areas was started in the spring of 1935, after a confidential instruction by G. G. Yagoda, people's commissar for internal affairs, dated March 25, 1935. By 1936, many settlements in the 20-km border zone had ceased to exist; many Lutheran churches had been razed to the ground. Then other people's turn came. As many as fifteen thousand Polish and German families (some sixty-five thousand persons) were deported to North Kazakhstan and the Karaganda region from the Ukrainian territory, adjacent to the Polish border. In September 1937, pursuant to the joint decree of the Council of People's Commissars and the Communist Party Central Committee "On the Deportation of Ethnic Koreans from the Far Eastern Border Regions," signed by Stalin and Molotov, 172,000 ethnic Koreans were deported from the Far Eastern border regions, as relations with Japan deteriorated. The deportation of "unreliable" people is usually connected with war preparations. The process of gradual abolition of ethnic regions and village councils outside the autonomous territorial entities of titular nationalities started at the end of 1937 and proceeded, along with folding up schools and publishing books and newspapers in national languages, outside the respective autonomous areas.

The Deportations during the Great Patriotic War

When the war with Germany was already on, the Presidium of the USSR Supreme Soviet by its decree of August

28, 1941, abolished the Volga German Autonomous Soviet Socialist Republic.

As many as 367,000 Germans were given two days to pack before being deported to the east—the Komi Republic, the Urals, Kazakhstan, Siberia, and the Altai area. Some of the Germans were recalled from the field forces. In 1942, mobilization of Soviet Germans reaching seventeen years of age was launched. They built factories, worked in mines, and fell trees.

People whose country of origin was part of the Hitler coalition (Hungarians, Bulgarians, and many Finns) were also deported.

Pursuant to the decision of the Leningrad Front Military Council of March 20, 1942, some forty thousand Germans and Finns were relocated from the area adjacent to the front line. Those who survived the war were again relocated in 1947 to 1948.

Mass deportations of the Kalmucks, Ingush, Chechens, Karachai, Balkart, Crimean Tatars, Nogaitsy, Meskhetian Turks, and Pontic Greeks were carried out in 1944. These ethnic groups in their entirety were accused of collaboration with the Germans. The territorial autonomy some of these peoples had been given was abolished.

A decree issued in 1948 did not permit the Germans and other relocated peoples (Kalmucks, Ingush, Chechens, Finns, and others) to leave the regions of their relocation and return to their former place of residence. Violation of this decree carried twenty years in a labor camp.

The conclusion to be drawn from the deportations carried out in the Soviet Union is that only deportations in the early days of the Soviet power were in the nature of reprisals. In this way, Soviet power punished its enemies. All the other deportations were part of war preparations or hostilities. The lame justification given for the relocation of Koreans in 1937 was that "they have the face the enemy has," that is, the Japanese with whom armed clashes occurred at that time.

As for the deportation of North Caucasian peoples and the Crimean Tatars, they were fully justified. But the way these deportations were carried out is also very important. Described below for the sake of comparison is the deportation of ethnic Japanese in the USA during the Second World War.

They Have the Face the Enemy Has

I am taking the USA as an example, because it is universally held up as a "paragon of freedom and democracy," the "defender of the human and civil rights." In early February 1942, the US authorities started the deportation of US nationals who happened to be ethnic Japanese. The first Japanese immigrated to the USA more than a hundred years ago. They made their homes mostly in Hawaii and California and worked at sugar cane plantations. They formed compact Japanese neighborhoods. The white, Christian, Anglo-Saxons did not welcome them, to put it mildly. The ill feeling that white Americans entertained for the Chinese already living there easily spread to include the Japanese, who looked very much like the Chinese. For all that, tens of thousands of Japanese moved to the USA before 1924, when their immigration was prohibited. Despite many obstacles, many of them managed to get US citizenship.

It looked like the Japanese—despite segregation—had a chance to emerge from the "melting pot" as a rightful element of the US nation. The Second World War, however, frustrated these hopes. On December 7, 1941, Japan attacked the US military base at Pearl Harbor in Hawaii, inflicting heavy losses on the United States.

Today, patriotism that united US citizens in the face of danger is called "everyday philistine racism." At that time, however, it was fostered by official propaganda. The Japanese had become an enemy. The anti-Japanese sentiments focused on the ethnic Japanese. On December 15, 1941, Congressman John Rankin said that he would grab all Japanese in America, Alaska, and Hawaii and put them in concentration camps.

Meanwhile, the data received by US counterintelligence showed that most of the ethnic Japanese were loyal to the Stars and Stripes, and their attitudes were essentially no different from those of other racial and ethnic groups in the USA. Even J. Edgar Hoover, head of the FBI, known for his being too ready to suspect everyone, was of the opinion that the Japanese community in the USA did not present any danger to the country's security. The logic of war, however, dictated otherwise. On February 19, 1942, President Franklin D. Roosevelt signed an executive order that allowed imprisonment and relocation without trial and investigation. It was pointed out that the decree had been prompted by security considerations. In this way, the military were given power over the civilians. Pursuant to this decree, ten concentration camps were established for relocated citizens. They were mostly put up far from the coast to make the country safe in case it was invaded from the ocean—in Arkansas, Idaho, Wyoming, Texas, and other states. The War Relocation Administration ordered the ethnic Japanese to report to the assembly places. They were given four days to get ready for the relocation. Their property and houses were sold for a song or just vacated. Over 120,000 ethnic Japanese—children, women, and elderly people included—were incarcerated in concentration camps. Two thirds of them were American citizens; the rest had valid residence permits. No attempts at escape or resistance were registered. Three people tried to contest the lawfulness of their relocation and incarceration in the US Supreme Court, as befits law-abiding citizens, but to no avail. Were inmates exterminated or bullied in these camps? No, they were not. There may have been cases of violence, but it was not part of a system. Even forced labor was not practiced. There were shops to make military outfits where the inmates were paid approximately half the average wages outside the camps. Families were not divided wherever it was possible. As a rule, a family occupied a separate cubicle in the common barracks. The rations of the inmates were the same as in the army.

The ethnic Japanese spent several years of their lives behind barbed wire, guarded by soldiers armed with Tommy-guns, the grounds flooded by light from the searchlights on watchtowers. No matter what justification for this decision might have been offered, it was incarceration of people who had not committed any offense.

Simultaneously, with the relocation of the ethnic Japanese, all servicemen of Japanese ancestry were discharged from the combat army. These people felt deeply offended and asked to be dispatched to the combat units as a sort of penalty. After some hesitation, in 1943, the authorities decided to heed these requests and began to form combat units that included ethnic Japanese volunteers. The first sessions of military training and instruction in handling weapons were closely guarded by armed escorts, as the ethnic Japanese were not yet trusted. Recognition of their combat valor came later. The One Hundredth Infantry Battalion and the 442nd Regimental Combat Team made up in large part of Japanese-American volunteers fought in Europe. In France and Germany, they took part in the liberation of the Dachau inmates. A few of them were in the Pacific Theater intelligence and counterintelligence units. No cases of desertion or defection to the enemy were registered. Moreover, during the war, 9,486 ethnic Japanese were conferred the highest US awards. While they were fighting, their families remained hostage in concentration camps.

Most of the ethnic Japanese were released in January 1945, when the end of the war was already near. In 1946–47, the last camps at Tool Lake in California and Crystal Lake in Texas were closed. Only about half of the Japanese returned to their former places of residence. The homeless occupied many of their houses. It took some time to have the deprivation of civil rights restored. Up to 1952, US citizenship was unattainable for the Japanese who had a permanent residence permit. They kept silent about it a very long time, as they did not want to reveal it to their children and grandchildren. During the war, most officials used euphemisms like "relocation" and "internment centers" for "concentration camps."

Many years later, in 1981, yielding to the pressure of the powerful movement for civil rights in which the US Black and Jewish communities were particularly active, the authorities set up a special commission to investigate the relocation and internment of civilians. The commission started gathering evidence all over the country. Proceeding from the results of this work, it was recommended that each victim of relocation and incarceration be paid $20 000 in compensation reparation. A US Congress committee, on inquiry into these events, came to the conclusion that the relocation and internment of the ethnic Japanese had been unjustified and was prompted mostly by racial prejudices and military hysteria and qualified these actions as a political blunder. In 1988, President Ronald Reagan signed the Civil Liberty Act and apologized to the Japanese Americans. The first reparation money to the oldest victims was paid in 1990.

Voluntary Deportation

In this case, quotation marks should go with the word "voluntary." No one would leave their homes and effects and flee unless threatened by pogroms and death. The end of World War II saw voluntary and forced deportation of Germans.

The Independence of North African Arab countries resulted in a "voluntary" flight of the French from these countries. The end of colonialist epoch in other parts of Africa also caused a "voluntary" exodus of the white population.

Today, Sergei Sumlyonny, a *Frankfort on the Maine* journalist, empathizes with the Germans banished from the East European countries sixty years ago (*The Expert* magazine, No. 30 (619), July 28, 2008). He believes that Germany's neighbors should realize that banishment was a tragedy for the Germans, not the other way around. This correspondent prefers to "forget" the enthusiastic welcome given by the Sudeten Germans to the invaders, the tears of the Czechs when the invaders marched along the streets of Prague, or that the Czech town of Lidice was razed to the ground and all its residents killed.

The journalist mentions the 1907 Hague Convention, which prohibited any transfer of civilian property (Art. 46) and condemned the principle of joint responsibility (Art. 50). The first to trample this convention underfoot were the Germans, who seized Jewish property and sent its owners to the death camps. The Germans introduced joint responsibility by punishing people just for being Jewish. What's the use of speaking of this convention today? The journalist recalls that in August 1945, the Nuremberg International Military Tribunal qualified deportation of peoples as a crime against humanity, but he seems to forget the old dictum that "victors are never judged." The victors do the judging. The Germans were tried for "crimes against humanity."

The carpet-bombing of Germany, Dresden in particular, by the Allies close to the war's end has not been forgotten. Day and night, British and American squadrons of five hundred planes each took turns in dropping their deadly cargo. Dresden, with its cultural heritage, lay in ruins. Just for the sake of comparison, he could have mentioned the Polish capital Warsaw, which also lay in ruins after the Polish uprising against the invaders was put down.

I would like to amplify on what I said above. During the war, operations of the carpet-bombing type were undertaken to "demoralize and intimidate." Victory alone is not enough; it is also important to break the spirit of the enemy, to suppress its wish to resist occupation and organize partisan or any other resistance detachments. It takes more than just inflicting defeat; it takes inflicting a *crushing* defeat on the enemy. We can see that the Allied operations aimed at "demoralizing and intimidating" were a success, both in Europe and in Japan.

The deportation of Germans from the East European countries was perhaps an act of brutal revenge, but it contributed to "demoralizing and intimidating." There remained no niche in Eastern Europe where the Germans could organize the slightest resistance. They were so downhearted that for twenty years, they had no recollection of their deportation. The wars waged today are different. The emphasis is on destroying military targets, while "demoralizing and intimidating" the civilian population of the enemy country is completely ignored. It is perfectly clear that by ignoring it, the victor loses its victory, as was the case with Israel after the Six-Day War and with the USA and England in Iraq.

After the war, fourteen million Germans were evicted from their homes in Poland, Czechia, Hungary, and other countries of Eastern Europe. Only twelve million survived the deportation. The tragedy of the deportation of German civilians is not seen as such by Germany's neighbors, even today. "Breslau, Oppeln, Gleiwitz Glogau, and Gruenberg are not just names, they are recollections that will remain alive in the minds and hearts of many generations. Renouncing them is treachery. The cross of deportation should be borne by the entire nation." FRG Chancellor Willy Brandt addressed these words in 1963 to the Germans, banished from the East European countries.

Symbolically, Willy Brandt included Gleiwitz in the list. It is a small town close to the old German-Polish border, which was the scene of a provocation that started the Second World War.

After the war, the worst lot befell the ethnic Germans who lived in East European countries. Despite the Hague Convention, effective at that time, which prohibited any transfer of civilian property and condemned the principle of joint responsibility, over fourteen million Germans, mostly women, elderly people, and children were, in the course of three years, expelled from their native parts and their property plundered.

The expulsion of Germans from Eastern Europe was accompanied by mass and organized violence, which included confiscation of property, incarceration in concentration camps, and banishment.

The Polish Disaster

The greatest number of Germans were banished from Poland. By the end of the war, there were over four million of them living in the country, mostly in the German territories that, in 1945, were given to Poland in Silesia (1,600,000 people), Pomerania (1,800,000 people), Eastern Brandenburg (six hundred thousand people), and in the areas of compact German settlements on Polish territory evolved over the centuries (some four hundred thousand people). Apart from these, over two million Germans lived in former eastern territories of Germany, which were annexed by the Soviet Union.

In the winter of 1944–45, the Germans residing in Poland began their flight to the West to escape the approaching Soviet troops, with the local Polish population starting their acts of mass violence against the fleeing Germans. In the spring of 1945, entire villages were engaged in robbing the Germans, killing men, and raping women.

On February 5, 1945, Boleslaw Beirut, prime minister of the Polish Provisional Government, signed a decree placing former German territories east of the Oder-Neisse line under Polish administration, which was an open claim to postwar territorial changes.

On May 2, 1945, Beirut signed a new decree, according to which all property abandoned by the Germans was to be taken over by the Polish state. In this way, it was planned to make it easier to resettle the population from Poland's eastern territories, part of which were to be given over to the Soviet Union.

Simultaneously, the Polish authorities treated the remaining Germans like the Nazi Germany authorities had treated the Jewish population. In many cities, ethnic Germans had to wear a white armband as a sign of identification, in some places with a swastika. Not content with that, in the summer of 1945, the Polish authorities began to herd the remaining Germans into concentration camps, holding from three thousand to five thousand people. Only adults were placed in such camps. The children were taken away from parents and put in orphanages or given to Polish families. In any way, their upbringing was fully in the spirit of loyalty to Poland. Forced labor was practiced with respect to the adults. In the winter of 1945–46, the mortality rate in such camps reached 50 percent.

The ruthless exploitation of the interned German population continued up to the autumn of 1946, when a decision on the banishment of the surviving Germans was taken. On September 13, a decree on "separating persons of German nationality from the Polish people" was issued. Still, inasmuch as the forced labor of the German inmates of the concentration camps was an important element of the Polish economy, banishment was postponed several times despite the decree. Violence against the German concentration camp inmates continued. For instance, in the period between 1947 and 1949, half the inmates died of hunger, cold, diseases, and brutality by the camp guards in the Potulice concentration camp.

The final deportation of Germans from the Polish territory did not begin until after 1949. According to the Union of Expelled Germans, some three million Germans died in the course of their deportation from Poland.

Truly Czech Meticulousness

Czechoslovakia was second to Poland for the sweeping character of its solution of the "German question." In prewar Czechoslovakia, Germans made up one fourth of the country's population. Most of them, as many as three million, lived in the Sudetenland, where they accounted for 93 percent of the population. A great part of Germans lived in Moravia (eight hundred thousand, or 25 percent of the population). There was a large German community in Bratislava.

These are not Jews driven to Auschwitz. These are Germans forced out of Czechoslovakia. Photo from Oestlichenachbam.bayern.de

Benes, the leader of the Czechoslovak government, as early as November 1944, presented the first action plan for the deportation of Germans to the Allies.

In 1938, following the go-ahead given to Hitler in Munich by the heads of the governments of Great Britain, France, and Italy, Nazi Germany occupied the Sudetenland and annexed the regions populated by Germans. In 1939, the German troops occupied the whole of Czechoslovakia and established the so-called Protectorate of Bohemia and Moravia in the territory of Czechia and the puppet Slovak Republic in the territory of Slovakia. The Czech government fled to London.

In London, the Czech government in exile first formulated the plans for a mass deportation of ethnic Germans after the war. Hubert Ripka, the closest adviser of President Edward Benes, entertained hopes of mass expulsion of Germans even back in 1941, expressing his ideas about "an organized relocation of peoples" in *The echoslovak*, the official newspaper of the Czech government in exile.

His ideas were fully shared by President Benes. In the autumn of 1941 and winter of 1942, Benes published two articles in *The Nineteenth Century and After* and *The Foreign Affairs* magazines, in which he developed the concept of "displacement of the population," which would supposedly bring order to postwar Europe. Uncertain of Britain's support for the implementation of its plans to expel the German population of three million people, the Czech government in exile addressed higher Soviet officials with the same aim in view.

In March 1943, Benes conferred with Alexander Bogomolov, the Soviet ambassador, seeking Soviet support for his plans for ethnic purges in postwar Czechoslovakia. Alexander Bogomolov skirted the issue, but Benes refused to be daunted and broached this subject during his trip to the USA in June 1943. He managed to secure the support of both the American and Soviet leadership for his plans concerning the deportation of Germans and started working on a detailed plan for ethnic purges. The Benes government presented the first action plan for the deportation of Germans to the Allies in November 1944. According to the Benes memorandum, the deportation was to be carried out in the regions where the Czechs made up less than 67 percent (two-thirds) of the population and would proceed until the German population was reduced to below 33 percent.

As soon as the Soviet troops liberated Czechoslovakia, the Czech authorities started to put these plans into practice. The spring of 1945 saw the first mass violent actions against the ethnic Germans, undertaken throughout the country.

The main instrument of violence was the First Czechoslovak Army Corps under the command of Ludvik Svoboda, the so-called Freedom Army. Ludvik Svoboda had some old scores to settle with the ethnic Germans. In 1938, after the Sudetenland was annexed by Germany, Svoboda was one of the organizers of the Defense of the Nation, a Czech guerilla organization. In 1945, sixty thousand Czech soldiers commanded by Ludvik Svoboda obtained an opportunity to take revenge upon the already defenseless German population.

Uprooting

Entire villages and towns populated by Germans were victims of Czech violence, aided and abetted by the authorities. All over the country, columns of Germans were formed and driven on foot to the border, nonstop. They were not allowed to take practically anything along. Those who lagged behind or fell were often shot down for everyone to see. The local Czech population was forbidden to help the Germans in any way.

According to various estimates, in the course of just a single of those "death marches"—expulsion of twenty-seven thousand Germans from Brno—some four thousand to eight thousand people died along the 55 km route.

The expulsion of Germans from Eastern Europe proceeded with organized brutality, confiscation of their property, incarceration in concentration camps, and deportation.

During the "customs clearance" on the border, these Germans were robbed of the few things previously unnoticed. The Germans who made it—robbed as they were—to the occupied zones of the former German territory envied those Germans who remained under Benes's rule.

On May 17, 1945, a Czech military unit entered the township of Landskron (now Lanskroun) and staged a "trial" of its residents. In the course of three days, 121 people were sentenced to death and immediately executed. In Postelberg (now Postoloprty), in the course of five days, from June 3 to June 7, the Czechs tortured and shot down 760 Germans aged fifteen to sixty, one-fifth of the township's German population.

A most tragic incident occurred in Prerau (now Prerov) on the night of June 18–19. Czech soldiers coming from Prague, where they had been celebrating the end of the war, came across a train taking Germans to the Soviet occupation zone; close to the end of the war, these Germans had been evacuated to Bohemia. The Czechs ordered the Germans out and made them dig a ditch for a mass grave. The elderly people and women could hardly do it, and the grave was not ready until midnight. Then the Czech soldiers, under the command of the officer, Karol Pasur, shot down 265 Germans. Among them were 120 women and seventy-four children. The oldest victim was eighty years, and the youngest was eight months old. After the execution, the Czechs took their belongings.

In the spring and summer of 1945, similar occurrences were common across Czechoslovakia.

"Spontaneous acts of retribution" reached their peak in June-July 1945. Armed Czech detachments scurried about the country bringing fear to the German population. The Benes government even established a special division inside the Interior Ministry, charged with ethnic purges and deportations, which was expected to keep the high pitch of violence. The country was divided into thirteen regions, each having an officer responsible for the expulsion of Germans. All in all, the Ministry of the Interior division dealing with deportation had 1,200 employees.

The rush in the escalation of violence elicited the Allies' displeasure, which was immediately countered by protests by the Czechs, who regarded the killing and deportation of Germans as their natural right. The note of August 16, 1945, in which the Czech government broached the question of final deportation of the 2,500,000 Germans remaining in the country, was the reply to the Allies. According to this note, 1,750,000 people were to be banished to the American occupation zone and 750,000 to the Soviet occupation zone. By that time, some five hundred thousand Germans had already been banished from the country. The negotiations between the Allies and the Czechs resulted in permission to banish the German population in an orderly manner and without outrages. By 1950, Czechoslovakia had got rid of its German minority.

Europe without Germans

Apart from Poland and Czechia, various degrees of violence against the ethnic Germans were also practiced in other East European countries. In Hungary, even before the war, relations between the authorities and the German minority were strained. Back in the 1920s, immediately after the establishment of a national Hungarian state, discrimination against the ethnic Germans began. The German schools were closed, and Germans were purged from bodies of government. There were no career opportunities for a person with a German name. In 1930, an order of the defense minister made it obligatory for all army officers either to change their German names for Hungarian names or to resign.

The position of the Germans greatly improved after Hungary became a satellite of Nazi Germany. Yet hardly anyone of them had any doubts that after the withdrawal of the German troops, the situation would change for the worse. That is why, in April 1944, the German troops undertook abortive attempts at the evacuation of the ethnic Germans from Hungary. The persecution of ethnic Germans began in March 1945. On March 15, the new Hungarian authorities approved a draft land reform providing for confiscation of the land belonging to the German organizations and individuals. However, even landless Germans were a thorn in the side of the Hungarian authorities, and in December 1945, a decree on the deportation of the "traitors and enemies of the people" was ready.

According to the decree, this category included not only servicemen from the German military detachments, but also those who, from 1940 to 1945, took back their German last names and those who, in the 1940 census, wrote that their native tongue was German. All their property was subject to confiscation. According to various estimates, from five hundred thousand to six hundred thousand Germans were banished.

Hardly a Hearty Welcome

The deportation of Germans from Romania proceeded with less violence than anywhere else. When the war ended, about 750,000 Germans lived in the country; many of them had been resettled to Romania in 1940 from the territories occupied by the Soviet troops (resettlement of Germans from Soviet Moldavia to Romania was governed by the USSR-German treaty of September 5, 1940).

After the capitulation of the Antonescu government and the entry of the Soviet troops, the new Romanian government refrained from harassing the German minority. Although in the regions of compact German settlement, curfew was introduced and cars, bicycles, radio sets, and other items regarded as potentially dangerous were confiscated; no cases of organized or spontaneous violence against the German population were registered. The gradual deportation of Germans lasted up to the beginning of the 1950s, and in the few preceding years, it took some effort on the part of the Germans to receive permission to move to Germany.

By 1950, the Germans banished from the East European countries had swollen the population, first of the Soviet and Western occupation zones and, subsequently, of the GDR and the FRG by twelve million people. They were distributed throughout all German regions, and in some of them, for instance, in Mecklenburg, they made up 45 percent of the population. There were just a few regions where this percentage was less than twenty.

Despite the scope of the deportation of the ethnic Germans from the East European countries, mention of the problems this posed was taboo in both Germanys. Up to 1950, first in the Western occupation zones and, later, in the FRG, the new arrivals were not allowed to organize any associations. Ingo Haara, a historian doing research into the banishment of ethnic Germans, holds that it was the start of the Korean War and deterioration of relations with the Soviet Union that made Western politicians admit the suffering of Germans and lift the taboo against mentioning the banishment of the ethnic Germans from Poland, Czechoslovakia, and other countries.

Today, the banishment of Germans from Eastern Europe still mars the relations of Germany with Poland and Czechia. According to sociological polls, more than half of the Germans still think of Silesia and Pomerania as German territories, although they are not eager to have them back as part of Germany.

The Poles keep expressing their attitude to the activities of the German Union of the Expellees by publishing collages on magazine covers showing its leader, Erika Steinbach, in an SS uniform. The opening in Berlin in the current year of an information center on the deportation of Germans from Poland elicited a protest from the Polish government. Even today, the pain and mutual grievances caused by crimes committed half a century ago make the neighboring countries wary of any attempt at recollecting what happened in 1945.

The Germans in Israel

On October 30, 1868, some people from Wurttemberg (southwestern Germany) got off a ship in the port of Haifa. They were members of the Christoph Hoffmann and Georg

David Hardegg families, who were leaders of the Templers, the Christian Temple Society. This society should not be confused with the Knights Templar Order, the valiant friars cum knights of the Temple in the time of the Crusades.

In 1861, Hoffmann and Hardegg established the Temple Society (Tempelgesellschaft) in the town of Ludwigsburg near Stuttgart. The objectives of this religious community, founded by evangelists who regarded themselves as successors of Jews, were to purchase land in Palestine's holy localities and to erect the third temple. Christoph Hoffmann, member of the Wurttemberg Parliament, a noted theologian, graduate of the Theological Department of the University of Tubingen and founder of the *Suddeutsche Warte* newspaper, was the rallying figure for the members of this Christian sect. The Templers saw their activities as a noble mission to save humanity, which was facing calamity and to put an end to the struggle between the followers of the various Christian beliefs and practices (it was the period of the Crimean War of 1853–56, in which the French—Catholic Christians—and the British—Protestant Christians—fought against Russian Orthodox Christians). To attain this objective, they decided to settle in Palestine and bring back holiness to this Promised Land abandoned by the Jews and, in this way, to speed up the advent of the Messiah and the construction of the Temple of the New Faith.

In September 1869, the foundation stone was laid on the slope of Mount Carmel in Haifa for the first German colony in Palestine, known as "Moshava Germanit" (the language of the Bible for "German Colony"). It was an important point on the way of pilgrims to the holy places in the Galilee and Lake Tiberias (also known as the Sea of Galilee). Before long, similar settlements sprang up in Jerusalem, near the place of today's Tel Aviv and in the Lower Galilee. Several settlements were also established in the Jezreel Valley close to today's Nahalal, in Nazareth, in the central part of the littoral plain (later developed into the German Sarona colony and, today, the location of the Kirya government township), Wilhelmina, near the town of Lod.

The industrious newcomers mostly engaged in farming. By the beginning of 1873, there already were over 250 settlers in Haifa living in some thirty houses with European-type conveniences. Most of them housed workshops, warerooms, trade outlets, bakeries, and the like. These strange people who abandoned their comfortable life in the Old World for starting everything anew in the ancient Land of Israel brought winds of change to the Middle East. They brought contemporary ways of construction, trade, farming, and handicrafts to the backward Turkish province, which Palestine was at the time. They brought the first diesel motor to pump water, state-of-the-art methods of winemaking and gardening, and organized the export of farm products, in particular to Germany. They bought olive oil from the Arabs, made soap, and exported it even to the USA, where it was in great demand and was called "soap from the Holy Land." They brought the first cows to this land, where people had had only sheep, goats, and camels. At the same time, the Templers led a secluded life. They did not allow mixed marriages and kept outsiders from settling in their colonies. The largest German colony in Palestine was in Jerusalem. Its most flourishing period was from 1872 to 1910.

During the First World War, most of the Templers who remained German nationals were banished by the British authorities in Palestine. Later, many of them—depending on their participation in the hostilities—were allowed to return. While in 1914 there were some 1,200 of them, in 1938 there were at least 1,500 of their descendants living in Palestine.

The Nazis coming to power in Germany wrought a radical change in the situation. Nazi emissaries became active in the German colonies. In the 1930s, a great section of the Palestine German population joined the Nazi party and hoisted flags displaying the swastika and Hitler's portraits on their houses. The Templers were German nationals and, as such, were called up for military training in Germany. In August 1939, all male Templers of conscription age received summons to report for service in the Wehrmacht. They fought in the Second World War.

By that time, the religious zeal of the members of the Temple Society had greatly waned, giving way to German nationalism. Their subversive activities compelled the British to banish them. In 1941, some six hundred of them were expelled from Palestine. At that time, most of the descendants of the first German colonizers were banished to Mauritius Island, New Zealand, and Australia. The British authorities interned many Germans. Yet when West German Chancellor Willy Brandt visited Israel, he was introduced to a "relic"—the daughter of the German architect who designed "Moshava Germanit" in Haifa.

In 1948, after a Jewish state was established in Palestine, their property was taken over by the Israeli government. In 1952, Israel and the FRG concluded a treaty on reparations, and the Germans claimed from Israel a fifty million-mark compensation for the land and other property lost by the Templers. The history of the German colony in Israel has some elements that resemble the history of the Japanese colony in the USA.

Lawful and Unlawful Deportations

In all the cases described above, the deportations were carried out within the law. In the Soviet Union, a relevant decree was issued; in the USA, the president and the Congress adopted a law on the deportation of the ethnic Japanese. The banishment of Germans was undertaken by the governments of their countries of residence after getting the approval of the Allies. An instance of unlawful deportation is the banishment of the American Indians from their territories to reservations. Further excursions into history may bring us to the days of Babylon captivity.

Today, the UN qualifies all these actions as crimes. Why this about-face? The answer may be found in the developments in Russia. During Stalin's dictatorship, deportations were a common practice. Today, they are considered a crime. This about-face was brought about by "democratization." During Stalin's rule, the country's citizens were golems who saw things as their leader saw them, while today, they see them in exactly the opposite light. This "opposite" depends on the degree of the society's cohesion. The deeper society's degradation, the greater the degree of the "opposite." What is the right thing to do?

It is society's degradation that made US President Reagan apologize to Japanese-Americans twenty years after the war ended for what President Roosevelt had done. Was Roosevelt a criminal? Certainly not. During the war, deportations were seen as a sort of a safety measure.

Some Costs of Democracy

For some time, sociologists have been trying to get at the causes of such social phenomena as genocide and deportation. In many cases, their answer is not exhaustive. *The*

Dark Side of Democracy: Explaining Ethnic Cleansing (2005) by the American sociologist Michael Mann can be taken as an example. He holds that mass ethnic conflicts is the price the contemporary world has to pay for the democratization process and that ethnic purges and genocide are part of the evolution of contemporary national states. According to him, the process of building a national state proceeded more smoothly in countries that had more advanced political institutions. However, he departs from this theory when dealing with a dictatorship, claiming that in such cases, exceptions in the form of spreading utopian ideologies to the state level take place. Stalin's ethnic crimes in the USSR can by no means be attributed to the democratization process.

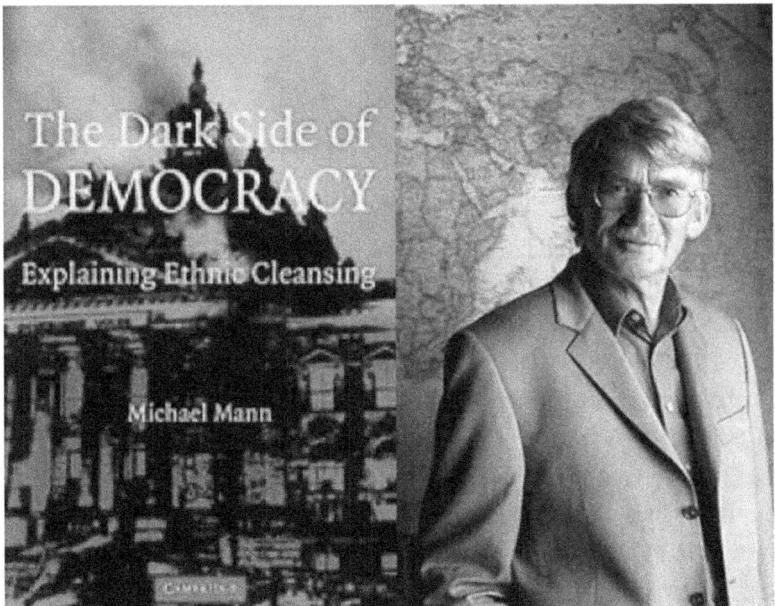

Mr. Mann's contention that genocide and ethnic purges are part of the evolution process is correct, but democracy has nothing to do with this.

✲ ✲ ✲

I mentioned Michael Mann and his work to underscore the gravity of the problem and the interest sociologists take in it. I leave it to the reader to compare his theory with mine and decide which of them is closer to reality.

Genocide

Genocide often accompanies deportations and reprisals and is the extreme form of such actions, inasmuch as they have identical social roots.

In spite of the fact that the UN General Assembly adopted a Convention on the Prevention and Punishment of the Crime of Genocide as far back as December 9, 1948, the convention failed to put an end to genocide. Below are some of the commonly known crimes of genocide: In Cambodia, the Pol Pot and Ieng Sary regime exterminated three million Cambodians over 1974–79.

Iraqi troops exterminated the Kurd population of Northern Iraq, specifically in the Anfal operation of 1987–89, when poison gases were used for the purpose. In 1994, in the genocidal war in Rwanda, Hutus killed eight hundred thousand Tutsis.

Actually, only the organizers of the massacre in Rwanda were punished following the ruling of the International Tribunal for Crimes in Rwanda, which began its work in Tanzania in November 1994. The persons under investigation were mostly former officials of the ruling regime at that time, who organized and masterminded the mass extermination of Rwanda citizens. Those found guilty were sentenced to life.

Why is it that genocide in Cambodia and Iraq has remained unpunished? Why were the International Tribunal for the former Yugoslavia and the International Tribunal in the Hague criticized and accused of partiality?

First, there is no international law enforcement body that could deal with a conflict the moment international law is broken.

Second, each country has its own degree of society cohesion and, consequently, its own norms and laws, which precludes interference in a country's internal affairs as, for instance, when Cambodians are being killed in Cambodia.

Chapter 10

How I Would Fight Arab Terrorism

At my lectures or on the Internet when I discuss terrorism and reprisals, I am usually asked how I would organize
the fight against Arab terrorism. My brief answer is that I
would emulate the *coup d'etat* staged by General Pinochet
in Chile. I would disband the Knesset, the Histadrut (a trade
union federation), Rashut Ashidur (the State Broadcasting
Service), introduce censorship, and carry out mass reprisals
in the country. General Pinochet's reprisals affected three
thousand people; the number of victims of my reprisals
would be around five hundred. It is only after anarchy is
put to an end in Israel and the rear has been strengthened,
that the fight against the external enemy—Arab terrorism—can commence.

Mass reprisals should be carried out among the Arabs;
namely, force should be used to disperse any protest march
or any other anti-Israeli mass rally. All privately owned firearms should be confiscated. Punishment of criminals should
include the punishment of the relatives of terrorists down
to the entire hamula (clan). The hostage system should be
introduced, if the situation calls for this step. Arabs should
be brought under Israel's rule at all costs. And the Arabs
should reimburse the costs. Terrorists, starting with their
leaders, should be eliminated. The Israeli army should stop
the unproductive "pinpoint hunt" for individual terrorists.
They would disappear after the reprisals.

All the prerequisites for mass reprisals are detailed in
the chapter on collective punishment.

Chapter 11

The War in Gaza

I had already finished my book *Military Sociology* by the time armed conflict blazed up in Gaza. It might be interesting to check against my book how the Israeli army fought. What did they achieve after the three weeks of war passed, apart from the death of ten soldiers?

Gaza is a coastal strip of land along the Mediterranean Sea, about forty kilometers long and twenty kilometers wide. Before the Six-Day War, this territory was dominated by Egypt. Then the Sinai Peninsula passed to Egypt, but the Strip was left to Israel. The border between the Sinai and the Gaza Strip was called Philadelphia Corridor.

The Arabs populating the Gaza Strip have become the overly united society (OUS). What pulls them together? Israeli generals called it "tashtit" (in Hebrew it means "the basis") and did their best to wipe it out in the course of the military actions. However, the generals are ignorant of sociology; that's why they confused religion with rockets, etc.

The "Tashtit" (the basis) of any society is its axis, something that conditions and unites the society. For the Arabs, it is Islam and those who profess it. That's what should be kept in mind in war. First, it is necessary to terminate Islam, or, at least, forcefully transform it to a less ascetic "Turkish" variant. The underground tunnels, leaders, and arsenal are of the second priority.

As I mentioned before, a member of OUS turns into the golem. The golem and his behavior are explicitly described in the book. Let me summarize the most distinctive features.

1. *Shahid.* The sociology classifies such suicide as "altruistic." It is the suicide for the good of the society.
2. Self-torture. That means the ascetic suppresses one's own mind and body. The golems enjoying themselves must be executed.

The key features and behavior of OUS are also described in the book. They are all present in the Gaza Strip. Let me reiterate of some of them:

3. Look how the Arabs pray. There are hundreds and thousands of golem bodies, spread-eagled on the ground.
4. The leader or the hero funerals turn into mass hysteria. The aggression of the OUS is one of its key features.

As soon as the Palestine autonomy including the Gaza Strip was declared, the conflict between the Arabs and the Jews settled on the vacant lands flared up anew. The Arabs fired at the settlements.

On one hand, the Israeli left wing dreamt of the Strip turning into the Middle-East Hong Kong; though, on the other hand, people said it was too expensive to keep the army for the settlers and the latter should be liquidated. In the end, the settlements were liquidated, and the settlers were forced to leave. The Israeli army left the Strip to the Arabs.

The Arabs celebrated the victory. They moved the attacks to the Israeli territory. The frontier towns and kibbutzes came under fire.

The fanatically religious party "HAMAS" seized the power in the Gaza Strip and, due to the financial support from Iran, started to take up arms. They established the rocket manufacturing of about four kilometers action range. Gradually, the construction was improved, and the action range increased. They illegally imported "Grad" rocket launchers. These rockets are a variety of "Katusha," though upgraded; they managed to reach the Port of Ashdod, the cities of Ashkelon and Beer Sheva. Such rocket launchers have low accuracy and no self-homing function. They are suitable for area firing.

Israel took protective measures and refrained from an active response. They established the warning system to locate the rockets and warn the citizens several seconds before they crashed to the ground.

The illusions of the Israeli left wing were shattered long before the war broke out in Gaza. The dream of Hong Kong was not meant to come true. As soon as the southern border of the Strip came under Egyptian control, the Egyptian troops flooded the Sinai, and the weapon transfers continued. The Gaza Strip was packed with rocket launchers and weapons. The Jewish settlements in Gaza served as the outpost and protected the Israeli cities; once they disappeared, those cities became the new targets.

After eight years of total inaction, the Israeli government decided to act. Initially, the aviation, as usual, made pinpoint strikes. Then the Strip came under artillery and tank fire. Then the tanks and the infantry entered the territory of Gaza. The army was given a mission to destroy "tashtit," the military basis of HAMAS. This was taken as the tunnels, arms, etc. Everything I wrote above, while the religion, excessive unification, etc., were never considered.

We should stress here that Israeli Defense Force (IDF or *TZAHAL* in Hebrew) repeated its mistakes. It is well known that in the course of the Six-Day War, the military power of the enemy was totally destroyed. However, Egypt managed to restore it in no time, through the help of the USSR. The Soviet Union supplied both weapons, including aircrafts and their pilots. This quick rearmament led to the "War of Starvation" that was also lost by Egypt, despite the strong support from the Soviets.

This time, IDF destroyed the military power of HAMAS in three weeks. Notwithstanding the promises of Egypt, the USA, and other countries, there are no obstacles to restore its weapons from Iran.

Why is Israel not able to protect itself? Why does it have to rely on Egypt, the USA, or the UN?

The War of Gaza did not finish with the enemy's capitulation or destruction. Surprisingly, Israeli mass media have never mentioned the Six-Day War of 1967 in the context of the Gaza battle. Everyone seemed to forget that HAMAS was created by Israel to oppose Yasser Arafat. If any parallels were drawn, they were the parallels with war against HEZBOLLAH.

Sobs and Moans

Here I would again quote Latsis, the assistant of
F. Dzerzhinskiy, the chief chekist:
"We do not recognize the old morals or humanity. We do not fight against certain people. We are wiping out the whole class of bourgeoisie. There is no need to search for the evidence to prove that the accused acted or spoke against the Soviets. The first question to be asked is the class he belongs to, his origins, his education or profession. These are the

questions that shall determine the accused destiny. Here is the essence and the very meaning of the red terror."

Just change the wording from, "we do not fight against certain people" to "we do not make pinpoint strikes," or change "the class of bourgeoisie" to "the Jews," and you will get the phrase that could easily be spoken by some Arabic organization. One may naturally ask a question. Why is the Jewish army fight against the gangs of terrorists so much disapproved of? Where does this admiration for gangs come from?

Why does Israel have to stick to "old morals and humanity"?

The war produced lots of sobs and moans about "poor kids" and "innocent civilians." The whole chapter of this book is devoted to "poor kids" to show that the OUS (abnormally united society) is capable of sending its children to war and sacrificing them for its own goals. The ends justify the means. "The kids grow and absorb the spirit of the OUS and become Golems and food for powder." Not only do they throw stones, but they also turn into shahids. Though once these kids become victims of war, people start sobbing and moaning. The dead bodies of "poor kids" or the kids themselves serve the advocacy goals. The humanitarians, pacifists, and human rights activists love to refer to the "poor kids." The kids' defenders extrapolate our morals to our enemy, who is totally immoral, who kills our women and children without a whisper of hesitation.

Nowadays, it is popular to divide people into civilians and warriors, into angels and devils, just as they did during Napoleon's time. Armies fight, while the civil people watch the battle from afar. We totally missed the lessons of the first and even the second world wars.

We should remember that the civil people are the source of armies. It is particularly obvious if the army is of a partisan nature. To see the mistakes, it is enough to analyze the USA and NATO's failed attempts to thrust its regime into Afghanistan or Iraq. Moreover, those blunders are aggravated by the endeavor to make these countries *democratic*. There has never been a flourishing democracy in an Arabic country. Arabs are just not ready for democracy.

Israel follows the USA's example and makes the same mistakes. The only difference is that the USA fights in foreign territory, while Israel fights at home and with poorer results.

None of the American soldiers has ever faced the International Criminal Court (ICC), despite the continuous wars the USA runs over the globe. The USA make their satellites sign the agreement under which the citizens of the USA are not transferred to the international court, but returned to the USA instead. There are sixty-eight agreements of this kind already signed. The US Congress passed a law on the protection of the American men-at-arms that forbids cooperation with the International Court and, obviously, allows violence aimed at protecting American citizens, brought to court. To grant the Americans immunity is to adopt the system of double standards: one standard is for the Americans, and the other standard is for all the rest. The Croatians find the position of the Americans strange, to say the least: the USA forced Zagreb to deliver war criminals to the Hague tribunal. Washington makes no secret of its double standard principle. *Quot licet iovi, non licet bovi.*

Here I'd like to remind you of the maxim that "the end justifes the means."

We cannot speak about pinpoint targets in the war against an EUS. The EUS itself is the target to be destroyed.

The EUS is not capable of work, but only to kill and plunder. If we do not destroy it today, it will destroy us tomorrow. That is the reason to fire the artillery at the squares.

How I Would Make War in the Gaza Strip

I would not enter the tiny territory of the Strip. The artillery, such as launchers of the "Katusha" type, would be located on the border of the Strip to fire at the area. I pause now and then to see if there were delegates with white flags. If no one wanted to capitulate, I would resume firing. I suppose the war would be over in two days, no longer.

To win a war, one should not only defeat the enemy's army, but also psychologically suppress the population of the occupied territories. How would I suppress them? Let's turn to the examples of the Second World War.

There were no problems with Japan. Colossal damage caused by two atomic bombs dropped on the country made the Japanese quite obedient. In the case of Germany, it is less obvious. Still, carpet-bombings of the allies in the last months of the war were impressive. No one seemed surprised to see the artillery and tanks firing in the cities. The drive to oust the Germans from the Eastern Europe, from Poland, Prussia, and Czechoslovakia, was just as impressive. About twelve million Germans were driven out of these countries, but only ten million reached the frontiers of Germany. The rest died on the way. Helpless German escapees deeply felt the rage of the Poles, Czechs, and other peoples. They took revenge for the destroyed Warsaw, Lidice, etc. The violence against or the murder of the German escapees was not a sin.

So what are the mistakes of Israel? They are the same. There are no innocent civilians (we call it "hafm mi pesha" in Hebrew). Islam tightly unites both soldiers and civilians.

Islam—is the "tashtit" to be destroyed by Gaza? What stops us from letting the heavy gas into the tunnels? It is not poisonous, but it displaces the air. We should never forget that the war means death and destruction. There are no other wars.

Strike the area!

One should look back at the way people fought during the Second World War and stop playing humanism. The Russians gave bread to starving Germans in Berlin only to show their blessings in the news films. There was no bread in the USSR.

IDF served as an example for the West, so let it be so. Now IDF has degraded under the influence of the left-wing ideology. My readers tell me about Israeli generals speaking of the "crimeful orders," and they are ready to break them. The breed of general Mitzn grows and multiplies in the IDF.

"Legal" Soldier Losses

Having achieved nothing during the three weeks of war, Israel lost ten soldiers, to say nothing of the wounded.

It has become fashionable to lose soldiers in the name of humanism, pacifism, and other *isms*. In 2004, Dov Vardy—the father of Moran Vardy, captain of IDF—accused the Israeli legal system of his son's death. He believes that the Israeli legal system does not provide the soldiers with enough latitude to fight the enemy, avoiding hazards to life. This leads to a waste of soldiers' lives. Dov says that the soldiers asked for permission to employ massive fire during the operation, but the command said no even without consulting with the higher commanders. Dov Vardy also claims that the soldiers were not allowed to launch a rocket at the house where the armed terrorist was hiding, the very terrorist that had killed Moran. He says that the decision was absurd, as it was quite obvious that the armed terrorist was hiding in the house; the terrorist that had refused to give up. Had the rocket been launched, Moran would have been alive. Dov came to the horrible conclusion that his son's death was in vain; it could have been avoided. For what did the soldier sacrifice his life? The commanders are gripped by fear that they will have to face the Israeli High Court of Justice. He claims that, nowadays, soldiers continue to act in excessively risky conditions.

I have already written about the rules of war. Since when does the Israeli High Court of Justice decide how the soldiers should fight? Let me remind the reader of my instructions to my grandson, a soldier: "I would prefer to defend you at court than to shed tears at your grave."

Ten soldiers died in the Gaza Strip. Some of them died from friendly fire. There would have been no friendly fire if we had not entered the Gaza territory.

Then I borrow materials from Guy Bechor, Ph.D., of the Interdisciplinary Center Herzilya, the center where there were no specialists capable of peer reviewing my book. These materials are published on his Web site http://www.gplanet.co.il/. Borrowing them, I primarily wish to show the way the Politburo corrupts the army. The society follows the downward path; its systems and the army, in the first place, break down. Regretfully, the Politburo and the Israeli Defense Force refuse to notice it.

How did it happen that the famous IDF, the dear creature of Israel, flee in terror from any armed conflict with the Palestinians in the Gaza Strip? How did we abase ourselves so far that our generals beg for a cease-fire extension and the head of the Joint Staff, General Gaby Ashkenazi, the general that brags about turning IDF into quite a different army, claims that Israel should avoid military actions in Gaza at any cost? Our army has not become worse; it simply does not want to fight, just as it was during the last war in Libya. The head of the Joint Staff had a detailed plan of land warfare with Hezbollah locked in his drawer, but the generals preferred to send in air forces to throw bombs on Libya. The same with Gaza: they send air forces, delivering a standard, mediocre, and thoughtless response, with no plan at all.

It is not the army that protects the country; it is the country that protects the army. If rockets strike the army base, the soldiers are evacuated to the deep rear, while the citizens are just left where they are. Israeli society believes that the life of the soldier is more precious than the life of its citizens; that's why they are taken so much care of. However, this is the Force to Defend Israel but not the Israel Defense Force! How do we abase ourselves so far as to let IDF become a nearly *political establishment that exercises its power over the politicians* in order to avoid fights on any front. For example, on the Syrian front, where the military authority pushes the government to negotiations with Asad and retreats from Golan—not to fight—this is their primary aim.

How can it be that our army has lost its killing instinct that used to be a distinctive feature of our self-confident commanders? Those who destroyed the Arab Air Forces so swiftly that not a single airplane managed to take off the ground!

How can it be that the army is petrified by the limited conflict with a small gang of terrorists and demand that the government extend the cease-fire period at any cost, even at cost of the state sovereignty and the peaceful life of its citizens?

Yearly, billions of shekels are spent on the army, so why does it not come up to the mark and its Joint Staff, dissolved in fat and drowsy from the endless budget, not want to take trouble and dream about retiring and about director chairs in private companies?

Legal bodies have interfered with the army too often, which in the end killed the IDF initiative. No one wanted to risk his life only to have his career shot down by the committee of Vinograd or Agranat after the war. Any war will end in investigative committees, as human losses are inevitable. No commander will ever take a risk; what's more, everyone now hurries to hide behind the lawyers. Will "mommy" let us bomb Gaza, or won't she? The head of the Joint Staff is not in charge of IDF anymore. It obeys the orders of the government legal adviser that dubbed the second Lebanon war as "the legal war." There is no place for ingenious strategic decisions and sudden risky operations in such wars. The lawyers' permission must be obtained in the first place. The Israeli High Court of Justice (BAGATZ) defeated the army.

In the past twenty years, IDF got all the human rights organizations on a string that does not bother about Israeli interests. They haunt the army from inside but are paid from abroad. With BAGATZ's support, the destructive effect of their activity might be enormous.

Nowadays, public opinion of Israel is influenced by the magnitude of human losses. They have become the single measure of military victories and defeats; that is why the army prefers not to fight—it is dangerous. The army is not afraid of the enemy; it is scared to death of mothers, by loud talk backers, by angry crowds, by Carmela Menashe (army observer of "Voice of Israel" radio station), by newspapers and TV channels. To lynch a general is considered to be a great achievement. Modern Israeli society thinks that the war is lost if there is at least one killed, for example Gilad Shalit.

During the triumphant Six-Day War, about eight hundred soldiers died within six days. In terms of modern concepts, this war was a catastrophe and a disastrous defeat. We report each death and return to this news every hour, which does not help but only demoralizes people and gives them the feeling of colossal losses. In 1967, the list of dead was announced after the war had been finished—and nothing happened.

The army knows everything, knows who they will have to deal with, and does not want to begin war—neither big nor small. No, it's not the enemy but the cries inside the country that will inevitably arise if, God forbid, there will be dead! Today, IDF tries to develop the strategy that will result in less damage after the loss; no one thinks of winning tactics.

Our enemy has noticed the strange feature of ours and successfully uses it against us. Thus, in 2006, when Nasralla hurriedly declared victory, we, overwhelmed by the defeatist feelings, only mournfully nodded to him in response.

We worry only about our personal interests, while the army and the state have moved to the background. Modern society does not believe in patriotism and love of the Motherland; the army has turned into something insignificant; it has become an unnecessary, stupid tool of "invasion." However, it is not only an Israeli phenomenon. It comes from the USA. Pacifism developed in the American mass media and cinema as a reaction to the wars in Korea and Vietnam.

Whole layers of our society have drifted apart from the army and from everything it represents. Now, a new group

of citizens do their job—they are religious Zionists, notably prominent in the army, and new repatriates that treat
the army as a symbol of social mobility.

The army command knows the way things are and
does not want to get where it found itself in the midst of
the second Lebanon war or to spend another eighteen
years in the Lebanon marshes, through the stupidity of the
political leaders of the country. The generals know that if
the army is stuck in Gaza escapees' settlements, the left
wing will oppose them and leave the army at the mercy
of the mass media and the numerous committees that will
tear it to pieces.

They know that the Israelis are ready to sacrifice Sderot,
Ashkelon, and other cities, so that the bourse go on working and gain profits. The army knows that it has no real
support in the rear. Modern Israel is based on personal ego.
The hell with solidarity, as though the Israelis do not understand that today they abandon Sderot and tomorrow
they will have to flee from Tel-Aviv.

These factors prevent the army from drastic actions.
The Modern IDF is not afraid to go forward, but it does not
dare to look back, at the rear, as it is afraid to be left alone.
IDF is not the people's army anymore. It's an army afraid of
people. However, we live in the Middle East where people
enjoy watching how we destroy and humiliate our army.
They do not have to stir a finger—we do the job better,
and we do it for them.

Lessons of War

I am not the only one to notice the failure of the Israeli Army. Regretfully, modern analysts tend to point out
other reasons for the defeat in the war with Hezbollah and,

consequently, draw purely tactical conclusions, not considering sociology.

The military sources thought that the main strategic lesson of the second Lebanon war was the inability to destroy short-range rocket launchers without ground forces. Nonsense. If Israel had dropped more bombs than leaflets, the rockets would have been destroyed.

IDF warned the houses' inhabitants over the phone about the strikes. This idea never occurred to anyone during the Second World War.

A one-ton bomb dropped in a pinpoint strike smashed the house of the head of the army of HAMAZ. The commander died. Thousands of its faithful soldiers came to his funerals. Israel got the splendid target and let it pass through its fingers. All police officers wait while the friends and enemies come to the funerals of a big mobster. IDF that performs the police functions lost the opportunity. These funerals once again proved that there is a EUS in Gaza. Any sociologist might have a look at the funeral's photo, conclude that the society is excessively united, and advise to strike the area. There are no pinpoint targets there. The whole of Gaza is the pinpoint target.

The events in the South of Israel proved the statements in my book. However, there are no military sociologists in Israel. Actually, the same mission was assigned in 2006 with respect to Hezbollah, although it was never achieved through the fault of the Politburo. Soldiers have died, but the Politburo has survived to begin a new losing war.

The Army of Nationalists

Why does the military academy invite Shulamit Alony and Asa Kasher but not me? Both are as thick as two planks and completely ignorant, but their ideology perfectly suits the aim of IDF demoralization. The degraded IDF has stopped thinking about victory.

Thus, during the war in Gaza, they did not plan to win; they hoped for help from abroad. The Israeli internationalists (the left wing) are very sensitive to the international reaction to their war. They begin fighting, but they do not wait for the enemy to capitulate—they wait for international public opinion instead. However, public opinion will not protect us. Remember the holocaust. Who gave a helping hand to the Jews? Why doesn't Israel protect itself? Why does it have to rely on Egypt, the USA, or the EU?

CHAPTER 12

Intelligence and Counter-Intelligence

As I have already mentioned in the beginning of the book that the military seem to be very enthusiastic about technical means and absolutely neglectful of sociology. Regretfully, in this chapter I will have to repeat what was already said on the subject.

Scientific and technical achievements allow distinguishing the smallest objects from the space. Where it is not enough, drone aircrafts will be able to complete the reconnaissance mission. At the start of my career I designed the eavesdropping devices.

With no aim to diminish significance of the state-of-the art scientific and technological progress, I suggest using it together with the sociological achievements. It is particularly reasonable as the information is still obtained by "old fashioned methods", through the spies, agents, prisoners' interrogation, etc. Then the special services have guidelines and instructions of all kind prescribing how to behave in different situations. Here is a good example: Russell C. E., Espionage and Counterespionage. — Garden City, NY: Country Life Press, 1926 (published in USSR by Voenizdat in 1938). Though the book is ancient, it may be successfully used by the special services as a valuable source of fundamental knowledge. It was published nearly one hundred years ago, but it is still relevant.

Apart from military intelligence, there are economic and industrial intelligence. Economic intelligence, naturally, pursue purely economic aims, including competitive wars, crashing rivals, takeovers, etc. Industrial intelligence deals with finding out and stealing technologies and things of that kind. There is a good example story of iconoscope. The Russian engineer and inventor of iconoscope for television Vladimir Zvorykin, who fled to the USA after the Bolshevik Revolution, once arrived at the USSR and told about his invention, though he did not revealed the iconoscope manufacturing process. The USSR had to spend a fortune to say nothing of the time to master the manufacturing of iconoscopes. If the technology had been stolen the country would have save a great sum of money.

The touched subject, particularly intelligence, deals with the illegal activity of state and private organizations. For this reason many aspects of this activity are enigmatic. At the same time intelligence and counterintelligence attracts trivial writers and movie-makers. Trying to please the public, they happily make up everything that is kept secret. That is why the truth cannot be easily found.

I am concerned only with the military area and my guidelines are aimed at extending the existing manuals. I assume my book is the only one that is based on sociology.

I have already described the social dynamics. According to my classification the society can be divided into three categories based on its cohesion level. Further I will use this classification.

Over-United Society (OUS)

The reader might notice that I often quote articles and documents from soviet sources. That is because the

USSR was the OUS and produced plenty of them. I have no doubt that any other OUS, particularly Arab countries, might provide me with similar materials. Though I neither speak Arab nor such documents are readily published. The communism crashed, the USSR broke apart and the documents appeared in the Internet.

This chapter is devoted to OUS. Over-United Society is the society where people spy upon each other and inform on each other. The security bodies of such society, for example, KGB, can easily summon citizens, interrogate them and instruct them to inform on their neighbors or whoever else. My sister complained that she was told to spy on her friend, a girl from Armenia, repatriated to the USSR. Out-and-out squeals. Espionage in OUS is not an easy task. Due to out-and-out squeals, austerity and poverty of OUS. The spy has nowhere to spend the earned fee. At the early stage of its degradation Interdevochki (international girls), a sort of prostitutes, appeared in the USSR. They catered to foreigners who paid for their services by goods, for example by beautiful blouse. Original imported clothes of high quality gave interdevochka still more chic and allure. Interdevochkas were a big problem for KGB as they were uncontrollable and competed with "swallows", sex-agents of KGB.

All military, underground, criminal and terrorist organizations belong to OUS. There are no exceptions. That's what differentiates military intelligence from economic one. In fact, there is no economy in OUS. It is impossible to bribe OUS members. They are ascetics that do not need either money or material goods. The OUS members are ready to commit so-called altruistic suicide that is a suicide for the benefit of their society. Obviously, even tortured they would never be broken down and provide the information.

They'd rather die than betray their friends. I know examples when members of underground societies, besieged by the police and military forces, killed their relatives and then committed a suicide. Remember the siege of Mossad Fortress built by Irod that was held by Roman legions in 73 A.D. When the Romans finally burst into the fortress, it was deserted. Only dead bodies of its defendants lied everywhere. The men killed their families and then killed each other. To do that they cast lots and chose ten people who should complete the mission. The last out of that ten should kill nine the rest and then commit a suicide.

The Federal Security Service (FSB) of Russia issued guidelines for citizens where among the specific features of the terrorists mentioned "absence of makeup on women except for the hair dyer". It is quite natural for women leading authentic life (OUS members, monks, kibbutz women).

Another feature, noticed by FSB is the special food, suitable for Muslims. Ideally, the suicider does not eat "unclean" food; the products should be bought only in special places. I have already mentioned that Islam makes people over-united, turns them into golems and terrorists.

OUS Members Interrogation

It is but natural that before interrogating **OUS members** or recruiting agents from them they should be brainwashed. The brainwashing is aimed at destroying the spiritual (ideological and religious) ties between the OUS member and their society. It is vital to shatter their faith and trust in OUS; to show the OUS member that the religion that unites them with their society leads to social stagnation, etc. It might be useful to show life in different countries, different societies.

What's more, the interrogated should be persuaded that their society turned the back on them and sees them as traitor. Here it would be appropriate to make a reference to the history of war between the USSR and Germany, when I. Stalin declared: "We do not have prisoners of war, only traitors". Maybe Stalin hoped to strengthen the moral of soviet soldiers, though it didn't work. Millions of soldiers got prisoner by the Germen due to his dull management while he decided to shift his blame on them. Freed soviet prisoners simply changed the German death camp to the soviet ones. It is useful to show that the society of the interrogated won't appreciate their sacrifice. No one is going to make a monument in their honour; what's more even their death will remain unknown for the members of their OUS. These statements should be illustrated by the examples from the USSR history, where the lost were remembered only 60 years after the war.

If the prisoners are exchanged, it might be useful to compromise those who are set free, for example by way of gossips.

Threats to friends and relatives are valuable tools to make the OUS member speak during the interrogations. One should find the relatives of the interrogated and hold hostage their families or friends. KGB once managed to recruit Svetlana Tumanova, hinting that in case of her refusal her family in the USSR would suffer.

Below is the recommendation for interrogating prisoners, given in the book of C. Russell:
"The prisoners' interrogation within your own army front requires deep knowledge of human nature and quick think. You should select people to be interrogated among prisoners that pass you by. Smart

questions and knowledge of human psychology will help you to obtain valuable information.

There were a lot of cases in the past when prisoners provided information of high value for the command. To achieve success you should know when the interrogated lie and when they tell the truth".

Smuggling the Agents

In the event when the agents are smuggled into the hostile territory, advice should be the contrary to that given above. The agents should have strong ties with their society, its ideology and nationality. The society and its leaders in the first place should never disregard the failed agents. It is necessary to take all possible measures to set them free, or to return them through exchange, escape or otherwise. This attitude will be a positive example for new agents, smuggled in the mist of enemies. At the time of the USSR the failed spies were often exchanged.

8. February 10, 1962. The USSR handed out to the USA an American pilot Francis Powers shot down over Sverdlovsk in exchange for Rudolf Abel, arrested by the FBI.
9. 1976. Upon the Chili's general Augusto Pinochet the soviet dissident Vladimir Bukovskiy was exchanged for the arrested leader of the Chili's communist Party Luis Corvalan.
10. June 12, 1985. Twenty three agents of CIA arrested on the East were exchanged for four agents of KGB arrested on the West.
11. February 11, 1986. Dissident Sharanckiy was exchanged for one of the soviet agents, arrested on the West.

As it is clear from the list, not only spies are exchanged, but also dissidents opposed to the leading power. In democratic society they are called "opposition".

KGB used to arrest tourists, for instance, from the USA and accuse them of some illegal activity. The relatives and the friends of the tourists started vigorous campaign, demanding from their government to free them. In the end the poor tourists were exchanged for some failed soviet spy.

Below is the decision of the Russian government to pay compensation to the families of special service agents for their death or injury in the course of carrying out their duties published in the Rossiyskaya Gazeta (RG) – tardy concern about their people.

They never returned from the intelligence mission

Published in RG (Federal issue) N3691 of February 4, 2005.

The government will pay a good compensation to the special service agents and their families for death and injuries.

Many are bewildered by the question "How much is the death of agent in roubles?" On one hand such questions sound like a blasphemy. On the other hand the government shall value those who sacrifice their life and health performing their duty.

Today Rossiyskaya Gazeta publishes an important document for the successors of Abel and Schtirlitz and their relatives. It is called "On the procedure of lump sum payments to the regular personnel of the external intelligence of the Russian Federation and their relatives, as per Article 22 of the Federal Law "On External Intelligence"". It is published together with the rules of providing those payments in case of injuries or death "through the performing the investigative activities", as it is said in the document.

These rules explain the procedures of payments and prescribe the fixed sums. It should be mentioned that the sums provided for the agents injuries or, as the document goes, "regular personnel" are quite substantial. They are not something to be ashamed of. The same may be said about compensations to the families of their external intelligence agents that lost their health through to the duties of head of the family. They are also subject to compensations. This is right as life of agents' wives and children is far from sweet and peaceful.

Now according to the new government statement, if the agent or a member of their family gets severe injuries at work and loses the labour capacity disabled for 2-4 months without getting the status of disability, they will receive a lump sum payment in the amount of 12 wages. This is a minimal rate. If they are ill longer than 4 months the rate is increased to 20 wages. If the injury has lead to disability - from 30 to 84 wages depending on the level of disability. In case of agent's death their family will receive the amount equal to 180 wages.

What are these amendments and additions to the Law "On External Intelligence" for? The matter is that the external intelligence agent was subject to two Federal Laws: "On state protection of judges, officials of law-enforcement and supervising agencies" and "On External Intelligence". These two Laws differ in many important, particularly financial, aspects, which led to legal lockup. Moreover these

Laws define people subject to state protection and, consequently, to insurance and compensations, in different manner. According to External Intelligence Law the payments shall be made only to the personnel of the agency and their families. The second law extends the protection to close relatives and in the exceptional cases just other people. The second part of Article 22 in External Intelligence Law only agents are subject to obligatory state insurance. It means that members of their families are not covered by such insurance.

RG Note

The real budget of the country's intelligence is kept secret. The same may be said about the wages of the agents. Some pieces of information sometimes leak into the Mass Media. Though are they reliable? There are secret funds used to finance special operations, pay to foreign agents and provide non-taxable compensations for the families of died special services agents.

Recently the veil of secrecy has been partially lifted by the government of South Korea. About one thousand of retired special services agents of South Korea participated in special operations against DPRK after 1953 applied for compensation from the official Seoul. The government expects applications from about 4700 people. The authorities of South Korea promised that each of them would receive compensation in the amount of 100-250 thousand dollars. In 2004 the government of the country passed the bill on compensation to retired agents and relatives to those who died during special operations.

Russia also lifts the veil of secrecy over its special services as the citizens should know how their money is spent.

The worst imaginable examples in this respect were provided by the leaders of German secret service who handed over their agents to the enemy during the First World War. The Heads of the German special services practiced rather peculiar punishments of their agents when they become too troublesome. For example, to get rid of the agent as soon as they got from him everything he could possibly give, the German did not hesitate to hand him out to the enemy. Most of former German agents were given away to the French counterintelligence by their own commanders, because they had become less effective or discredited the Service.

Russian Intelligence also «uncovered» its good-for-nothing agents, who tried blackmailing or, possibly, acted as double-agents. Though this behavior was justified as the Russian agent colonel Redel was the head of counter intelligence office in Austrian-Hungarian army. To supply Redel with good-for-nothing agents meant to cement own positions.

OUS Degradation

The OUS degradation always comes hand in hand with special service agents' treasons and escapes abroad. During the USSR degradation the citizens of the country were eager to escape to the West. Many people did not return home after tours abroad. There was even a popular joke then: «What is a quartet? - «It's a grand orchestra after the tour abroad»». Surely, the KGB and intelligence agents participated in that grand exodus. The administration of the

USSR played an important role in special services escape and degradation, as they ordered their employees to take part in the parade on the Red Square in Moscow in 1990. GRU (Main Intelligence Directorate) colonel Oleg Penkovs-kiy and KGB general Oleg Kalugin are worth mentioning in the context of high-profile scandals that accompanied the USSR degradation. Mr. Penkovskiy handed over to CIA about 10,000 documents that helped the USA to avoid war during the Cuban missile crisis. Mr. Kalugin uncovered both intelligence service operating procedures and names of soviet agents. There were so many line-crossers after the so called «perestroika» initiated by Gorbachev, that it won't be an overstatement to say that Russian special services collapsed.

The memories of Oleg Tumanov (they can be found on the web-site http://www.agentura.ru/phpbb/viewtopic. php?t=1800&start=30) are of great interest. By the order of KGB Tumanov, 21 years old, escaped from the soviet military ship in the Egyptian port. Then pretending to be a refugee he found a job at the German radio station «Radio Liberty». The radio broadcasted on the territory of Eastern Europe in different languages, but mostly in the USSR and in Russian. In the USSR the radio was jammed as its programs were clearly anti-soviet. During 25 years at the radio station Tumanov climbed the carrier ladder from an announcer to the head of the department. Upon the KGB order he identified people with anti-soviet feelings that fled from the USSR to the West. KGB and special services of other countries got rid of them. The death of Bulgarian writer Markov was the event that captured the headlines. Someone injured him with an umbrella. The injury proved to be fatal. The investigation showed that someone implanted one millimeter capsule with strong poison, castor oil into his leg. It is suspected that the writer Alexander Galich and many other were killed the same way.

On one hand due to Perestroika initiated by Gorbachev, the USSR broke-down and KGB agents' flight to the West foreign radio stations jamming stopped, Radio Liberty even opened news office in Moscow. On the other hand the line-crossers gave out Tumanov to the Western counter intelligence services and he had to flee for life to the USSR.

That's where the most interesting starts. Tumanov realized that everything he had done for the KGB had been worthless and even wrongful. His memories are full of bitter disappointment.

Censor

The censor ceased to exist in Russia after the USSR breakdown. That's when it became clear that life without censor is next to impossible.

In Israel religious Jews build their own Internet networks without even a hint of pornography. There are some other limitations as well there. Though we will slip ideological and moral aspects, as we are interested only in military issues.

Scientific and technological development provided the counter intelligence services with excellent means of eavesdropping and peeping, and at the same time created a huge problem of security leakage. It is nicely illustrated by the passage bellow:

«IDF: «Odnoklassniki» won't live a long life

Sunday, August 16, 2009 http://news.israelinfo.ru/technology/26302

IDF's web-site published an article titled "Social networks become out of fashion" about special subdivision, engaged in activities aimed at preventing confidential information from distribution over the Net.

It is devoted to the issue, raised by the army several months ago. With world-wide known Facebook in English and its peers in different languages such as Mekusharim in Hebrew and Odnoklassniki in Russian gaining popularity, information that is not supposed to be disclosed by the military flooded the Internet. There are photos of military objects, descriptions of the departments, composing personal pages as military divisions, and so on.

Amir Kidon writes in the article that life of the head of the computer systems security department in IDF would be much easier if the Internet was what it was supposed to be: means of communication and data exchange in the American army.

In the past, if a soldier published confidential information in a newspaper and signed by his own name, he would be held for court. Today thousands of soldiers do the same on the pages of the world-wide-web.

Anyway the security department believes that pure restrictions won't produce the desired results. The head of the department stresses that nowadays nearly all draft-age men, except those from special layers of the society, have their personal pages in the social network. It has become as natural as having a mobile phone. To forbid pages is as good as to forbid mobile phones. But the security department believes that soldiers should be aware of "shadow issues". They should be able to distinguish personal content and the army.

So what can be put in the network? For example, communities may be divided upon the forces types, such as Air Forces, Ground Forces Sea Forces, etc, but not upon military divisions, special courses or special qualifications.

It turns out that the members of the networks use special codes of the divisions instead of their names to prevent the leakage. It is a gross mistake: should any of them write anything that might disclose them, the whole division would be identified.

How is the army going to fight the data leakage in the social networks? 90% is explanatory work and only 10% is monitoring information in the social networks.

People are beginning to understand that they do not have to expose whole their lives on the social networks just as they don't have to answer each mobile call."

As the OUS breaks down and large-scale squeals stop, the intelligent services and counter intelligence services in particular, have to face an issue of information gathering from the citizens. Thus informators appear. They replace those who were previously called by the contemptuous word "secsot" (abbreviation from a Russian equivalent of "security officer"). The informators are to be paid and, according to BBC, very well paid.

The British police paid millions to the informators.
BBC article of 29-07-2009
According to BBC journalists during the past fiscal year the British police paid over £6 mln. (About $ 10 mln.) to people who supplied them with the information concerning criminal activity.

The representatives of the Police Administration Association underlined that the existing system of attracting informators is "very important for the purpose of delivering criminals up to justice."

The expenses of the Police related to the informators were disclosed for the first time in accordance with the Freedom of Information Act.

The local police representatives refused to explain how these funds were spent, but they assured that they were needed to clear a number of criminal activities.

A former senior police officer that had been working with the informators for over 20 years, told BBC than most of them receive £50-2000 for the supplied information, and a limited number of special informators supplying very important data were paid about £100,000 per year ($600,000).

According to Gevin Lee, officially the police have spent over £6 mln, though the real scale of informators usage by different security services is far greater than that.

The fact is that the police may offer the informators assistance in reducing the potential prison term.

The deputy head of the Mercyside police Patricia Gallan said that informators are very important for solving crimes of different nature - from robberies to criminal underworld.

"Informators are valuable source of information. Their use is justified and adequate in comparison with other techniques employed by the police.» she added.

The Army and the Society Demoralization.

Let me quote Pavel Sudoplatov and his book "Special Operations":

Those who was so eager to lavish solicitude on democracy in the countries "behind the Curtain", actually sanctioned the USSR repressions on their political enemies abroad. It is an unheard-of   violation of the international rights fundamentals. Does anyone still believe that the state interests of the Western countries still leave the room for their "sincere concern" of democracy in Russia and other CIS countries?

During the Cold War European offices of BBC, Radio Liberty and Voice of America broadcasted in Russian. The USSR jammed them all. There was a transmitter somewhere near Moscow that worked on the same frequency as BBC and transmitted noise so that soviet people could not understand what Mr. Goldberg, the anchor man was speaking about.

The hunt for anti-soviet emigrants was initiated to stop the hostile voices.

I suggest using an army as a model of OUS to see how it is influenced by the anti-war propaganda of pacifists. Then the result can be easily extrapolated on any OUS. Carrying out the experiment, one should bear in mind that the strength of army is not only in its weapon but also in its discipline. The army's unity shall be as close to 100% as possible. While the optimal society's unity is about 50%.

The history offers plenty of examples. It is easy as pacifism is very popular among the left wing (internationalists). Let's refer to the history of Russia. Remember that "Bolsheviks" declared the First World War imperialistic and "**fought for the defeat of their government**" "**Peace to peoples, bread to the starving, land to the peasants**" – that was their motto. I would also remind that it was Germany that gave Bolsheviks a helping hand in their strive for peace, the Germany, that was at war with Russia. Not only did the German allowed the railcar with Lenin V.I. and other leaders into their territory, but also provided them with a pretty handsome sum of money. That fact permitted the Interim

Government of Russia to declare that Lenin was the German spy.

The Bolsheviks carried out their anti-war propaganda in 1917 when battlefield was already on the territory of Russia. So called "Parvus Plan" used by Bolsheviks in 1916 consisted of "… destroying defeat of Russia with the subsequent revolution! The whole world is in danger if Russia is not decentralized and democratized". A unique agreement was achieved among Bolsheviks and the German authorities with respect to "world propaganda" issues (that's how it was called in Berlin when this touchy question was raised). It was no mere chance that after the February Revolution Bolsheviks started to publish newspapers, leaflets and brochures in heaps. In July, 1917 the circulation of newspaper "Pravda" reached 90,000, and there were 40 more newspapers in different languages with total circulation of about 320,000. Large print shops were bought. No contributions from the party men could possibly provide enough money for such printing flood. The Plan worked. Russia was defeated, "decentralized and democratized" and later choked with blood of millions…

It is clear that "pacifism" was just another word for "decentralization and democratization", or Russia breakdown.

Germany was at war with Russia and highly interested in its breakdown. Germany backed up pacifists.

The events that happened in the USA during the war in Vietnam were purely suicidal. When the war began (1964), there were plenty of   supporters in the American society. But in the late 60th and early 70th the USA were swept by the large-scale anti-war movement. So the American army had to flee from Vietnam, leaving all their machines and weapons.

Something similar happened to Israel when the army under command of the Minister of Defense, "soldier No.1" Barak, run away from Libya.

What are the roots of this behavior of the USA and Israel?

The society degradation in these countries increased over optimal 50%. As a result, the society broke in two opposite camps: republicans (nationalists) and democrats (internationalists). They are united only by slimsy notions of "freedom and democracy", which they try to thrust upon everyone unhappy enough to fall within their eyesight. The USA is still degrading, which is proved by the fact that Barak Obama was elected as the president.

All the above said can be applied to Israel.

In the environment of no censor and worshipped freedom the American Mass Media painted vivid pictures of cruel bombings, replicated interviews with shot down American pilots returned from the Vietnamese prisons of war, where the pilots heavily criticized the "malicious war". Comparing the facts from history, one cannot but believe in the thesis that modern democrats are similar to Bolsheviks of 1917, they also don't care about their country

Pacifism is the ideology of opposition that affected different countries in different times. Pacifism is the denial of any armed protection of the state interest. Here is another fact:

Anti-war propaganda made the Ukrainian army unpopular. Such statement was made by the head of the territorial administration of the South operational command, general-major Alexander Rosmasnin. According to the major-general, in 2008 the competition in the military educational institutions did not exceed 1.02 applicants per place.

Protect your country with the CENSOR and your Forces with the military censor!

ANOMIA

Espionage is flourishing in the society broken in two opposite camps. The left wing supporters (international-ists) hating their country and their people, will willingly dis-close secrets of their motherland and spy selflessly, purely out of the ideological believes. There are a lot of examples of such volunteers. The most famous of them are the so called "atom spies", the Rosenbergs in the USA, Claus Fooks in the UK and Mordekhay Vaanunu in Israel[1].

1   That's how British radio station BBC describes Mordekhay Vaanunu. "A 47-years old technician convicted to 18 years in prison for disclos-ing the Israeli nuclear program. Today he is one of the most famous political prisoners in Israel and in the world. He was born in Marakesh, in Morocco. In his childhood he lived in Dimon in the family of 13 souls. He attended yeshivah and in a religious school, then he studied ge-ography, physics and philosophy in the Universities of Tel-Aviv and Beersheba. During his academic years he was an activist of students and pacifist movement. In 1986 he concluded that the nuclear reactor in Dimon is dangerous for the Israeli citizens and neighboring coun-tries, and he told the journalists of British Sunday Times that nuclear weapon was manufactured in Dimon. Vaanunu insisted that "reactor in Dimon was the second Auschwitz for the citizens of Israel and their neighbors". After those revelatory publications he was kidnapped by Mossad agents in Italy and brought to Israel upon personal order of the Prime Minister of that time Shimon Peres. The court procedures were closed and their details were kept secret until 1999. Vaanunu was

Atomic espionage

Mr. Rossel pays special attention to the weapon of mass destruction (WMD) in his book. At that time it was poison gases (PG). Below is the abstract from the book. Replace "poison gases" for something more up-to-date.

"Being proud of inventing new and powerful poisoning gas, an indiscreet worker will eventually spill the beans and provide food for gossips. The newspapers responsible for supporting the public sentiments will publish ambiguous articles about new invention. All these will help to find the direction for the research. As soon as you have enough materials that require confirmation, put aside everything else (if you do not have special tasks) and concentrate efforts and attention on this issue.

Try to prove gossips as soon as possible: time is vital when the enemy prepares a surprise attack. Having heard of a new invention, send a report to the commandment, stating, however, that this is only a gossip. The report should be made immediately as any delay may cost lives of many people and the victory. Having sent the first report, go on proving

_____

convicted to 18 years in prison for espionage (for whose benefit?). During his imprisonment he was subject to emotional abuse."

It seems that BBC forgot that physic Claus Fooks was convicted in Britain for disclosing country's nuclear secrets to the USSR, just as Vaanunu purely out of the ideological motives. Noone ever dreamt of granting Fooks with the Nobel or any other Prize for his treason. No one declared that Fooks was the peace champion and saved England.

So there is a double moral with respect to one and the same phenomenon. It is important to see both sides of the medal and know how to turn it.

gossips until you find the facts. As soon as you discover the true plans of the enemy, make all haste you can to report them to the commandment. The information about possible poison gas attack is so important that you may desert your post to report personally if you doubt timely delivery.

Remember that accurate information about military chemical service of the enemy are of the highest value and you are allowed to bear any expenses to obtain them.

The required information may be obtained from three main sources: the first one – chatter in officers' clubs and hotels; the second – talks of soldiers in cafes and camps; the third – prisoners."

So far we have discussed single traitors. But the Left are capable of creating organizations, including political organizations that act against the interests of the country and its people. What's more they can descent to blackwash their country and their people to earn financing from abroad. Often the left-wing political parties are just legal cover for illegal terrorist organizations.

There are lots of pacifist and anarchist organizations in Israel nowadays. They are complemented by "fighters for human rights", while they consider humans only among the Left. The Israeli organization Shalom Akhshav (The Peace Today) can serve as a good example. Hiding behind the slogans of Peace, they play the game of Arabs as the fifth column. They spy on the Right and supply the information to the USA and Europe. Such organizations are nothing more than commonplace traitors.

They receive financial aid from different international funds. While the funds are fed by the Arab sources. Thus ex-president of the USA Jimmy Carter gave the "human rights fighters", the Betzelem organization 15,000 US Dollars received from Saudi Arabia.

The fight with voluntary espionage is complicated by the fact that the Security Service or the court system might be headed by the same left-wingers.

Considering the above said we can conclude that the country should never be brought to the conditions when it may break down. However the existing system that is called democracy will inevitably lead the country to the breakdown and collapse.

Juvenile espionage

I have already explained how children are used in military actions. I have mentioned about using children for total spying, firstly on the parents, and reporting to the authorities. The best and the most well-known example is famous hero pioneer Pavel Morozov. I have also told about using Arab children as terrorists.

Now I am going to explain how children are turned into tools of terror and intelligence.

Associated Press and eurosmi.ru reported on august, 6 in 11:08. following the fights in the Swat valley the Pakistani army discovered 20 children in the Taliban camp, they were studying in the school of suicide bombers. The terrorists trained the children to be fighters, snoopers and suicide bombers. The journalists were shown 11 boys, the youngest of them was seven years old. The Talibs were known to use children during military operations in Afghanistan, though the information about the similar practice in Pakistan was unveiled only recently. http://www.nomad.su/?a=15-200211270007

The agent Leonard Rembitskiy was caught by Russian counter intelligence officers near one of the troops unit.

Rembitskiy spoke willingly and gave lots of details. He told how he had been forcefully recruited by the German to spy in the rear of the Russian troops. Rembitskiy was ordered to obtain information about the artillery units in Riga and about prices for food. After he had been forcefully recruited, the German sent him to school of espionage in Warsaw. The Counter intelligence officers listened very attentively, forgiving the captured agent for his fidgetiness and inconsistency of thought. At that time agent Rembitskiy was 12 years old. There were 72 boys and 300 girls and several grown-up girls in the school for juvenile spies where Rembitskiy came from. Like him, they were forcefully recruited from the day Warsaw was captured. No one found this story funny. Everything was more than serious. To be sure that the juvenile spies would carry out the task and turn back, the German took hostage their parents and close relatives and threatened to shoot them if the children ran away or consciously sabotaged operations. Young spies sent to operations were entitled to special allowance; boys received 15 roubles, girls - 20 roubles. They were not given any documents. Their working outfit was quite monotonous. Boys were dressed in black school coat with white buttons or in short black jacket with breast pockets, high black boots, grey school shirt with two white buttons, pants of the same colour, and high black astrakhan hat with woolen pointed top. There was inner cartoon insertion over the upper and the lower edges of the hat to keep notes; girls were dressed in black slack coat, similar dress, black shawl and black boots with buttons and lacquered noses; or blue duffle coat, dress of the same colour, white scarves and black boots; grown-up girls wore short black coat or a bit longer blue coat, brown dress, lacquered shoes with white buttons, black hat with small brims and a feather in front.

In the end of education in the spy's school the juvenile spies were attached to the Russian troops units. The number of the unit a child was attached to served them as the pass when they returned from the operation. The children educated in the school for juvenile agents were sent for the intelligence operations either in groups or solo, mostly to Petrograd and Moscow.

Under the guise of escapees the juvenile spies easily penetrated to the deepest rears of the country and were able to obtain the information for the German, first of all about railroad movements of the Russian troops. The soldiers missing their families took fancy for poor little boys who often became so called sons of regiments. Discussing the latest awful train blowup and patting some snappy little Vasya, the soldiers could hardly imagine the blowup was organized by that very Vasya.

Lots of sabotages were carried out by young hostile agents in the depth of Russia during the First World War. Those little «death angels» set fires on defense plants and factories, indent depot with feed, timber-works; blew trains, throwing mines camouflaged as a piece of coal in the furnace, etc. In addition those little agents were actively engaged in military espionage. A war uglifies and turns everything upside down. There was another group of dangerous spies that completed the transformation of axiom «save children and women» into «save yourself from children and women».

Sex espionage

Love affairs help James Bonds to climb the career ladder and ruin Mata Haris

I will start this section with a description of women's functions. They are simple. A woman has to seduce and compromise a certain person. For these purposes she does not have to be either highly educated or competent. It is enough to be womanly. Having achieved the success the woman gives a code signal and a crowd of «witnesses» barge into the room where the compromised person is. They recognize this person and take photos. The woman's job is done. Then the compromised person is blackmailed and recruited.

Swallows

One of the most powerful special services that prepared women trained to seduce men functioned in the USSR. Such women were called «swallows». There are stories of a line-crosser from the USSR in the history of sex espionage. She told how KGB recruited cute schoolgirls, promising them beautiful life, high salary and all sorts of privileges if they would agree to fulfill their «civic duty» and become secret sex-agents.

The girls were taught to get rid of shame or shyness, they practiced different sex techniques, constantly watched pornography with various perversions. They should be able to complete any task. One of the practical classes was devoted to the lesbian orgy with teachers participating. The orgy was recorded and then thoroughly analyzed at the group discussion.

«We were told that we are soldiers», the cross-liner said, «that our bodies are our weapon that we are on the front line. By the end of training we became cynical and very experienced girls, ready to go to bed with anyone and make him the happiest man on the earth». The objects of sex attack were carefully studied to identify their sexual fancies, so that no one could come off the hook. The acquaintances looked natural and never arose any suspicions, but they always ended in blackmailing. The object was politely explained that they did not have another alternative except for cooperation with the soviet intelligence. The most successful operation of the swallows is considered to be the seduction of the American soldier who kept ward in the USA embassy in Moscow. The swallow that worked in the embassy on a low position managed to seduce the soldier. In the end the soldier switched off the security alarm system and let the «swallow's uncle» in. The false uncle mounted the eavesdropping devices in a special room for secret negotiations.

Though sometimes things went contrary to the expectations. That's what happened with famous seduction of Indonesian President Ahmed Sukarno. He was known as a great lover of bedroom mischief. That is why KGB sent him a group of young sirens during his visit to Moscow. They got acquainted with the president as a group of stewardesses from Aeroflot on the plane from Jakarta. Then he invited the girls to his hotel room in Moscow and arranged a great orgy. It was recorded from all possible perspectives by two cameras installed behind the mirrors. The best colour tape was used.

Everything seemed to go without a snag. Before the blackmailing, Sukarno was invited to a private cinema room and was made a «gift» in the form of a porno-film with him as the main star. The KGB agents supposed that he would get frightened and consent to cooperate. No such luck! Sukarno naively believed that the soviet government made him a true gift and asked to make half dozen copies for him to take home and show in the cinemas.

«My people would be proud of their president when they see this», explained Sukano to the startled agents.

The atom spy Mordkhey Vaanunu moved from England to Italy thanks to the efforts of his «girlfriend of straw». In Italy he was twisted, made an injection of sedative and brought to Israeli steamboat. In Israel the «pacifist» was brought to court and imprisoned.

Clever women know how to use their looks and get even more, evading from men's embraces, than falling into them too quickly.

The intelligence services in Eastern Germany reached new levels of sex espionage implementing the plan of seducing lonely secretaries form important state institutions of Western Berlin and FRG. The plan was developed by the head of the GDR intelligence office Marcus Wolf. The first contact usually took place somewhere on a bus stop or in a cafe during the lunch time. The «Romeo» agent started the conversation accidentally on purpose and went on with the seduction. There was such a trick. A man with a bunch of flowers calls the door of a single woman and pretends that he has got the wrong address. Apologizing, he presents the woman with the flowers and the acquaintance begins. Before the operation the agents knew about the woman even more than her close relatives. The seducer should not have the looks of a Hollywood star. It would be suspicious if he started to take interest in a single unimpressive woman.

The men chosen for sex espionage were trained in special centers by beautiful teachers.

The secretary problem became so serious that there appeared posters in NATO headquarters in Brussels that encouraged women to hold their hearts locked.

Wolf confessed that sometimes such operations failed as people fell in love with each other and it became difficult to control them.

Though I am not going to list names of successful agents and sex spies, describing their adventures. It is more important to underline their virtues and drawbacks as special service agents and compare them with male agents.

Women achieved success in intelligence services due to their natural charm and appeal. There is a saying in the intelligence that «when women undress, men start to talk». Though these are not the only virtues of female agents. There are other features inherent in women. I have noticed their excellent memory, accuracy, carefulness and, finally, artistry. Everything that is listed below is taken from different sources. The list includes unconventional logics, cunningness, and tendency to intrigues.

Women can hide their true face far better than men. Working on invisible from women revealed enviable insistency and dedication that deserves respect. The female agents are not apt to drinking and non-marital relations. In addition they are better masters of dramatic identification than men; they warm to a new role easier. The women's intuition is better developed and it is very important for the intelligence. Another women's advantage is their overwhelming vanity that is absolutely different from simple men's ambitions. If men often break the conspiracy rules to satisfy their ambitions (to boast before the friends, to impress a lady, etc.) women find other ways to satisfy their vanity: through their looks, beautiful clothes, etc.

A spouse as a cover

Abroad the agents often use their spouses as an operational cover during the investigative trips. During such trips a whole range of investigative issues can be solved. These are visual investigation, identification of the required address, drop of correspondence, studying the route to be checked, signals and special devices installation. Spouses can withdraw the surveillance attention, they support the agent's legend, carry out counter observation, and, where necessary, separate outside surveillance, take pictures of the route and its landmarks. Sometimes they check the hiding places.

Wives of residents

Both before and after war wives of soviet residents used to be agents of special services themselves. It helped their husband, the agent, to control his subordinates. He was aware of all embassy gossips.

In the USSR it was prestigious to marry an intelligence agent. High salary, trips abroad, relationships, cars, flat, clothes. Those who married lieutenants hoped to become wives' of generals some day. Only later did they realize that they had chosen a hard life of a thread that always had to follow the needle. Before the husband's infiltration the wife receives special training and actually becomes an agent herself. And here we go: he is on operation - she is covering him; he is withdrawn after the failure - she goes with him; he is arrested - she won't escape interrogations, and sometimes even imprisonment, either. Indeed, husband and wife live the same life! If he showed the white feather and betrayed his country, the wife has to decide whether to follow the treacherous husband or to remain faithful to her motherland.

Women that worked for the German intelligence during the First World War mostly were the women of pleasure. Though not every cafe singer or narrow-minded hooker had a chance to become a spy. The German chose beautiful, exquisite and interesting women.

There was a special Central Bureau on top management of espionage in Russia established in Berlin. The German special services organized two spy schools on the territory of Warsaw county: in Lublin and in Lubish. The Lublin school trained both male and female spies. Mostly all trained women were prostitutes. The German sent them to the rear of Russian troops to use the same skills. All spies sent to operations were supplied with forged passports, bombs, 20 pounds each to blow the royal train and bridges in the district Zamorie-Stolbtsy and special saws to spoil telephone and telegraph cables. In case of arrest they were advised to simulate insanity.

There was a three-week course in Lubish. The officers taught the future spies to use topography, distinguish forces based on the types of armory, remember the numbers of troop units, and carry out sabotages in the rear of Russian army. After the training the spies were sent to Russia to carry out investigative activity and sabotages. Just as Lublin spies they were supplied with 20-pound bombs to blow the royal train.

It is quite clear that the German did not bother with deep researches. Accordingly, they could not expect much from such female spies.

Women's drawbacks

All heads of the intelligence offices agree that women have three common drawbacks: firstly, their reports, particularly on the military units, tends to be inaccurate and exaggerated: secondly, women get tired faster than men, they cannot stand either long periods of emotional stress or long periods of monotonous peace and quiet. And, finally, they fall in love, and often with the man they are supposed to be shadowing.

The prejudice against women in the intelligence has a long history. Event the famous soviet spy in Japan Rihard Zorge believed that women were absolutely ill-fitted for intelligence operations. They were poor in political and military issues.

To crown it all women are too emotional, sentimental and unrealistic. The First Chairman of KGB general Ivan Serov treated women in intelligence only as a source of serious personal security threat. When he headed the office it was forbidden to appoint women to the positions of operative intelligence officers in KGB subdivisions. He reasoned his position that women were deceitful and uncontrollable.

Why do women look for troubles? After all, married couples of agents are always at risk. The history of special services is only too full of examples when a husband-agent ruins the life of his wife. Especially when he manages to annoy the enemy greatly enough. If the injured party fails to get the "offender", they will want to take revenge. In this respect the wives are the weakest link. They died through the murderous assaults of the fighters, sent by those who could not catch the successful spy red-handed. It is quite common for the special services to put the evasive threat to the national security out of the by way of engineered accidents (car accidents or air crashes).

The wives of underground agents are under special threat. There is no reason to leave them at liberty. They may warn the Center and the operations would be wrapped up ahead of time. At the very least she would be accused of entrance to the country with forged documents or prosecute for a failure to report a crime. But the counter intelligence often manages to prove the fact of direct complicity. In this case a wife will get a term, though a bit shorter that her husband. In 1960-th in London a station agent Lonsdale Peter Kroger (Morris Cohen) was sentenced to 25 years in prison, while his wife Helen Kroger (Leontina Cohen) – to 20 years in prison. When this happens at wartime, wives are shot for the espionage together with their husbands. The higher the husband's positions, the higher the risks for his wife. It is believed that the wives of security agencies' ministers N. Ezhov, N. Schelokov, B. Pugo and deputy minister of foreign affairs A. Shevchenko who had become the CIA agent, committed suicides.

Femme Fatal

The Major Karin, officer of the War Department of the Austro-Hungarian Empire was recruited by the Russian intelligence in the beginning of XX century. His beautiful wife played a fatal role in his life. To be able to buy her glamorous dresses, the loving husband became a traitor and sold Russian intelligence confidential information that he obtained being an insider.

There is a nice joke on the point. A question to the Armenian radio:

"What bride is better: stupid or beautiful?" The answer: "Of course stupid! Beauty is a non-durable quality, while stupidity is eternal."

Unconventional Sex

For some time the intelligence services of different countries actively used services of homosexuals. Though it is necessary to consider the attitude to unconventional sex in the country the object has come from. There is a story about a French diplomat who set sights on a security officer of the embassy, which was noticed by a KGB agent. The Frenchman was entrapped and KGB managed to photograph the compromising scenes. But when they tried to recruit the diplomat showing him the pictures, he laughed. It turned out that his sexual orientation was not a secret in the embassy.

Terror and Anti-terror

I have already explained the roots of terror and described the psychology of terrorists in my book "Civil War, Terrors and Gangs". Though there is a form of terror that is closely connected with the special services of a country. Particularly such services organized in other countries, to discriminate the government of hateful regimes. Or to destroy the enemies of their own regime. I have not touched upon theses issues in my book and now I am making up for it. Let me quote an abstract for the book "Special Operations" of a great specialist in this field, Pavel Sudoplatov:

It is indicative that all scandalous political murders of XX century both in Russia (attempt on Stolypin's life) and abroad (Trotskiy murder, Mussolini kidnapping, murder of Kennedy, Indira Gandi. U. Palme, I. Rabin, etc.) were committed to some extend by people related to special services of their respective countries. It is important to mention that, according to unquestionable facts received from reliable sources, the terrorists-executors that shot at the state figures, "had got out of control" of their former masters and right under the influence of extreme political groups that by no means wanted to be identified with the terrorist acts.

Besides, true facts about executors of political terrorist acts are usually unavailable for public. The political fight allows various provocative methods of creating favorable conditions for extreme terrorist actions. The tragedy of the situation intensifies due to the fact that special services usually operate in the regime of power, which allows to manipulate visible circumstances of the political murders, conceal personal or political motives in the murderer's actions and, consequently, unleash political terror, as it happened after Nikolayev's shot at Kirov.

Those who was so eager to lavish solicitude on democracy in the countries "behind the Curtain", actually, sanctioned the USSR repressions on their political enemies abroad. It is an unheard-of violation of the international rights fundamentals. Does anyone still believe that the state interests of the Western countries still leaves the room for their "sincere concern" of democracy in Russia and other CIS countries?

When I read the book "Aquarium"of Victor Suvorov (true name is Victor Bogdanovich Rezun) where he described the selective and training procedures for future soviet intelligence agents, I knew how to react to Putin's nomination for presidency: "That is the right man for Russia."

A terrorist act is prepared by classical rules of secret intelligence but at the last stage it is made widely known and even advertized. A terrorist, being a member of some organizations, is eager to glorify themselves and their organization, where the Mass Media turns out to be of great help. I will pay special attention to woman's terror and single out its peculiarities. But at first…

My Colleague Luis Mercader

There were two murder attempts on life of ever-being red commissar Leo Trotskiy, committed upon the order

of his worst enemy I. Stalin. The assassinations were organized by Pavel Sudoplatov, who explains in his memories
that Trotsky's murder was necessary because the international conditions required unity. While Trotskiy planned to
create the 4th International (FI), which would lead to inevitable breakdown. Sure enough he saw himself but not Stalin as the leader.

Trotskiy lived on a villa of a famous Mexican artist
Diego River. The assault was organized by another Mexican artist David Alfaro Siqueiros. The villa was attacked
by 20 people armed with assault rifles and bombs. Led by
Siqueiros, dressed in Mexican major's uniform, they cut off
the telephone cables and burst into the inner yard – patio,
the "major" and brothers Arenal opened fierce fire on the
house and primarily on Trotsky's bedroom. The bedroom
was fired from three directions. Three hundred bullets
were shot, but all in vain. Trotsky's wife hid him in the cor-
ner under the bed and covered him. The ever-being commissar survived.

Thus the second plan of liquidation was initiated. According to this plan Trotskiy should be killed by Ramon
Mercader. Mercader del Rio, aka Ramon Ivanovich Lopes,
agent of NKVD (People's Commissariat for Internal Affairs),
Hero of the Soviet Union and Spanish communist. He had
been recruited by his mother Maria Karidid[2], also NKVD
agent. Ramon Ivanovich prepared the operation and on
August 20, 1940 he hit the leader on the head with an ice-
axe and gravely wounded him. Ramon was arrested, he refused to make any statements and was sentenced by the
Mexican court to 20 years in prison.

---

2   As we can see mother sent her son to death. This case is not unique.
There will be further examples of terrorist mothers who throw away
their children. They do not have mother's instinct.

Mercader did not feel any discomfort in prison. He lived in a spacious separate cell with all convenience including TV. His wife visited him twice a week. Several times the police got to know about the plans of escape. Though Mercader bluntly refused to runaway. After Stalin death no one ever offered him to escape and the prisoner praised himself for clever cautiousness. It is entirely possible that the survived executor bothered someone, thus it was planned to kill him under colour of the escape. Mercader served his time. In 1960 he was released, transferred to Cuba and then, by steamboat, to the USSR.

I had a chance to work with the younger brother of the murderer, Luis Mercader. I am writing memoirs about his brother as I want small sparkles of his glory to dust on me. Luis has already written memoirs about his brother. Now it is my turn. By the way, I am not the first trying to exploit Luis.

I worked with Luis in Research and Development Institute (R&DI). We were both engineers and specialized in wireless engineering. He graduated from Moscow Institute of Energy. There he met his future wife Anzhelika. We worked with engineers that had studied together with Anzhelika and knew her well. By the order of GRU we developed an eavesdropping station. It was located in two lorries with Austrian registration numbers. When the station was ready, a platoon of soldiers arrived headed by the major and his assistant in the rank of senior lieutenant. The lieutenant had a personal auto and he took our women shopping. The soldiers came every day, we taught them how to use the station and they disappeared in the evening. "Where?" we asked. "To New-Vasuki"[3], joked the lieutenant.

---

3   It is an allusion to the a virtual city "Old Vasuki" form the classic satirical novel "Twelve chairs" by Ilf and Petrov.

I lived on the street where our R&DI was located. Within 15-minute walk from work. That's why colleagues often gathered in my flat to read poetry. Our cheerleader was Jack Ruby. That's how we called our mathematician Rubinstain after the murder of the President of the USA Kennedy. He managed to get poems of Rilke and other then rare poets. Lucia Nortsova was the reciter:

So I took her to the river
Believing she was a maiden,
But she already had a husband.
    Where did Lucia get the reciter's talent? Anyway she recited Federico Garcia Lorca magnificently.

Luis wanted to write a thesis and become PhD of Technical Science There were already six PhDs in our department. It was the cleverest one in the R&DI. Though that fact never saved us from being sent to "potato gathering" every autumn. Only Boris Ruvimovich, secretary of the Party organization in our department stayed at home. He had already settled down and even published a book about theory of probability in wireless engineering.

We were dislocated in the farmers' houses, and had to sleep right on the floor. Women were lodged apart from men. Once I woke up in the arms of my male colleague. To my surprise I found out that our technician was thoroughly enjoying himself in the comfort of a widow's bedroom. He was rather shy and I would never expect anything of the kind from him. Our duties were limited to gathering potatoes that had been already dug out, shaken out and thrown back to the soil by the potato-diggering machine. Autumn rains pushed the tubers back into the ground. We did not bother with digging them out, caring about our hands, and took only those tubers that lied on the surface. In the evening we went to "the spot" at the edge of the village. It was a grassless place in the form of a big circle. There the "aborigines" danced and sang chastushkas. Tangos or foxtrots were out of place. They even sang a chastushka in our honour:

We are kissing and hugging from dawn and to dusk
And R&DI engineers digging potatoes for us.
Other chastushkas were pretty dirty, but made us laugh.

A week passed and we returned to Moscow. It was a warm sunny autumn day and we went to the river. Watching calm waters of the small river from the high bank, I decided to swim. I took off my clothes and jumped into the water. The water was cold. It was autumn after all. I swam to the river bank. "How's water?" Luis shouted from the bank. I mumbled something unlanguaged. He rapidly took off his closes and jumped from the bank into the river. How he shot out of the water! Cursing me he swam to the bank. Under the chorus of loud laughter from the observers. Obviously, the Spanish blood was not accustomed to Moscow-area climate.

Spanish blood blew in Luis's veins. He spoke too fast. spattering and cluttering. His voice was dominated by high tones and his laughter turned into shriek.

I knew that Luis had come to the USSR as a child after the failure of Republicans in the civil war in Spain. I knew that his mother had a high position in the Catalan Communist Party but her whereabouts were unknown. Trotsky's murder was never mentioned in the USSR at that time.

Hot Spanish blood made Luis very popular among women. Working in the laboratory we often heard a burst of laughter and happy shrieks of Luis. It meant that he caught and hugged a woman. Tamara, our secretary, was his favorite victim. She sat in a small room with a window. Every morning she gave us our working notebooks from this window. In the end of the day we handed them back to her. Tamara was a Tatar. Her round face was exceptionally beautiful. Obviously, Luis achieved success. Tamara divorced her husband and left the Institute. She was replaced by Galya. Luis switched to Galya. The history repeated and Galya also disappeared.

Our new secretary lived far from Moscow, somewhere in Zagorsk. I do not remember her name, but clearly recall a special thing about her. It was a strong scent of sweat. When she opened the window a thick waft of odor hit our nostrils. The shrieks stopped.

Our department transferred into a new R&DI and we moved to new premises closer to the center of Moscow. I did not want to move and parted with the brother of Leo Trotsky's murderer and a great womanizer Luis Mercader.

Luis managed to return to Spain in 80-th. There he worked as a teacher in the University of Madrid and published a book about his brother. Though I left the USSR for Israel earlier than Luis.

Women-Terrorists
JUDITH

The first woman-terrorist is considered to be the biblical Judith who sneaked to the camp of the Assyrians and cut off the head of their leader Holofernes. Judith packed the head of the victim in a prepared before hand traveling bag and went to Yuahudis (or Jews) to prove that she had really murdered their enemy. As the legend goes, Assyrians, petrified by Judith act of brevity, ran away.

This biblical legend has been reflected in many artworks where beautiful Judith is shown with the head of Holofernes, and in the opera of Russian composer Alexander Serov, a father of a talented artist Valentine Alexandrovich Serov.

I would not label Judith's act as terrorist. I'd rather say that it is a brilliant military operation.

It is worthwhile to analyze the attitude to the story of Judith. Initially it was included in the TANAKH (Five Books of Moses), but excluded afterwards. There is even no such story in Hebrew. The story was excluded on the ground of its "amorality" that was felt in the methods the woman used to sneak to the enemy's camp and do away with their leader. She used tools most typical for women and intelligence: deceit and cunning. Those Yuahudis (Jews) who decided what should be included in TANAKH probably were people of high moral. And narrow-minded at the same time. The war boils down to the ability to outsmart, cheat and destroy the enemy. The Christian religion that received the Old Testament translated in Greek left the story in the Bible. Though, Protestants threw it away again.

What is so special about the religions as some delete the story and some prefer to keep it? Judaism (Jew Religion) prohibits asceticism. The Christianity, on the contrary, based on asceticism. As compared to the Jewish society, asceticism leads to greater unity and OUS generation. As a result, a person turns into golem, while morality disappears together with personality. The act of brevity for the benefit of the society, or the altruistic suicide is typical for the OUS. Thus Judith became a Christian heroine. The Protestants religion implies the denial of asceticism, liberation of the personality and return to morality. Naturally "moral society" denies amoral behavior. That's where the moralists made a gross mistake. At wartime the society shall be strongly united while all the morals shall be forgotten. Judith's act shall become a synonym for military brevity, not terror, and serve as a lesson for "pacifists": there are no rules and no morals at war.

Vera Zasulich

Vera Zasulich was born to noble parents in 1849. In eighteen she graduated from a woman's boarding school and became a teacher. She also attended obstetric classes. Her two sisters were married to the members of terrorist organization «Popular Will» (Narodnaya Volya) and Vera herself held mostly popular views.

In December 1876 during a youth meeting in Saint Petersburg, a student Bogolubov, was arrested and sentenced to hard labour. During the examination procedures the chief of the city Trepov visited the Saint Petersburg preliminary detention house where the prisoners with respect to this case were kept. In the yard he accidentally met Bogolubov who greeted him politely. They walked around the building and met again. That time Bogolubov failed to greet the important visitor. Trepov was furious and ordered to wipe the rebel in public and then lockup him in the isolation ward, which triggered the prison upheaval. In the end the upheaval was put down and Bogolubov was wiped until unconsciousness. When Ms. Zasulich heard of that she made her mind to shoot at the chief of the city.

Corporal punishment was considered to be something quite outstanding in Russia of those days; the youth believed that rod belonged the times of Ivan the Terrible. Bogolubov's wiping was seen as the outrage against human rights. People waited for Trepov to be punished but that did not happened. So then angry Ms. Zasulich decided to shoot at Trepov in a desperate attempt to draw attention to the event. She bought a revolver and came to see him. Entering his office she shot at random. The bullet got him through the pelvis. She dashed the revolver aside and simply waited for what was about to happen.

Trepov survived the shot. Ms. Zasulich was arrested, accused of attempted murder and supposed to be imprisoned for twenty years. The investigations were carried out very swiftly. Judge Anatoly Kony presided in the court, Mr. Kessel, a friend of the Petersburg district court prosecutor, was counsel for prosecution, and lawyer Mr. Alexandrov was the attorney. The authorities demanded guilty verdict from Kony, though he was not inclined to give it.

Ms. Zasulich's guilt was obvious. Even her attorney admitted that she fired conscious of her intend and ability to make it a fatal shot. The prosecutor's speech was anything but bright, while Mr. Alexandrov made a brilliant eloquent speech. The Judge Kony tried to shelter him. From the very beginning the attorney stressed that Trepov himself did an ugly thing, while Ms. Zasulich, being a woman, simply could not but sympathize with poor ill and beaten prisoner.

The jury pledged Ms. Zasulich not guilty. She was freed in the court and her friends helped her to escape to Sweden.

This very shot and the subsequent not guilty verdict triggered a breach of terror in Russia. This was clear immediately after the court. It seemed that people perceived the event that happened in the court as a mockery justice and Law. She shot at a human being, she wounded him badly and she was pledged not guilty and set free. No one ever mentioned of «inadequate response» or «excess act of force». Many Moscow journalists wrote that the experiment with juries (started in Russia not long before the described events) was a complete fiasco.

There is a chapter devoted to the judicial system in my book "Civil War, Terrorism and Gangs" that explains the way the judicial system collapses. The collapse of judicial system is the omen of the whole ruling regime breakdown. Truly, Ms. Zasulich was put on trial on 31st of March in 1878, while the first armed attempt of dethronement was made in 1905. In February 1917 the Russian Tsar voluntary abdicated the crown. In October 1917 the Bolshevik Revolution was carried out. Thus it took 39 years for the first symptom to develop into the Bolshevik Revolution.

So how did it happen that Ms. Zasulich was justified? The reforms of Alexander II (or Alexander the Liberator) prompted rapid degradation of the Russian society. It was losing unity and in the end split into the left wing and the right wing, or, speaking in terms of that time, into Slavophils and Westernizes. Thanks to the Judge's support and the prosecutor's negligence the attorney managed to choose the Westernizes to the Jury. All the rest was the nothing but natural.

It might be useful to compare Ms. Zasulich trial with the contemporary Israeli justice. The principle of the punishment equal to the crime (eye for eye, blood for blood, death for death), written in Torah, was abandoned under the pressure form all kinds of left-wing organizations. The death penalty was abolished. Terrorists and murderers are sentenced to life in prison, two lives in prison... Such indulgence, just like in Zasulich case, encourages terror. What's more, the Arabs bend over their backwards to get living

Israeli to exchange him for the imprisoned terrorists. They are changed one to one thousand.

Miss killer

(http://cn.com.ua/N182/lukomorie/terror/terror.html)

According to the statistical data, women equal men in terrorist activity. The Executive Committee of terrorist organization "Popular Will" consisted of 29 members, ten of them were women. Here is ten-year statistics of SR (Social Revolutionary) terror, particularly, its Battle Group (BG). The SR Party was established after the defeat of "Popular Will" that followed the murder of Alexander II. SR members declared themselves executors of mass terror. In this organization women were no longer associates, but immediate executors of terrorist operations.

During 1901–1911 SR members carried out 263 terrorist operations. Their victims were 2 ministers, 33 governor-generals, governors and vice-governors, 16 heads of the cities, 7 generals and admirals, 26 police agents and provocateurs.

Among 78 members of BG there were 25 women. Totally, according to the American researcher of women terrorism Ami Knight, there are 44 documentary confirmed cases of women terrorists. In reality there even more of them than that. Below are two examples of female SR members:

Maria Spiridonova. The most popular woman terrorist in Russia after Sophia Perovskaya. She was born to noble parents and studied in gymnasium where she joined the SR Party to become a terrorist. In 1905 she assassinated Police Inspector General Luzhenovsky. She was severely beaten and raped during inquest. She wrote open letters and gained popularity. She was sentenced to death penalty, but later the sentence was changed to hard labours in exile. After the Bolshevik Revolution she was triumphantly freed and became a member of VtsIK Presidium (All Russia Central Executive Committee). In 1937 she was arrested and executed. – Bad end!

Anastasia Bitsenko. She was born to farmers, studied in gymnasium and joined the Party in 1902. She became a member of a flying squad and assassinated General Sakharov, who tried to suppress rebellion among farmers of Samarskaya County. She was arrested and sent to hard labours in exile. After the revolution she became deeply involved in politics, supported Soviet government. In 1938 she was arrested and executed. – Not a nice end either!

They are the brightest stars of SR terror. Female terrorism flowered in Russia in the beginning of the century. Several research papers are devoted to the problem of Russian women in terrorism. Above mentioned Ami Knight wrote that female SR members were closer to upper social layers, contrary to the popular belief that the terror roots in poverty. To justify the terror ladies invented an excuse: they wanted to pay their tribute to people[4]». Ami Knight analyzed biographies of 44 female terrorists and came to the conclusion: Out of 40 female terrorists with proved social background, 15 women were born either to noble parents or merchants; 4 women from the families of intellectuals, 11 women came from bourgeois, one girl was a priest's daughter and 9 women were born to farmers. And even those farmers' daughters were not farmers to the full. Anastasia Bitsenko and Zinaida Konoplyannikova got education and became teachers. 11 terrorists had higher education, 23 – high; 6 – family education and only 3 – primary. One girl said that she was self-taught. There were

---

4   Nonsense. What were the motives of Che Guevara when he exported revolution to the South America?

9 teachers, 8 students and only 4 workers among female terrorists. Their average age was 22 years old. For the sake of comparison: out of 131 male terrorists 95 were workers and farmers. At the same time there was no such thing as sexual equality in the society, even if revolutionary circles tried to follow the principles of equality.

Over 200 women became suicide bombers during the period of 1985–2006. They carried out 15% of all suicidal terrorist acts.

A feminine image faded away. After every terrorist act committed by a woman only one question hangs in the air: WHY.

According to Interpol about the half of wanted terrorist-killers are women. The British journalist Eileen MacDonald published interviews with 20 female terrorists in her boot "Shoot the Women First". Though the Introduction to the book is probably even more interesting that the book itself. The author claims that the title for the book was taken from the Interpol Guide for anti-terror special services. Obviously, the specialists believe women to be more dangerous than men, that's why they are to be shot first. Surely, there is a beginning with every thing. But now, after more that a hundred years of female terror, can we believe that Vera Zasulich's shot was a mere coincidence?

Frustration

The desire to explain the situation has led to the suggestion that the reason is "unbalanced psyche of these women". This theory is supported by many suicides committed by female SR members. Rashel Lurie, Esther Lapina, Sophia Khrenkova and many others committed suicides. One of the most famous terrorists among women wrote in her memories that she wished she had been killed at the place of terrorist act, than the effect would have been greater.

In my book "Civil War, Terror and Gangs" I explained where the terror comes from. A human is a collective animal. A human has a special feeling "hevraav" that helps them to understand the level of the society unity. When the unity decreases, some humans become frustrated ("tiskul" in Hebrew). There are only two possible outcomes: depression or aggression. Depression ends in suicide, which Emil Durkheim called "anomy" Aggression leads to terror. The when terrorists are not tortured by ethical issues, because they are members of OUS, deprived of moral. To abandon their own children or to kill other people's children – doesn't matter. They are golems.

Women are more sensitive to the decrease of unity in the society than men. Normal women then get interested in makeup, clothes and try to show off. Golem women feel frustrated in the environment of society degradation. They are sooner than men run into depression and aggression.

I won't describe various terrorist gangs, such as German RAF (Red Army Faction) also known as Baader-Meinhof Group where 80% of members were women, Japanese "Red Army" and AUM Shinrikyo, Italian "Red Brigades", etc. They are no different from each other and operate according to similar scheme.

Islam

On November 2005 the Belgian citizen Muriel Degok turned to Islam and joined one of its radical streams. She blew herself up in a car in Iraq. The same very day Sacide Atrus al-Rishavi failed to detonate the bomb fastened to her belt at the wedding in one of the Amman hotels.

What is so special about Islam that it turns everyone in terrorists?

Islam is based on ascetics, on suppressing personality, on turning people to golems. A man is a herd animal and a religion is aimed at uniting people into society. Though speaking about the unity of the society one should consider how strong the religious ties that unite people. They may be too strong and then people lose their idiosyncrasy and turns into golems. The golem has nothing personal and is bound up by the society. These people are ascetics suppressing their own Ego by any means. Look how low the prayers bow or how well a woman is hidden under the clothes to see the degree of suppression. The personality is suppressed by self-sacrifice and self-torture. Wild crowds of men go into the streets and violently beat themselves with the chains. Islam forbids drinking wine and the drunk shall be beaten with stones. The Muslims applies equally Draconian rules to women. At the age of six girls have their clitoris cut, so that a woman cannot feel pleasure. She is shrouded from head to foot in veil so that she cannot suggest wicked thoughts to good Muslims. A woman committed offence shall be executed. She is killed by her own relatives for «ruining the reputation of the family».

The Islam has gained popularity in Europe and America during the last decades. Not only does it spread with the Arabs flooded the Western countries, but it is also adopted by the golems, by those who needs it, by Afro-Americans, by people like the above mentioned Belgian woman, Muriel Degok. They need the religion with strong ties. If they are not strongly united they grew frustrated.

What is so attractive in Islam? A religion that can strongly unite people has one special feature: it relieves them from reflections and ensures emotional stability. Such people suffer from infantilism. They do not know halftones. Things are clearly divided into black and white, people can be either good or bad, either trusted friends or outsiders. An outsider is an enemy!

Due to Muslim need for unity all Arab countries are one-man rule countries. Only iron hand of a dictator can ensure the unity the Muslims need.

As ascetics do not need material values, they are not motivated to work. That's the reason why all Muslim countries are among the poorest in the world. The returns of Saudi Arabia and Arabian Gulf countries are based on proceeds from oil.

They do not want to work, but how do they manage to survive, particularly those who do not have oil? The OUS and golems are very aggressive. They are always ready to fight and rob. This aggressiveness eventually turned into eternal civil wars in Afghanistan, bloody wars of Iraq with its neighbors and endless wars of Israel with Arab countries.

So how should we treat Turkey in the light of the set forth? This country does not suit the given description. The time was when the Turkish janissary were as frantic as talibs. Turkey had a vast territory. Then Young Turks under the leadership of Kemal Ataturk defeated the sultan's regime and established Turkey as the democratic republic. The Islam was shown its place and the fanatism began to show signs of strain. This outcome helped Turkey to lead its economy out of lethargic dream.

Now let's imagine that the Muslim society degrades and its unity starts to drop sharply. The members of the society feel frustration. If the OUS is aggressive by its nature, the frustration turns the aggression and hatred against those who, in the view of Muslims, are responsible for their degradation. In other words, they begin to hate the Western liberty and culture. Hiding behind the slogans of freedom and independence, Muslim fanatics sow terror all over the world.

Leaders in some countries in an attempt to keep good relationship with Arabs try to separate terror from Islam. I would suggest that they should study sociology and stop thrusting democracy upon Muslim countries.

Leila Khaled

Leila Khaled was born in 1943. She studied in the USSR on the faculty of journalism in the Moscow state University. The foreigners studying in the USSR had hard times back then. They were children of communist leaders. On one hand children were kept hostage in the USSR, on the other hand they were trained as the fifth column in their respective countries. Thus the son of Israeli communist leader Meir Vilner (Ber Kovner) got a military education in the USSR and the rank of lieutenant. They were sent by communist or similar party of this or that country. The students received a profession and a good ideological brainwashing.

Since 1969 Leila Khaled became an active terrorist and a member of the PFLP (Popular Front of the Liberation of Palestine). She was a part of several bold hijackings. So student years in the USSR were not spent in vane.

On September 6, 1970 the Arabs hijacked 4 planes at once. They demanded to release their fellows, imprisoned in England and Israel. At first the British government did not make concessions. Leila Khaled, the head of the gang, was overpowered during on of the attacks. The Front demanded to free the terrorist otherwise they threatened to hijack more planes. In a couple of days they kept their word and hijacked the plane from Bombay to Beirut. The British got 72-hour ultimatum.

English diplomats managed to extend the term. The terrorists released several hostages, mostly children and women. But then they felt tired to wait and blew up three planes in the Jordanian desert.

Israel insisted that they should not make any concessions. But, naturally, the British thought about their hostages and began secret negotiations with the terrorists. On September 13 it was agreed to change hostages for Leila Khaled.

We should thank the Arab terrorists for thorough inspection of the passengers and their luggage in the airports.

Leila Khaled was backed by extensive military forces of terrorists. Initially created to fight Israel, they might change their targets at any moment, which actually happened. They landed and blew up the hijacked planes in Jordan. They attacked the units of Jordanian army and threatened the King of Jordan Hussien with the upheaval. The Jordanian King Hussein declared war against the Palestine Liberation Organization (PLO). Israeli planes smashed tank columns of Syria that supported PLO and saved the King of Jordan. Trying to escape from repressions of Hussein, a lot of terrorists ran to the territory of Israel and yielded themselves prisoners to the Israeli Army. The PLO was driven out from Jordan to Libya.

Now the war has moved to Libya.

Anti-terror

If the terror is caused by the society degradation and the decrease of its unity, then how can we fight terror?

First of all I would recommend making every effort to prevent the breakdown and the collapse of the society. For

that purpose I wrote a guidebook for leaders "The Art of Government: A Guidebook for Leaders"
http://www.authorsonline.co.uk/New/synopsis.asp?eBookID=449 .

When the terror is still weak and limited to the gangs like the Japanese «Red Army», or the Italian «Red Brigades», they can be fought by the police. Though even in these cases some human rights activists perceive this fight with terror as the violation of laws, rights, etc. Here is the BBC report:

The fight with terror undermines the international law

Published on 2009/02/16 12:48:44 GMT Address of the article on bbcrussian.com

http://news.bbc.co.uk/go/pr/fr/-/hi/russian/international/newsid_7892000/7892686.stm

By Frank Gardner

BBC security issues observer.

The UK and the USA «actively undermine» the international law with their attempts to fight the international terrorism, declared the report prepared by the lawyers and judges.

This conclusion drew the bottom line under the three year research of the International Legal Commission.

The legislators believe that the significant achievements made in the last century in relation to the human rights were destroyed within the latest seven years.

This report will surely put a lot of leaders on both sides of Atlantic out-of-position.

Having thoroughly investigated the situation in several countries the lawyers and judges concluded that the international laws that had existed before September 9, 2001, were sound and effective.

Lack of control

The researchers believe that the contours of the international law are being eroded by many countries, headed by the states with well-developed democracy, such as the USA and the UK.

A lot of anti-terror actions are illegal and counterproductive, the report says.

The specialists are also concerned about lack of control, weak diplomatic guarantees with respect to the decisions about departures and arrests without any charges being served.

I do not think that the groans and moans of the human rights activists should be taken seriously enough to stop the fight with terror. If rules are out-of-date, they should be replaced or cancelled. Otherwise the scale of terror will only grow bigger. We should never forget that the terror knows no rules or laws.

Now the terror is growing to an international scale. The Islam is spreading all over the world, so is the terror. As I have already mentioned, they are inseparable. That is why more drastic actions are needed. First of all concepts of «freedom and democracy» should not be thrust upon the countries that need dictatorship regime, namely, Islamic countries.

Let me remind you how the dictators opposed their rioters and united their people. Communist religion is as good as the Islam.

The farmers outbreaks against the Soviet government robbed them of absolutely everything (so called «prodrazverstka») were violently crushed. No one knows even approximate number of victims.

In 1921, RSFSR was seized by anti-Bolshevik farmers' outbreaks, with the largest movement of the European part of Russia were formed in Tambovskaya County. In the beginning of May, considering the outbreak in Tambov as a serious threat, the Politburo appointed Tukhachevskiy as the commander of Tambov troops and instructed him to liquidate the outbreak as soon as possible. Due to the plan, developed by Tukhachevskiy, the outbreak was mainly suppressed by the end of July in 1921.

From Tukhachevskiy order No. 0116 of July 12, 1921:

I HEREBY ORDER:
10. The forests where the the bandits are hiding should be cleared by poison gases. The cloud of the choking gas should spread all over the forest and kill everything hiding inside.
11. The artillery inspector shall immediately deliver the required amount of balloons with poison gas to the specified locations, and provide necessary specialists.
12. The Head of the areas of operations shall be insistent and strenuous in fulfilling the order.
13. To report on the actions taken.

The Commander of Troops, Tukhachevskiy,
The Chief of the Joint Staff, Kakurin.

The order of the Decision-Making Committee of VTsIK about the procedure of clearance in rebellious volosts and villages.
No. 116, Tambov, June 23, 1921.
The clearance of the first area has proved the effectiveness of the following method aimed at fast clearing known regions from bandits. When the most rebellious volosts are specified. The representatives

of Politcommission, special department and RVT department and commandment are sent there together with the units, appointed for the clearance operation. As soon as they arrive, the volost is closed off, about 60-100 people are taken hostage. It should be forbidden to leave or enter the volost during the operation. Then the general meeting of the volost is called, where orders of 130 and 171 of Decision-Making Committee of VTsIK are read together with the sentence for the volost. The people are given two hours to give away weapon. Bandits and their families. They are informed that in two hours time the hostages would be executed should they refuse to provide the required evidence. If people failed to give away weapon and bandits within two hours, the meeting is called again and the hostages are shot before the eyes of the villagers, new hostages are taken and people are again asked to give away bandits and weapon. Those who are willing to obey shall be separated, divided into hundreds and each hundred are interrogated by the investigative committee of RVT special department representatives. Everyone shall testify and not to pretend being unaware. If people do not want to submit to the orders, new hostages should be executed, etc. Upon the processing the information, obtained during interrogations, expedition teams are formed, which include those who provided the information and other local people; the teams are sent to catch bandits. When the clearance is over, the state of siege is cancelled, revolutionary committee and militsia are established. Upon the Decision-Making Committee of VTsIK order this document shall be accepted as exact guidelines and executed.

The Chairman of the Decision-Making Committee of VTsIK Antonov-Ovseenko
The Commander of Troops, Tukhachevskiy,
The Chairman of the Executive Committee of the County Lavrov
RGVA, F.235. Op2. D.13, L.25. Certified copy.

The Order of the Decision-Making Committee of VTsIK about taking hostages and their execution in case of bridges destruction.
No. 189, Tambov, July 9, 1921

The defeated bandits hide in the forests and try to work off their rage on local people, by burning bridges, destroying dams and other people's values. For the purpose of preserving bridges the Decision-Making Committee of VTsIK orders: 1. to take at least five hostages from all villages located near bridges and immediately execute them if the bridges are destroyed. 2. to get the local people establish the bridges defense from bandits and to get them responsible for restoring the destroyed bridges within 24 hour period. 3. to bring this order to notice among the villages.
The Chairman of the Decision-Making Committee of VTsIK Antonov-Ovseenko
The Commander of Troops, Tukhachevskiy,
The Chairman of the Executive Committee of the County Lavrov

RGVA, F.235. Op2. D.13, L.27. Certified copy. There was an original text of the order, amended by Tukhachevskiy on July 7, 1921, Resource Center of Recent History of Tomskaya Oblast, F.235. Op1. D.213, L.25. copy

Undeniably, Tukhachevsky's orders contain a complete set of international crimes: usage of chemical weapon, hostages, execution without judicial safeguards. Besides Tukhachevskiy only Saddam Hussein used chemical weapon against people of his own country. Taking hostages is forbidden by the Hague Convention of 1907 and considered to be a severe military offence.

On June 12, 1937 «Tambov Punisher» aka Marshal Michael Tukhachevskiy was executed, but not for his crimes. He had just fallen out of grace with Stalin.

The documents I am citing here were written in Arab and would have never been published if the dictator of Iraq Saddam Hussein and his handy men had not been hung. There are two documents provided in the report «Human Rights Watch» devoted to «Genocide in Iraq». They defined the powers of «Chemical Ali» (al Majid). Decree 160, signed on March 29, 1987 that orders all state authorities - both military and civic - follow the instructions of al-Majid. And Directive of Saddam Hussein of April 20, 1987 ordering «Chemical Ali» to establish budget of the Committee on the Northern regions issues. Actually the revolutionary committee headed by Saddam Hussein gave him absolute power and total leadership in operations for two years form 1987 to 1989. During this period Ali Hassan al-Majid carried out campaign called «al-Anfal» and a number of other operations against Kurds rebellions. He used all military troops and all special services dislocated in the North of the country.

Under one of his first decisions the military commanders were ordered «to fire at «forbidden zones» at any time of day or night. The zones we created by the Iraq government to desert Kurd's territories in near-border and other strategically important territories. The Kurds should have been driven out of those territories with the help of aviation and artillery. » (Order SF/4008 of June 20, 1988). The same order underlines the necessity to destroy all men of Kurds from 14 to 50 years old.

Al-Majid actively developed and carried out «al-Anafl» operation aimed at squeezing Kurds out of the Northern Iraq. al-Anafl» consisted of eight stages that were implemented from February to September 1988. It implied mass destruction of hundreds of people, complete demolition of more than 3 thousand villages, tenths of cities and countless civil objects, including masjids, robberies, expropriations, large scale arrests and tortures, forceful movement of hundreds of thousands Kurds to «living quarters» in the South of Iraq, destruction of economy, agriculture and infrastructure of Kurdistan. In the course of this operation the troops demonstrated outstanding violence and used only too cruel methods, including chemical weapon. On March 16, 1988 Ali Hassan al-Majid sanctioned chemical weapon employment against citizens of Halabja that caused death of at least 5000. Those who survived suffer form the consequences of chemical weapon employment.

Many countries consider these events to be the act of genocide against Kurds. Though at the time of «al-Anafl» operation both the USSR and the Western countries preferred to ignore this fact in order to satisfy their geopolitical interests. Al-Majid was named «Chemical Ali» for using chemical weapon. In 1989 the Kurds position in Iraq worsened every day.

Earlier only villages had been attacked, but then even pretty large cities were also exposed to strikes. About half a million people were forcefully driven out of their houses. That nightmare finished only with the beginning of another military operation - Iraq assault at neighboring Kuwait.

There is a difference between Tukhachevskiy and the Chemical Ali. Tukhachevskiy poisoned Russian men, robbed by the Soviets. The Arab Ali poisoned some Kurds.

Obviously, no one care about international laws. In Africa and other countries the justice is severely violated every day.

With the view of the above said, I would remember Israeli settlement in Eastern part of Jerusalem. The USA, Russia and other countries seem to be annoyed even if people take houses that are legal property of Jews. Maybe it would be better to repeat the «deed» of Chemical Ali. Then everybody would have pretended that they had seen nothing.

In the end I would underline that the Arabs are tightly united by Islam that is why they need massive repressions and dictator.

Conclusion

*One has to be a potentate to grasp the character
of the people, and one has to be one of the people to
grasp the nature of potentates.*
Machiavelli

In 1988, I took up sociology and wrote the book *Civil War, Terrorism, and Gangs,* in which there is a section entitled "The Collapse of the Judicial System." Courts of law and justice are a function of the level of society's cohesion. I defined the level of cohesion at which the judicial system as such disappears. The degradation of society is accompanied by the degradation of all its systems, including the courts of law and the army.

Something of the kind happens to society leaders. They lose both power and brains and turn into impotents pursuing their own interests to the detriment of the interests of society. The courts of law, the army, the leaders—all systems become politicized, criminalized, impotent, and ineffective after society develops a rift. The Israelis can see for themselves what is going on in their government, the Supreme Court, and the IDF.

I have no doubt that the Israeli leaders are so aloof from their people that they cannot grasp its character.

However, I am one of the people, and I have grasped the "nature of the Israeli potentates" by a very simple method. From time to time, I send them a strong insult or threat and evaluate their response.

I tested my experiment on Ezer Weizman, the president of Israel. I sent him "a light insult," then a stronger one, and a still stronger one. He was adamant and did not respond to any. I thought it was not enough and addressed it to "all." A week later, they took away my computer and returned it after another two weeks; the case was dismissed as we have "freedom of speech." I made it a habit of sending "something" and waiting for the response. There was "freedom of speech." But there was neither power nor leadership in Israel. I could not grasp the "nature of the potentate." During my latest arrest, newsmen and paparazzi surrounded me at the entrance to the courthouse. I asked, "How can we get rid of Olmert? Just shoot him?" None of the papers that came out with my photo quoted these words.

In June 2007, after another of my experiments, the police confiscated my computer again. In the previous cases, they had returned it rather quickly, but this time, something went wrong. The 180-day period set by law had expired, and still I did not have my computer back. I had already written half of my *Military Sociology* and could not finish it without the computer.

The prosecutor's office brought no charges against me, but the investigating officer told me that I would be accused of something like instigation to revolution (*hamrada, hasata, iumim* in Hebrew). What had they done these past 180 days? Everything could be found in my book. They could have filed their charges right off.

I do not know what they found in my computer. I think that the investigating officer did not read any of my writings, even those that are in Hebrew. He admitted as much, saying he had no time for reading. During our talk, he called me a racist (*gezani* in Hebrew). This seemed to be the reason for confiscating the computer for good and bringing charges against me. I am not a *gezani*, I am a *gezi* (purebred). The Jewish poet Nathan Alterman is my uncle from my mother's side and nationalist Berl Kaznelson, from my father's side.

I did not care what the police or the prosecutor's office thought of me, but I could not allow them or anybody else to dictate to me what and how I should write. Yosi Sarid, ex-member of the Knesset, tried to make me behave. He lodged a complaint against me with the police. He did not like a section in the book, "Can Yitzhak Rabin Be Assassinated?" My answer was anything but polite: I used the term "idiot" referring to him many times. The new ideologues also tried to fit me into their mold.

I sent a letter to the prosecutor's office, warning them that unless my computer was returned, I would sue them and claim damages. They did not return the computer but retaliated by suing me in an attempt to impart legitimacy to their actions.

To make a long story short, ultimately, Haifa's deputy prosecutor sent me a letter saying, "the case which was opened against R. Raikhlin on suspicion of crimes, threats, instigation, etc., has been dismissed." There would be no trial. My instigations would go on.

My experiments with leaders have shown that **Israel has no leaders, either in the rightist or in the leftist camp.** The position of the head of government is filled by impotents concerned with nothing but their private affairs, mainly lining their pockets.

I have made it crystal clear that degradation of society ends at the anomie stage. The degradation of society is accompanied by the degradation of all its systems, mainly its armed forces. At the degradation stage, a citizen or a sect may depose the leader and stage a revolution. Reprisals are bound to follow the revolution, which will put an end to anomie and create a new society. We have either to wait for the time our oligarchy is dispersed and our leader is gunned down or take an active part in this process. *The sooner we end this power vacuum, the better for us and our society!* The Israeli armed forces are incapable of protecting us from our enemies. Perhaps it is still capable of ending anomie, assuming power, and putting our country in order.

1. These figures were made public by the Israeli television on April 30, 1985. See: Ruth Linn, "Conscientious Objection in Israel During the War in Lebanon." *Armed Forces and Society* (USA) 12, no. 4 (1986), p. 490.